THE BOOK OF FINE PRINTS

Books by Carl Zigrosser

FINE PRINTS OLD AND NEW 1937
SIX CENTURIES OF FINE PRINTS 1937
THE ARTIST IN AMERICA 1942
KAETHE KOLLWITZ 1946
CAROLINE DURIEUX 1949
MASTERPIECES OF DRAWING IN AMERICA 1950

THE BOOK
OF FINE PRINTS

An Anthology of
Printed Pictures
and Introduction
to the Study of
Graphic Art in the
West and the East

by Carl Zigrosser

CROWN PUBLISHERS, INC. · NEW YORK

TO LAURA

PRINTED IN THE UNITED STATES OF AMERICA

AMERICAN BOOK-STRATFORD PRESS, INC., NEW YORK

Foreword

This is a postscript to serve as a foreword. Most forewords, as a matter of fact, are written after a book is finished. This one is frankly so. To mark the fourth edition of a work first issued in 1937, it seems fitting to review the state of graphic art at the mid-century mark. Difficult as it is to evaluate the salient features of a movement from the viewpoint of a contemporary, one feels nevertheless a certain obligation to do so, and thus to attempt, in the light of the past and with the perspective of a half century, to come to terms with our own turbulent and exciting XX century.

One conclusion seems plain and indubitable: that there is a new orientation for printmaking in the XX century. It has, one might say, attained its majority and graduated from a minor craft into a full-fledged art. Since the utilitarian and strictly reproductive functions of graphic art have been taken over by the photomechanical processes, printmaking is becoming a major vehicle for creative expression. By and large, prints of today have a different purpose and justification from those made in the past. If the artists of our time are aware of this new orientation—and I believe that they are becoming more and more so—unfortunately the world at large is not. It is a paradox that, with the spread of democracy as a social and political institution, printmaking, the one medium dedicated in principle to the production of many originals at a moderate price, should not have experienced a corresponding growth in popular esteem. Easel painting is still more or less a vested interest as far as public recognition of creative work and prizes are concerned, with sculpture and graphic art lagging far behind. The *snobisme* of exclusive possession still seems to be potent in the motivation of a collector.

Once we have granted that painting and printmaking are on a par as effective vehicles for creative expression—the only difference being in the number and availability of originals—it might then be well to define the scale and type of expression most appropriate to the graphic arts. Prints today may be roughly classified in two groups according to their general interest: hand prints and wall prints—hand prints, small in size and designed to be looked at in the hand; and wall prints, larger in size and predominantly decorative in the best sense of the word as wall decoration, in the way that mural and easel paintings are used. The hand print is in the great tradition of graphic art, closely related to the book, since the printed picture has always been linked with the printed word. As black and white designs eloquently expressive of humanity in all its aspects, they represent the tradition of Mantegna, Dürer, Rembrandt, Goya, Blake and Daumier, to name but a few of the great masters. Such prints are usually kept in boxes or portfolios and brought out to be studied and enjoyed on occasion. One is reminded of that wonderful drawing in the Louvre by Daumier of *Les Amateurs d'estampes* where the print lovers are discussing Raffet's *Revue Nocturne;* or of Goethe's after-dinner discourses over the open print portfolios, as recorded by Eckermann. Today, alas, there are practically no portfolio collectors; and consequently there is relatively little demand for the hand print as such. Which is a great pity, for such prints do function as a sensitive reflection or index of our emotional and mental climate. Prints, by reason of their intimate scale and their intense concentration within a small space, are much better adapted to precipitate and record the profound as well as the fugitive intuitions of mankind than are wall paintings. There are so many things to be said, or rather depicted—the spontaneous sketch, the intimate tone, the ironic or reflective comment, the flash of psychological insight, even the austere beauty of geometric design—which seem out of place, day in and day out, on a wall. At present such works find their home chiefly in museum collections; yet they should be in the portfolios of countless cultivated amateurs.

By contrast, the wall print seems to enjoy more widespread popular favor for various reasons. In the first place, most wall prints are in color; and the public at present prefers color to black and white. Furthermore, modern prints are becoming larger and larger in size, and are definitely intended to be framed and hung on the wall, thus rivaling easel painting in general effect. In fact, one might say that prints are the poor man's easel paintings. It is the younger generation— thoroughly acclimated to the modern style, and as yet without a great margin of affluence for the purchase of paintings—who buy prints to decorate their walls. It is unfortunate that they cease to collect when their walls are filled. How can they be transformed into portfolio collectors? Prints are ideally suited to function in both ways. It is merely a question of demonstrating to the public how simple it could be. The practice, among the Chinese and Japanese, of showing only a few pictures at a time and storing the rest, gives a clue to the solution. Prints in standard size mats can be fitted into frames so designed that they can be easily changed, thus providing a rotation of pictures on the wall. The reserve can easily be stored in print boxes or portfolios.

Because printmaking is now a creative medium, more and more painters or sculptors are making prints, and therefore contributing a fresh point of view— the artist's as opposed to the craftsman's—which has influenced even those few who are exclusively printmakers. It seems obvious that the painter, in taking up a new medium, would carry over into it his habit of thinking in color, and of working on a scale more comparable to that of a canvas. Furthermore, the painter, accustomed as he is to working for unique effects, would be reluctant to spend much time printing large editions of such prints, with their subtle textures and complicated color printing techniques. Whatever the reasons, the fact remains that more and more color prints are being produced today, large in size, complex in technique, and few in number of edition—a tendency which, if developed to its ultimate conclusion in the attempt to rival the easel painting, would eventually negate the principle of the cheap multi-original, which is the core of graphic art. If the demand were greater, the artist might possibly be interested in making larger editions.

There is a factor in the new orientation of printmaking which may ultimately help to increase the prestige of this art, namely the fact that it is now exclusively

2

an artist's medium. It has happened before, and may well happen again, that artists have set a fashion and molded taste well in advance of popular acceptance. If enough distinguished artists continue to devote much of their energy to printmaking, their influence will ultimately make itself felt, and it will be difficult to ignore their contribution to graphic art.

The great impasse in the print field is distribution and sales. Theoretically, fine prints can be offered at very low prices if the editions are large enough. The practical difficulty is caused by the high cost of distribution. Several solutions to this bottleneck suggest themselves. Print clubs on a yearly subscription basis, modeled on the big book clubs, have been started in the United States and in other countries, such as Holland and Switzerland. Prints have also been sold through the existing machinery of mass distributing agencies, such as book clubs and greeting card manufacturers. Artist organizations sometimes offer annual gift prints to their patrons or lay members; and museums and print clubs sometimes circulate exhibitions of prints which are for sale. All of the above methods seem in line with the trend toward mass distribution techniques engendered by the increasing mechanization of our cultural life. In prints the business has not been carried as far as it has been in certain other arts. Thus the chief burden of distributing fine prints still rests upon the enterprise of relatively few galleries and print shops in the big cities, with the result that the artists are not too greatly subjected to the pressures of mass appeal; but on the other hand they do not make much of a living from their prints either. There is need for a concerted program of education to make fine prints better known, and to raise the public interest in them to the level of appreciation now enjoyed by music and literature. Above all, to spread the idea that a fine print is an original work of art and, as such, has a vitality of its own, a continuing source of esthetic satisfaction that far outlives the superficial appeal of photomechanical reproductions.

During the XX century, printmakers have been much concerned with technique and technical innovations. In all mediums technical manipulation has been developed and raised to new levels. Experiments have been made with materials other than wood, such as lucite and other synthetic products, for relief printing. Textures derived from impresses on soft grounds have been explored in wide variety by Atelier 17. Aquatint has been given a greater freedom of manipulation through the sugar-lift process. Printing by intaglio and by relief from the same plate have been combined to produce new effects. Encaustic or wax pigments, instead of the regular printing inks have been used to make color prints from only one plate (Milton Goldstein). The carbograph has been devised as a quick method for producing a mezzotint ground. Another old and little used method, the stencil, has been transformed into the serigraph with unlimited possibilities for color printing. And finally, as the latest word in our atomic age, there are "electron prints," developed by Caroline Durieux and H. E. Wheeler, that make use of radioactive isotopes as the image-making agent. All of this would indicate an overbalance of interest in technique and textures to the detriment of communication and ideas. Could it be that this concern with technique or with *minutiae*, this multiplicity and confusion of aim in contemporary printmaking, merely reflect the uncertainties and conflicting standards of value in our society at large? Such analogies can be strained too far. It remains true, however, that only when

3

an artist has nothing in particular to say, does he lavish so much of his energy upon technique and style.

At this mid-century mark one may say that the influence of Rembrandt on printmaking—so widespread for centuries—seems to have diminished considerably. Artists of today are inspired by theories of abstraction, expressionism, and surrealism; and the abstract vanguard has broken away completely from the tradition, dominant since the Renaissance, of the picture forming a window into an imaginative and idealized world, a perspectively ordered universe, still bearing some faint resemblance to Nature. In the new esthetic, pictures are constructed with flat or linear patterns or with abstract forms floating freely in space.

Today, then, the so-called modern movement reigns supreme. All youth speaks in a modern idiom; the older or conservative artists are definitely on the defensive. In the past decade the new movement has spread like wildfire in the United States, Europe, South America, and Japan. At the moment there is rivalry between the "humanists" and expressionists on the one hand and the non-objectivists and a new *avant-garde*, the abstract expressionists, on the other—but with abstraction and distortion taken for granted by all. Although creative individuality and experimentation are the order of the day, paradoxically enough a great deal of contemporary work is done under the external prompting of fad and fashion. There almost seems to be a coagulation into collective art groups, a compulsion to climb on board a band wagon. It is the rare artist who is willing or able to go it alone. With our accelerated facilities of communication and publication—"museums without walls"—influences travel fast; minor styles flourish and decline in bewildering rapidity. There seems to be almost more activity than meaning. Could it be that the painter puts too much emphasis on creative individuality and too little on communication and social responsibility? If the artist's voice goes unheeded today, is it because he speaks for himself alone and not for his fellow man? More than ever, the artist has lost touch with his public. If he chooses a big canvas upon which to wrestle with his creative soul, does it follow of necessity that the public should be concerned? In their use of symbols so personal as to become a private code, some extremist painters have practically become solipsists. It is, of course, theoretically possible for a solipsist, as one completely engrossed in his own world, to paint or draw solely for his own need or pleasure without concern for a public. A printmaker, however, can never be a solipsist, for a print implies a plural audience and a message.

The question arises whether the so-called modern movement is only a passing fashion to be supplanted by some unknown future style, or whether it is here to stay and grow perhaps in scope and influence. One is inclined to hazard the prophecy that it will endure, though perhaps in a modified form. An international style seems to be in the making. It is sometimes hard to tell whether an abstraction was made in Europe or North or South America. There have been other styles which have transcended national boundaries: the Gothic, for example, which endured for several centuries. Analogies from the past, however, can throw little light on our own present and future, both because the tempo of our civilization has accelerated so much more rapidly, and because there are no longer, as there were in the past, racial areas of unknown potential. The modern style, in its broadest aspect, seems on the way to becoming, if not universal, at

4

least international outside the communist orbit. What culture is independent and strong enough to withstand its widespread crystallization, even eventually behind the iron curtain? There may appear, from time to time, minute variations and manoeuvres backwards and forwards, but the main body apparently is proceeding toward a basic common denominator. This common denominator, insofar as it will be expressed in art, may well have an abstract basis for several reasons. Photography has effectively eliminated the mirror image of man and nature as the goal of art. Our scientific civilization, as Roderick Seidenberg has pointed out, tends more and more to displace Nature and create its own environment—based not on the diversified aspects of Nature but upon the uniform laws of science—resulting in the subordination both of natural background and of individual idiosyncrasy. Thus the language of modern art, by reason of its abstract and impersonal forms, seems appropriate to express that trend toward collective uniformity which appears to be one of the characteristics of modern society everywhere. Barring miracles or cataclysms, an abstract art, not necessarily solely geometric—emphasizing the universal and gradually overlaying national idiosyncrasies and the conventions derived from Nature—may eventually become the art of the future. This, admittedly, is the long, long view.

Meanwhile, much has happened since the last edition of this work. Some distinguished artists have passed away, and numerous new stars have appeared on the horizon. Among the obituaries should be noted those of Matisse, Léger, Ensor, Beckmann, Orozco, Sloan and Marin. In England there has been a revival of interest in color lithography through the work of Henry Moore, Sutherland, Colquhoun, MacBryde, and Piper. In Italy such artists as Giorgio Morandi (in etching), Massimo Campigli, Marino Marini, and Renzo Vespignani (in lithography) have begun to achieve international renown; in Switzerland, likewise, Hans Fischer and the intensely personal sculptor Alberto Giacometti; in Holland, W. Ellenbas, M. C. Escher, and H. van Kruiningen. The Norwegian, Rolf Nesch, has produced striking effects through the use of welded metal plates for intaglio printing. The international style has found spokesmen in France and Germany in such artists as Alfred Manessier, Gustave Singier, Hans Hartung, and Fritz Winter. The influence of Kandinsky seems to be growing as one of the prime movers in the development of non-objective art.

In Japan there seems to be a resurgence of activity in printmaking, stimulated largely and influenced by Western Art. Among the leaders of the movement may be cited Hiratsuka, Onchi, Munakata, Saito, Sekino, and Kitaoka. Mention should also be made of the Chinese artist, Zao Wou-Ki, residing in Paris, whose prints likewise show Western influence, notably that of Paul Klee.

In the United States many new voices are to be heard. Three of the most powerful in the field of woodcut are Antonio Frasconi, Misch Kohn, and Leonard Baskin. To these should be added that of Adja Yunkers, now residing in this country. Other artists working in wood are Bernard Reder, Worden Day, Louise Kruger, Seong Moy, Helen Siegl, and Carol Summers. The practitioners of the intaglio processes are many; there is space to name but a few: Milton Goldstein, Edward Colker, Morris Blackburn, Karl Schrag, Rudy Pozzatti, Ynez Johnston, André Racz, Sam Kaner, Lee Chesney, and Gabor Peterdi. Among new lithographers may be cited June Wayne, Ralston Crawford, Jerome Kaplan, and Martin

5

Jackson. The imaginative and technically proficient printmaker, Harold Paris, is working effectively in all mediums. André Girard has produced several books entirely in serigraphy, notably *Heraclite*, one of the most distinguished illustrated books of the XX century. Others who have worked fruitfully in serigraphy are Dorr Bothwell, Louis Bunce, Sister Mary Corita, Henry Mark, and Dean Meeker. Certain mature painters have started to make prints with noteworthy results: Franklin Watkins and Karl Zerbe (woodcut), Eugene Berman (lithograph) and Ben Shahn (serigraph). The above outline represents a brief and necessarily limited review of new personalities in the graphic arts. Most of the artists mentioned in the body of the book are still busy producing. The American school of printmaking seems to be one of the most vital in the field today.

Such, then, is the state of graphic art at the mid-century mark. Printmaking can be said to be flourishing among the artists—if not so vigorously for the public at large. With the artists it is necessarily a labor of love; and one can ask for no more favorable atmosphere for creation. In the more public art world there may be turmoil and confusion; controversies may rage and manifestoes be issued. Conflicts, after all, are a sign of life, and manifestoes a sign of youth. Youth, producing the while, will grow up and become the embattled conservative to the vanguard of another generation. In the field of prints these alarms and excursions somehow seem more muted and less acute. The extremes seem easier to take in small doses. The printmakers—most of them level-headed and mature beyond their years—go along on their diverse ways, giving out the best that is in them.

Sources and credits for individual illustrations are indicated (gratefully) in the picture index. In the preparation of the present work and of the original edition, I have had help from many persons and many sources. My sincerest thanks go to them all for their generous and unstinting cooperation.

CARL ZIGROSSER

The Philadelphia Museum of Art, 1956

6

Contents

8

1. Introduction

THIS is the story of certain scraps of paper—scraps of paper, some old, some new, with curious marks of ink on them, but rare and precious in men's eyes, scraps of paper treasured in museums and cherished by collectors in many lands. These prints, for such they are, must indeed have something provocative and mysterious about them despite their ubiquity and matter-of-fact presence: they seem to be woven into the very fabric of our culture and civilization. What is this mysterious something that enhances so greatly the value of prints? It is not the intrinsic value of the paper and ink, for that is negligible. It is their power to move the beholder, not only to amuse or instruct him but also to stir the wellsprings of his being, to speak to him poignantly of his inmost thoughts and feelings, of religion, of sex, of war, of pride and pomp and power, of freedom and justice, of order and beauty. Prints share this power of evocation and inspiration with other great forms of visual art, but with the added virtue that, the print being a democratic form, its examples can be owned and enjoyed by many instead of a few.

Prints have had many apologists and defenders, but none more charming than the anonymous author of *Sculptura-Historico-Technica*, or *The History and Art of Ingraving*, of 1747:

When I reflect on the Usefulness of this Art, I am surprized to find so few Gentlemen professed Admirers of it. It requires a large Fortune to make a fine Collection of Paintings, and great Judgment to avoid Imposition, and understand their Beauties; but Prints are adapted to all Ages, all Ranks of Men, and all Fortunes; they cost much less than Paintings, the Knowledge of them is more easily attained; and they comprehend all Sorts of Subjects, they are equally as useful as entertaining. . . .

Prints divert Youth, and instruct them at the same Time, by the lively

9

Impression they make on their Minds; and this Instruction is not only more readily received but is more durable than that conveyed by Words. If you have a Child learn any Passage in Sacred or Profane History, by amusing him with a Representation of it, and explaining the Subject, he will rarely forget the Impression the different Characters that compose it will make on him. . . .

Prints are also as useful as entertaining; they represent absent things to us, as if they were present; they convey us instantly, without Hazard or Expence, into the most distant Countries, and make us as well acquainted with them as with our own; they communicate to us the Knowledge of many beautiful Objects in those Countries, which we must have been ignorant of, without their Assistance; and make us Contemporaries (in a manner) with the greatest Men of past Ages by giving us their lively Resemblance. . . .

Nothing is more proper to form a Taste than Prints: they give us a Tincture of the fine Arts; they assist us to arrive at the Knowledge of Paintings; for if we examine them attentively, they make us easily discover the different Manner affected by each School and Master. . . .

Lastly, there is hardly any Subject, with Regard to which we cannot either acquire some Knowledge, or enlarge that we already have, by the Help of this noble Art.

When our old author mentioned that prints can be both useful and entertaining, he hit upon a characteristic which distinguishes prints from most of the other forms of the visual arts—their potential duality. Prints, like literature and the printed word, can serve both science and beauty, in Coleridge's famous distinction between science and poetry, as the communication of truth and the communication of immediate pleasure (in its widest sense as emotive power); or, as Erasmus put it in praising the prints of Dürer, the natural aspect of a thing and the perfect symmetry and harmony. I am far from asserting that all the visual arts have a literary or didactic or scientific purpose—they have conventions peculiarly their own—but the graphic arts * are on the border line between science and art, and function in both. Fine prints as a class can serve beauty in a timeless way. They have an intrinsic appeal entirely

* The term, graphic art, is used strictly in this book to mean art forms produced by printing methods.

apart from the question as to whether they were made in the fifteenth or the twentieth century. They possess uniqueness, magic, a spiritual impress, the stamp of vivid personality, a singing quality of line or mass, some telling economy of expression that satisfies in a flash of immediate comprehension. But just as a work of art can splendidly evoke almost the whole gamut of the emotions, so it can also diagram or illustrate an idea. It can organize a group of facts into a telling picture. It can add to our knowledge in a graphic way. It can document contemporary life. Indeed, much of our knowledge of the past, its life, customs, manners, fashions, comes from the prints and illustrations of the time. In this respect photography has made an enormous contribution since its perfection less than a hundred years ago. In the past, prints were the only medium for illustrating flowers, birds, and other forms of natural history, maps and city views, pattern designs for lace, furniture, costumes, goldsmith's work, and all kinds of ornament in applied art and architecture. Graphic art is also the accepted vehicle for satire, caricature, humor, propaganda—all the various forms of comment and persuasion in pictures.

But what are prints anyway? The word, "prints," like charity, covers a multitude of sins. To some people prints mean mechanical reproductions in color, used for decoration, which one can buy, neatly framed, in drug or department stores. To others prints are the innocuous etchings that are given again and again as wedding presents. To still others they are the photographs that are pasted in snapshot albums. To others, again, they are textiles with designs applied in color, such as chintzes or cotton and silk dress goods. Prints, especially when prefaced by the word "public," are sometimes used to mean newspapers and magazines. In a specialized sense, however, fine prints usually denote the etchings, woodcuts, and lithographs which artists make for esthetic or other reasons. They are usually called fine prints to distinguish them from prints in general. All of the above meanings are strictly correct, for as a matter of fact, "print" stands for anything that is printed. That the word has so many and so varied connotations, merely emphasizes the extent that prints have permeated and become part of our daily life. Indeed it would be amusing to speculate on how barren life today would become were all prints removed. All books and newspapers, all of photography including the movies, most of the intellectual life, science, philosophy, social science, most of music except that played by ear or from manuscript, and most of graphic art would disappear.

The graphic arts, which include fine prints, illustrated books, and photography, are a great cultural force in our lives; indeed they rank as one of the three principal spheres of art activity in general, the other two being the art of personal adornment, costume, etcetera, and the arts that cluster around the home or around public buildings (including churches), painting, sculpture, furniture, and all the applied arts. To put it in a catch phrase, art is focused at three essential points—the Body, the Building, and the Book. Practically every branch of art can find its expression and use within these three categories. Since the Middle Ages, with the development of the democratic idea, the graphic arts, summarized in the last great B, the Book, have become a major art. It is only in recent times, however, that the real importance of prints has been recognized, when it was discovered how closely their development coincided with the rise and development of the bourgeois or middle class. When the graphic arts will have become so widespread as to touch and speak to every man, woman, and child in the community, then it may be said that they truly have become the art of the people.

Just as people in speaking of prints often mean quite different things, so also, when referring to fine prints in the specialized sense, they like them for various and sundry reasons. There is no doubt that there are many different incentives to own prints, some of which have little to do with art or esthetic standards. There is, for example, the incentive to own religious images or icons, which was most powerful during the Middle Ages. Sometimes a person likes a print because it recalls pleasant memories of a holiday spent abroad or of a hunting or fishing trip. Sometimes a person collects prints because it is the thing to do. (There used to be a saying current that no wedding was legal unless a print by a certain etcher was present among the gifts to the happy couple.) Sometimes, again, because a person sees a picture in the possession of another whose taste he values. Sometimes, following Veblen's theory of conspicuous consumption, because a person desires to show that he can afford expensive things. Sometimes, a person buys a picture because he thinks, or has been told, that it is a good investment, and will enhance in value, just as stocks and bonds sometimes do. But, sometimes a person owns a print just because it appeals to his esthetic sense: because he gets a unique pleasure from a particular pattern of black and white, or a delicious bit of fine draughtsmanship. Or because he is moved in a special way by the intensity or grandeur of a visual idea. Or because he is amused by a portrayal, whether benevolent or malicious, of some aspect of the *Comedie Humaine*. Because, in short, some element in the picture haunts his memory like a phrase of poetry or a strain of music.

Finally the critics by their varied approaches contribute their testimony to the conclusion that art is not any one thing but a vastly intricate complex as elusive as the secret of life itself. Most critics, sitting in judgment on the art of the past and present with one or another of their measuring rods, remind one of the fable of the seven blind men and the elephant. Each one of them was sure that he was right in his report about the elephant, and strangely enough he was right—they were all right. A work of art, like a fact of life, has a certain being of its own—it just *is*. If it be great and vital enough, it will have a long life, and each generation will look at it anew and interpret its virtues and defects according to the prevailing taste of its time.

The pictures which make up the main portion of this book, form an anthology, as it were, of ten centuries of fine prints. Out of the millions of prints that have been made in the course of time, six hundred and two have been chosen for reproduction. It is hoped that they can be looked at with pleasure apart from the text as a portable, so to speak, exhibition of art. The groupings were made with a view to harmonious and significant arrangements on the page. In the selection an attempt has been made to maintain a balance between two different attitudes: that of the historian who searches for what is typical, average, and expressive of the time, and that of the artist who is interested in what is unusual, heightened, and timeless. In some rare instances, it is believed, these seemingly divergent aims have been united in one and the same print, that is at once timeless and nobly expressive of its time. Furthermore the attempt has been made, as far as it is possible in the brief space

13

allotted, to project prints against the background of history, to synchronize their production with that of the other arts and sciences, with the events of war and statecraft, economic and social life; in short to try to see them as their contemporaries saw them as well as in the perspective of time. There is a give-and-take between the artist and his age: he leaves an impress on his contemporaries, and contemporary influences leave their impress on him. All this is mirrored dramatically in his works, more especially in such a medium as the print, which, being widespread and popular, reflects more accurately contemporary conditions. Two great factors have molded the actions of all men, economic conditions and ideology, stomach and mind. These inevitable strands of warp and woof are as evident in the tapestry of art as they are in the other activities of life. Art is one of the noblest of man's endeavors, but it is not mysterious; it is still essentially human, the product of his hand and brain.

II

Just as the connoisseur of food is interested in cook books, in how the delectable dishes are prepared, so the print lover is interested in the technique of the graphic arts, the "cookery" of fine prints. Therefore it might be well to explain briefly how prints are made. There are three general methods of reproducing designs: the first the "relief" method usually employed on wood; the second the "intaglio" or "incised" method on metal such as copper or zinc, or for very brief periods on iron or steel; the third the "planographic or chemical" method on stone or zinc or aluminum. The relief method or woodcut is the oldest in point of time. The technique is relatively simple. The artist takes a block of wood, cut along the length of the tree and planed smooth, and proceeds to cut away all those portions of his design that he does not intend to print black. When he has finished cutting on the wood, his drawing stands complete in relief with the rest of the block cut down to a depth of about one eighth of an inch. The artist then inks the surface of the block, lays a sheet of paper over it, runs it through a press, and the composition appears complete on the paper. The earliest woodcuts were printed not in a press but by rubbing with a spoon-like

14

instrument on the back of the paper in the way that all Japanese prints are made. In early times too there generally was a division of labor, the design being drawn on the wood by the artist and the cutting away being done by a professional woodcutter.

There is a variation and development of woodcut technique called wood engraving. In this instance the artist works on a block cut from the cross-section of a tree (thus avoiding the difficulties of cutting against the grain) and uses among others a burin or engraving tool which makes a white line against a background of black. There is some confusion and difference of opinion as to the exact meaning of woodcut and wood engraving. Some hold that the difference lies in the artist's fundamental conception of his picture: in a woodcut he conceives of the picture in terms of black lines against a background of white; in a wood engraving in terms of white lines against a background of black. It sometimes happens that the artist uses both methods in the same picture, and then it becomes difficut to say which predominates. The other school holds that the difference between the two lies in the technique. Woodcuts are printed from blocks sawed along the grain and cut with knives and gouges; whereas wood engravings are printed from end-grain blocks cut with a burin. This classification as least has the virtue of not being ambiguous; the artist cannot combine end-grain and along-the-grain on the same block. But it is not always easy to tell what kind of wood was used just by looking at a print. Dürer's woodblocks and Japanese prints are typical woodcuts. Bewick's blocks and Urs Graf's *Standard-Bearer* are examples of wood engraving. An early development of wood engraving is seen in the prints in the "dotted manner" or *manière criblée*. In these white line engravings, the solid blacks are often broken up by means of little white dots executed with a punch. Most of them were printed from metal blocks, such as copper, tin, bronze, or lead. Indeed the distinction between the two great processes of relief and intaglio lies not so much in the material as in the way of printing. Eric Gill has printed etchings, or rather engravings, from wood blocks, and William Blake etched copper plates for his "Songs of Innocence and Experience" in such a way that they could be printed as woodblocks. Still another variation of woodcut technique is seen in the "chiaroscuro" prints perfected at the beginning of the sixteenth century. This form of color printing involves the use of several blocks, a black and white key block, and one or more tone blocks in which the high-lights are cut out in order to increase the range of tonal relations.

The class of intaglio print includes metal engraving, etching, dry-point, mezzotint, stipple engraving, aquatint, and soft ground etching. In engravings the lines are incised into copper or other soft metal by means of a burin or graving tool. The technique of etching was per-fected early in the sixteenth century in order to lighten the labor of cutting into the metal with the burin. It was discovered that it was possible to dig out the lines by chemical means instead of by the sweat of one's brow. Therefore over the polished surface of the metal, a thin coating of an acid-resisting ground (consisting largely of wax) is laid; the artist makes a drawing upon the plate with a needle and thus lays bare the surface of the copper. The plate is then laid in a bath of acid (commonly nitric) which attacks the metal wherever it is exposed. It is this method of "etching" lines in metal that gives the process its name. One great advantage of etching over engraving is the greater freedom it gives in the drawing of the lines, since all manner of way-ward and curved lines can be laid, which are exceedingly difficult to execute with the burin. Furthermore by "stopping out" some of the lines with an acid-resisting varnish and again inserting in the acid bath, it is possible to vary the biting and consequently the depth and quality of the line.

The printing principle of an engraving or etching is exactly the reverse of a woodcut. In a woodcut the lines stand out in relief and become the surface which is inked and printed. In an etching or engrav-ing the lines are incised in the metal; the ink is forced into these lines and the surface of the metal is wiped clean. When a dampened sheet of paper is laid on the plate and the whole run through a press under considerable pressure, the paper is forced into the lines and picks up the ink therein; and the whole design is printed on the paper and be-comes an impression, or proof as it is sometimes called, of an original etching. In an impression of an etching or engraving, the lines are ever so slightly raised above the surface of the paper, as can be proved by running the finger very lightly over the proof (though this action will grieve the true print lover!). This fact and the noticeable impression which the edge of the copper plate works upon the paper, called the plate mark, are among the features which help to distinguish an etching or engraving from the woodcut processes. Etching is primarily a line technique, that is to say the etcher builds up his design by means of lines bitten at various depths. To amplify the technical means at the etcher's command, the Frenchman, Le Prince, invented in the late eighteenth century, the process known as aquatint. The technique is complicated but the principle is simple. By its use the etcher is enabled to draw not only with lines but also with washes or areas of tone with varying degrees of dark and light, thus adding a certain richness and variety of tonal color to his linear composition. Since both are etched with acid, it is easy to combine pure etching and aquatint. Aquatint was used to hold and define areas of colored ink in French eighteenth century color prints; but even before its invention, roulettes, moulettes, and similar instruments were used to produce grained surfaces for the same purpose.

There is still another intaglio method designed to reproduce tones and not lines, namely mezzotint. A copper plate is covered with a multitude of tiny indentations made with a special instrument called a rocker. The plate if it were inked at this stage would print uniformly black. The engraver by means of special instruments scrapes away and burnishes out at will the minute indentations to establish his high lights, and working from dark to light, gradually creates a complete pattern of light and dark tones. It is a process particularly adapted to reproducing oil paintings, and was used almost exclusively for that purpose. It is printed like an engraving but does not yield as many impressions. Another technique, used largely to reproduce drawings and paintings, is stipple engraving or, similarly, engraving in the crayon manner. It is a variation of etching in which the design is built up by minute dots produced by means of a roulette and similar instruments. It can reproduce the texture and grain of a crayon drawing with great fidelity, but owing to its softness and lack of definition (even the lines are made up of tiny dots like a modern halftone) it found its widest use in sentimental and "fancy" subjects. Still another variation is soft ground etching. A special and rather sticky ground is laid on the copper plate and upon this is laid a sheet of paper or silk or other textile. The lines are drawn over this, and when this is lifted off, the ground sticks to it wherever it was drawn upon. The plate is then bitten in the regular way. By this means a considerable variation in the textures of line work can be produced. It is sometimes used in conjunction with aquatint since its rather crumbly line is in keeping with the grained surface of aquatint. Lift-up soft ground can be used to produce areas as well as lines in varying textures. The possibilities of this method have been explored in recent times.

There is another modification of engraving called drypoint. Where the lines of an engraving are cut into the metal with a burin, in drypoint they are scratched into the surface with a steel needle or diamond point. In the process a furrow or shaving of metal is raised beside the line, called the burr, which catches and holds more ink than the ordinary engraved line and imparts the rich and velvety black characteristic of the drypoint line. This burr soon wears down and few good impressions can be pulled unless the plate is steel-faced. The technique was known in early times, Dürer and the Master of the Amsterdam Cabinet having both made drypoints, but Rembrandt was the first to use the medium with a full realization of its possibilities. Drypoint is often used in conjunction with etching to give added richness and color to a composition.

The third great graphic method is lithography. It makes use of still another principle of printing. Its lines are neither incised in metal nor raised in relief on wood. It is called surface or chemical printing, and was invented around the beginning of the nineteenth century by a German, Aloys Senefelder. The process is based upon the well-known antipathy of grease and water. The artist draws with a greasy crayon on a slab of special limestone (found only in Bavaria) which has been grained to a requisite degree of fineness. When the artist has finished his drawing, the stone is turned over to a lithographer for printing. By a series of chemical steps which it will not be necessary to elaborate here, the greasy content becomes fixed in the stone. The stone is then moistened with a sponge. Wherever there is a greasy spot or mark the water will be repelled, but everywhere else the stone will absorb water and become damp. The stone is now ready for printing. A greasy ink is rolled over the surface. Wherever there is a greasy mark the ink will take, wherever the stone is damp and clear the greasy ink will not take. A sheet of paper is placed on the stone and the whole run through the press, with the result that an exact replica of the drawing appears on the paper. A certain kind of zinc plate can be used in place of the lithographic stone with equal success. Lithography is an exceedingly flexible medium with an enormous range of effects; lines with crayon or pen, washes, stump work, tonal values of all kinds can be rendered with fidelity and subtlety. **For this reason many modern artists use lithography** in preference to the other graphic media.

Still another duplicating principle has been used sporadically throughout the ages, and has recently been perfected for artists' use with such efficient simplicity that it bids fair to become of major importance. It is the "stencil", or hole in a masking surface. If any shape is cut in the masking material (such as a sheet of thin copper or celluloid or even paper) and if that sheet is laid over a piece of paper, and if some pigment is brushed over the whole, an exact replica of the shape of the hole will appear on the paper beneath. This method, called *pochoir* in French and *Schablone* in German, has been used for the coloring of prints in quantity for many centuries in Europe and China (the red and yellow colors on illustration 542 were probably applied through stencils). The crucial improvement of the process came about by fastening the master stencil to a piece of silk stretched on a wooden frame. The open mesh of the silk allowed the pigment to flow through freely, yet the silk, wherever attached to the stencil, gave it firm support on the delicate strips and promontaries which otherwise were easily torn. By this device one could anchor an island of opaque in a sea of open mesh—which was impossible to do in a regular stencil. The essential characteristic of the cut stencil—and its great limitation—was sharpness of outline. Subtle blending of tone and freehand irregularity of outline were impossible to achieve. The next great step in improvement was to dispense with the cut stencil entirely by creating its equivalent directly on the screen itself in the form of an opaque coating of glue or lacquer. The artist, for instance, draws his design on the silk with lithographic tusche or crayon, coats the whole screen with glue, and then dissolves out the tusche with a refined form of kerosene. By this last step the glue which covers the tusche areas is also disintegrated, because it no longer has any support; and thus a replica of the original design appears in the open mesh of the silk, bounded on all sides by the opaque coating of glue. Another method for creating stencils directly on the screen has been perfected by Otto Linstead. It makes use of the property, possessed by potassium bichromate, of hardening upon exposure to light. The drawing is made on the screen with opaque crayon or ink; the screen is coated on the reverse side with glue mixed with bichromate, and exposed to light. The parts unprotected by the drawing will harden, whereas the protected parts will be soluble in hot water, thus creating the stencil. Finer lines and detail can be obtained by this method, also areas of textural variation by a further extension of the rayograph principle. In all methods the registration of successive color separations is a relatively simple problem. The techniques of silk screen stencil printing as adapted for artists' use have been given a distinctive name—serigraphy, and the finished prints are called serigraphs.

One final word on the use of the word, "original." Since it is used in two different senses, confusion sometimes ensues. It is used as an adjective in contradiction to "reproductive." An original etching is one which the artist has conceived and executed himself. A reproductive etching is one in which the etcher has copied another artist's design or painting. This distinction has lost much of its force in the last fifty years since photography has taken over the reproductive function of prints. In any case the distinction is invidious because some so-called reproductive engravings, by Raimondi after Raphael for example, are infinitely superior to a multitude of original etchings by mediocre artists. When used as a noun, original refers specifically to a print. Some people have the mistaken notion that all prints are copies of some hidden and mysterious original. Every single impression of a woodcut, etching, or lithograph is an "original," the final and complete embodiment of the artist's intention, of which the plate, the paper and the ink are the preliminary steps. The miracle of the process is that there are not one but many originals—the incarnation of the democratic ideal.

20

2. The End of Gothic

DURING the fifteenth century—as far as it is mirrored in the history of prints—one great epoch ended and another began. In the northern countries, France, Germany, and Flanders, the Gothic era ended and the Renaissance began; in Italy the Renaissance was in full bloom. In one sense, however, the classifications of Late Gothic and High Renaissance are relatively minor distinctions: the very idea of making prints, a cheap multiplication of originals, like the idea of printing from movable types, was an event of the greatest cultural importance, and one that marked the transition between the medieval and the modern point of view. "The Gothic sun," as Victor Hugo said, "set behind the colossal press at Mainz." It was during the fifteenth century that both woodcuts and copper engravings in any quantity began to be made and printed and sold.

It is interesting to speculate why the idea of making prints should have been carried to a practical conclusion at that particular period in the annals of European history. It was not that the idea or the technique of engraving was a new one. There exist incised drawings by primitive man on mammoth tusks capable, when inked, of producing prints in our sense of the word. Likewise the Greeks sometimes engraved designs on the back of their bronze or silver mirrors which could easily serve as printing plates. And there are examples of Romanesque art such as the famous Chandelier of the Emperor Barbarossa at Aix-la-Chapelle of the twelfth century, parts of which contain metal plates with incised designs, as if made to order for the production of engravings. About a century ago when this chandelier was taken down to be cleaned, some one conceived the idea of inking the plates and striking off a small number of impressions from them. One of these prints, the *Nativity*, in circular form is reproduced in this book (illustration 142). The result might easily be taken for a true engraving in Romanesque style some three centuries before the earliest known engraving. Likewise, the technique of designing and cutting a wood block had already been perfected for the printing of textiles. There exist Coptic textiles of the sixth century which are stamped with wood blocks (illustration 107). Printed textiles were common in the Middle Ages. Cennino Cennini describes the technique in his *Book of Art* at the end of the fourteenth century.

One of the chief reasons why prints were not produced in the twelfth century was the fact that there was no cheap and efficient reproducing medium such as paper. Paper, to be sure, was known in Europe at the time. The earliest extant document on paper in Europe is a deed by King Roger of Sicily written in Arabic and Latin and dated 1109. Paper is officially recorded as having been invented in China in the year 105. It remained a Chinese secret until its manufacture in Samarkand in 757 and in Bagdad in 793 through knowledge gained from Chinese prisoners. This knowledge was later transmitted to the Saracens in Spain in 1150. The first paper-mill in France was established at Hérault in 1189, in Italy at Fabriano in 1276, in Germany at Nuremberg in 1391. Much of the paper used in Europe, however, was still imported from the Saracen mills in Spain and Damascus, and it was not until the middle of the fifteenth century that paper was in general use in Europe. "There were few in Europe who could read," as Carter points out, "and the demand for a cheaper writing material, until the advent of printing, was small. It was the coming of paper that made the invention of printing possible, yet it was the invention of printing that made the use of paper general."

Thus it is to be seen that a plentiful supply of a cheap reproducing material such as paper was a conditioning factor in any widespread production of woodcuts and engravings. There was, however, still another factor to be considered, namely the demand on the part of the people. In the early Middle Ages the standard of living was very low. In this age of scarcity there was little demand for such marginal luxuries as pictures or the written word. In so far as a demand for pictures existed it was satisfied by the church, which was the meeting place and treasure-house of the whole community. Most of the people were scattered on the

22

land; very little of the population was concentrated in towns. Furthermore there was little trade. Each community was a self-contained economic unit. It produced, with considerable effort, all that it required for subsistence; there was no surplus. It is difficult for us in this day and age to visualize such a state of society. There were no books or newspapers, no ready-made clothes, and few utensils, no shops or stores, few artisans who practiced their trade exclusively. There was practically no money: almost all trade was effected by barter. There was very little travel. The roads were bad, and there were many knights and nobles who made common practice of out-and-out brigandage, or, with some show of legality, of the exaction of tolls. A great many of the people could not travel at all since they were bound to the land as serfs or tenants. The standard of living in the manors and castles was more sumptuous but not much higher.

It is small wonder then that in such a milieu there was small demand and no place for "art in the home." There were, however, several major historical developments which eventually succeeded in breaking up the stagnation of the feudal or manorial system. One of these was the Crusades; by increasing travel they introduced new ideas and cultivated a taste for the comforts and luxuries of the Orient. Another was the rise of Free Cities, which either retained or acquired exemption from feudal obligations incumbent on the peasantry. Concomitant with the growth of Free Cities was a vast extension of trade both with the Orient and with various parts of Europe. The Italian cities, Genoa, Pisa, Amalfi, and chiefly Venice, grew rich through the Crusades and the oriental trade. The cities of Flanders, chiefly Bruges, were the meeting place of the northern and southern maritime trade, and at the same time the center of the woolen-weaving industry of Europe. Augsburg, Nuremberg, Ulm, Basel, Mainz, Frankfurt, and Cologne were cities that waxed prosperous along the overland trade routes from Venice to the north. All of these engaged in manufacture and trade—activities of the middleman as opposed to the agrarian and producer-consumer economy of feudalism. Their merchant and artisan guilds became wealthy and powerful, and their citizens acquired a taste for art and other luxuries. Albrecht

23

Dürer, in his diary of his journey to the Netherlands in 1520, recounts how he was received in Bruges in the height of its prosperity:

Then they prepared a banquet for me, and I went thence with them to their guild hall; there were many honorable men gathered together, goldsmiths, painters, and merchants, and they made me sup with them and they gave me presents and sought my acquaintance and did me great honor.

And thus he describes a festival in Antwerp:

The Sunday after the Feast of the Assumption I saw the great procession of Our Lady's Church at Antwerp, where the whole town was gathered together, with all the trades and professions, and each was dressed in his best according to his rank; every guild and profession had its sign by which it might be recognized. Between the companies were carried great costly gold pole-candlesticks and their long old Frankish silver trumpets; and there were many pipers and drummers in the German fashion; all were loudly and noisily blown and beaten. I saw the procession pass along the street, spread far apart so that they took up much space crossways, but close behind one another: goldsmiths, painters, stonecutters, broiderers, sculptors, joiners, carpenters, sailors, fishermen, butchers, leather-workers, clothmakers, bakers, tailors, shoemakers, and all kinds of craftsmen and workmen who work for their livelihood. There were likewise shopkeepers and merchants with their assistants of all sorts. After them came the marksmen with their guns, bows, and cross-bows; then the horsemen and foot soldiers; then came a fine troop of very gallant men, nobly and splendidly costumed.

It was in such free and vigorous city life that the practice of printmaking in the North took hold and spread rapidly. Prints, being produced in relatively large quantities, require, if not trading, at least an organized distribution over a wide area. Furthermore a prosperous middle class, which made up the urban population, was then and for many centuries to come the best customer for prints. The peasant and laborer never had any margin above subsistence to buy more than an occasional religious image. And the nobles and the court circles, notably the Burgundian court of the fifteenth century and the rulers of the Italian cities, bestowed their greatest patronage on painting, sculpture, miniature painting, and architecture.

Of the two great genres of printmaking the woodblock was the

24

first to be developed. Its actual beginnings are lost in the obscurity and anonymity which surround most popular art. Popular art, the obvious and omnipresent thing, the cheap common object, is generally quite literally worn out in use; little value is attached to it at the time and it is preserved only by some happy chance. Those prints which have come down through the ages have sometimes been found in out-of-the-way places, pasted inside the bindings of old books, or pasted on doors and walls like wall paper. Occasionally they are found pasted on the insides of little trunks or traveling cases (illustration 133). These boxes, as Hind suggests, were probably used by lawyers or merchants for their documents or accounts, or by priests to carry their breviaries and other requisites on their journeys. It is obvious that with such great lacunae in the record, the history of the woodcut in its origins is hard to determine. It is probable, however, that the idea of printing impressions on paper to supply a demand for a cheap multiplication of designs first gained currency around the beginning of the fifteenth century. And demand there was, on two separate counts. One was for playing cards. Although there are no examples of woodcut playing cards extant before about 1450, cards by their nature being apt to be worn out, there is every reason to suppose that there was a flourishing production of playing cards from the beginning of the century in Germany and Italy. An example dating from the second half of the fifteenth century and signed by J. de Dale of Lyon is reproduced as illustration 56. The more primitive cuts were in outline only and were designed to be colored either by hand or through stencils. An early representation of card playing, with a glimpse of the cards themselves, is given in illustration 6, from a book printed in Augsburg in 1472 by Gunther Zainer.

The second great demand for prints was for religious images, pictures of the saints, illustrations of the life of the Virgin or of Christ. Some of the early woodcuts were probably produced in monasteries by the monks themselves. The monasteries enjoyed immunity from guild restrictions, and at the beginning there undoubtedly was opposition by the guilds of artists and illuminators to a technique which threatened their livelihood. To a certain extent printmaking in these early times labored under the stigma of being a counterfeit or illegitimate art. The

25

great bulk of the work, however, was either made by regular artists by direct commission from monasteries or produced with an eye to the religious market at the great centers of print production, such as the cities of Ulm, Augsburg, Bamberg, Nuremberg, Cologne, Dijon, Avignon, Bruges, Salzburg, etcetera. The religious orders and the churches, in any case, were among the chief customers for such prints. Hind quotes Luther's complaint against the Pope, in his pamphlet, *An den christlichen Adel deutscher Nation:* that he granted the revenues of a convent to some cardinal, who would leave a single monk in charge, one of whose chief duties was to sell pictures to pilgrims. The artists and printers also sold directly to the people at their shops or at the fairs. Dürer, when in Venice, wrote back to his friend, Pirkheimer: "Now I commend myself to you, and tell my mother to be ready to sell at the Crown Fair."

A characteristic example of primitive woodcut is reproduced herewith as illustration 19. The Buxheim *St. Christopher* was for a long time famous as the first example of a woodcut actually bearing a date, namely 1423, though further research has discovered an earlier print, the Brussels *Madonna* bearing the date 1418. It was discovered in the binding of a book in the Carthusian monastery of Buxheim and is probably of Bavarian origin. It is a dramatic rendering of the Christopher legend and is full of simple and naive charm. In addition to the date below there is a Latin inscription which may be translated as follows: "On whatsoever day thou hast seen Christopher's face, on that day, to be sure, thou shalt not die an evil death." This inscription furnishes a clue to the extraordinary popularity of images of St. Christopher: the sight of him was talismanic and insured if not against death, at least against an unshrived and unsanctified death—according to popular superstition. It is interesting to discover in a painting of the Annunciation by Robert Campin, the Master of Flémalle, in the Brussels Museum, a print of St. Christopher hanging (with charming disregard for historical sequence) over the chimney. It illustrates the way in which these prints, unmatted and unframed, were used in the home, and also demonstrates why so few of them have survived. The anachronism of displaying a print of St. Christopher in a room where the Archangel Gabriel is foretelling to

26

the Virgin the miraculous birth of Christ is characteristic of the age. This disregard of the unities of time or place is mirrored in our print of St. Christopher itself: various incidents in the life and miracle of St. Christopher are telescoped into one picture. The intention of the artist was not realistic but symbolic. The realistic touches that do appear in the picture are in the nature of corroborative or decorative detail. This approach to the solution of an artistic problem has been widely used by artists of all ages, including the twentieth century. Another very early woodcut, possibly around 1420-1430, is the *Madonna surrounded by Saints* (illustration 133a). Its rounded forms are characteristic of the earlier phase of fifteenth century Gothic art. The *Onuphrius* and the *Nativity* (illustrations 132, 133) are examples of single woodcuts of the second half of the fifteenth century. Still another "*Einblattdruck*" is reproduced, more realistic and satiric in subject matter, and executed on metal in the dotted print manner. It probably dates from about 1490 of German provenance. The subject is a satire on *Gossip during the Celebration of Mass* (illustration 18). The technique of *manière criblée* undoubtedly grew out of the metal worker's use of punches of various sizes and shapes to build up a design, often of great richness and delicacy. The subject is unusual and is executed with great spirit.

The so-called block-books form an interesting phase in the development of the woodcut. In block-books text and pictures were combined in one impression, and the lettering was cut out of the same block as the picture. At one time the importance of these books was greatly exaggerated when it was thought that they formed a connecting link between the graphic arts and the printing of books. Subsequent research has demonstrated, however, that the perfection of the art of printing proceeded quite independently of the block-books. As works of art they have relatively little merit, with the possible exception of the *Ars Moriendi* and the *Canticum Canticorum* (illustration 29). They were nevertheless very popular in their day and many successive editions have been recorded.

Not so many years after the invention of printing, the printers saw the possibility of using woodcuts for illustrating their books and thus

27

competing more advantageously with the illuminated manuscript. From about 1470 on, woodcut books began to appear with increasing frequency in all the leading centers of book production. William Morris has written with appreciation of these early books:

The invention of printing books and the use of woodblocks for book ornament in place of hand-painting, though it belongs to the period of the degradation of medieval art, gave an opportunity to the Germans to regain the place which they had lost in the art of book decoration during the thirteenth and fourteenth centuries. This opportunity they took with vigor and success, and by means of it put forth works which showed the best and most essential qualities of their race. Unhappily, even at the time of the first woodcut book, the beginning of the end was on them; about thirty years afterwards they received the Renaissance with singular eagerness and rapidity, and became, from the artistic point of view, a nation of rhetorical pedants. . . . It may surprise some of our readers, though I should hope not the greatest part of them, to hear that I claim the title of works of art, both for these picture-ornamented books as books, and also for the pictures themselves. Their two main merits are first their decorative and next their story-telling quality; and it seems to me that these two qualities include what is necessary and essential in book pictures.

It would not be possible in so brief a space to make a complete survey of illustrated incunabula, and a few typical examples will easily do service for the whole. From Ulm three examples have been chosen: Johann Zainer's edition of Boccaccio's *De Claris Mulieribus* of 1473 (illustration 7) cited by Morris as a special favorite of his; Lienhart Holle's edition of *Bidpai* of 1483 (illustration 20), a collection of Oriental fables also known as the *Panchatantra*, compiled by Anthonius von Pforr from a Latin version based upon a Hebrew version in turn based upon an Arabic translation of the original Sanskrit; the third Dinckmut's edition of Terence's *Eunuch* of 1486 (illustration 22). In the last mentioned woodcuts, the houses and windows have been conventionalized into a delightful pattern of black and white. It is interesting to compare this early print with a recent print by Niles Spencer where the modern artist has also made a lively abstract pattern by conventionalizing house forms (illustration 439). Another revelation of the medieval conception

28

of Terence and the theater is given in illustration 21, after a woodcut from a Lyons edition of 1493. The designer has presented a view of the theater as a whole including the audience, and below has portrayed the *"Fornices"* or "Stews" with the daughters of joy plying their trade.

Two examples of Netherlands presses are given: the *Chevalier Delibéré* (illustration 23) printed in Gouda in 1485, a ponderous pane-gyric on the exploits of Charles the Bold; and the cut of *Sir Hercules Fighting Three Lions* (illustration 30) from the *Histoire van Trojen* printed by Bellaert in Haarlem in 1485. This woodcut, with its highly decorative pattern of black and white, is conceived in a sort of heraldic style with artistic conventions familiar to all students of heraldry. It is interesting to note that the hero wears the plate armor which replaced the old fashioned knee-length coat-of-mail around the beginning of the century. It was this style of armor that brought about the use of a separate upper and nether garment, shirt and hose or trousers, which has remained characteristic of male attire ever since.

The introduction of printing and the expansion of the forces which led to the Reformation focused much attention and interest on the Bible. Not only were various editions of the Latin Vulgate printed, but many translations into Dutch, French, Italian, Czech, German (notably Luther's of 1522) were made and printed during the fifteenth and six-teenth centuries. The authority of God's Word in the vulgar tongue (as interpreted by each individual conscience) was invoked to contro-vert the authority of the Catholic Church in matters of salvation. One of the articles of the Schmalkaldic League, a league of Protestant princi-palities, specified that "the articles of faith shall be based upon God's Word and that of no one else, not even an angel's." Many of these popu-lar Bibles were illustrated with woodcuts, some of only archaeological interest, others famous for their beauty and design. Three characteristic examples are reproduced herewith as illustrations 5 and 8 and 50. The first is the *Adam and Eve and the Expulsion from Paradise* from the Cologne Bible printed about 1479 by Quentel. It was the most ambitious undertaking made up to that time and the blocks had considerable influ-ence on other artists; Koberger borrowed them (a not uncommon pro-cedure of the day) to use in his edition of the Bible at Nuremberg in

1483, and both Dürer and Holbein borrowed and transformed some of the designs in their own series of Bible illustrations. The other woodcut is from the Bible printed in Lübeck by Steffen Arndes in 1494. There are certain realistic touches and a certain interest in the psychological interplay of the characters—the embarrassment of Joseph's brothers in the presence, as they suppose, of a high Egyptian dignitary—that strike a somewhat new note in German illustration. Most early German illustration is schematic, a sign-post, as Kristeller called it, a symbol rather than an illustration in the true sense of the word. They presented the bare bones of a subject but seldom clothed it in flesh and blood. The pictures were subordinate to the text and served as a quick method of locating a particular chapter or subject. In the *Nuremberg Chronicle*, for example, one and the same portrait cut was used to represent Thales, Paris, Anastasius, Odofredus, and Dante. The Lübeck Bible illustrations foreshadowed the time, soon to come, when the artist's illustrations would have an importance and validity equal to that of the text. Another famous book which initiates a more modern attitude is Breydenbach's *Voyage to the Holy Land*, Mainz 1486 (illustration 28). It is the first illustrated book in which the designer's name is mentioned—Erhart Reuwich. The author took the artist along on his journey, and he made many drawings, translated into woodcuts, of city views and sketches of foreign peoples, Turks, Saracens, Jews, etcetera. There is also a page of animals including a camel, monkey, giraffe, crocodile, and, believe it or not, a unicorn; underneath is an inscription saying, "These animals are accurately drawn as we saw them in the Holy Land." In spite of such occasional lapses, the book is not only lively and entertaining but surprisingly accurate. It is the first work of travel and geography that is based not on Aristotle or Ptolemy but on independent observation, and it inaugurates a long line of views and maps in printed form that were to extend man's knowledge of the globe.

Not only Bibles but other religious books were adorned with woodcuts, Missals, Psalters, and Books of Hours. A cut depicting the *Celebration of the Mass* from the Paris Missal of 1481 printed by Jehan du Pré, is shown in illustration 15. It is the earliest illustrated book printed in Paris, and it set the style of French illustration for some time to come.

It contains more sensuous imagery than most of the German work; more of the élan of the actual scene is carried over into the picture. With it all, the artist has succeeded in illustrating literally, after the fashion of the Middle Ages, the image of the priest lifting up his soul to God. Another charming example of French engraving is the *Bible en Françoys* printed for Vérard about 1505. Its *Adam and Eve* (illustration 50) affords an interesting contrast to the similar subject from the Cologne Bible. The emphasis of the German work is on the moral question, whereas that of the French work is on a naive delight in the wonders of a terrestrial paradise. Among the most beautiful and touching productions in the whole history of prints were the *Horae* or Books of Hours, printed in Paris in the two decades just preceding and succeeding the turn of the sixteenth century. These *Horae* were prayer books chiefly for the laity, designed as cheap substitutes for the manuscript *Horae* which had been current for hundreds of years. They usually contained the Kalendar, extracts from the Gospels, the Canonical Hours or daily offices of the church, various other offices including the Office of the Dead, the Litanies, and the Penitential Psalms, and the whole furnished with a host of charming designs and pictures, following out the Latin proverb, *"Pictura est laicorum scriptura."* There might be large cuts of the Visitation, Nativity, Adoration of the Shepherds, and the Magi, Flight into Egypt, Dives and Lazarus, David and Bathsheba, and similar subjects traditionally associated with certain portions of the text. And there would be borders made up of small cuts of Gothic designs, scenes from the life of the Virgin and of Christ, the story of Susanna or Joseph and his Brethren, images of saints, the procession of the *Danse Macabre*, the occupations of the months, glimpses of huntsmen and stags and dogs, of lovers and fools, of griffins and mermaids—a veritable kaleidoscope of imagery, austerely religious or enchantingly secular, to strike the fancy and delight the eye. The essence of the Middle Ages is distilled in these pages, the faint perfume of incense, the quiet and the coolness of churches, the perennial magic of an ancient legend sweetly told, a gallimaufry of sublime and grotesque. A page from the *Horae* printed in 1498 by Philippe Pigouchet for the bookseller Simon Vostre is reproduced as illustration 16. The dramatic story of Dives and Lazarus is set

31

within a frame of beautiful Gothic ornament and this in turn is surrounded by a border of small cuts depicting the Cumaean Sibyl, the Marriage of Joachim and Anna, and three scenes of the Dance of Death, the Pope, the Emperor, and the Cardinal. These books of hours were very popular at the time, about six hundred editions by various French publishers having been preserved and recorded, in addition to countless others that have been lost. They were one of the last fine flowerings of the Gothic spirit, and their popularity was short-lived. The impact of the Renaissance created an entirely new style of ornament and design, which is reflected in the *Horae* designed by Geoffrey Tory and printed by Simon de Colines in 1525 (illustration 60). Tory, famous humanist, typographer, and designer of type and woodcuts, author of *Champfleury*, was thoroughly imbued with the ideals of the Italian Renaissance. But these ideals were not in the long run sympathetic to a mode of expression so essentially medieval as the books of hours, and they eventually ceased to have any influence in the lives of the people. Though this later *Horae* does not suggest the religious feeling of the fifteenth century book, from a typographical standpoint it is a beautiful work, the Renaissance ornament and open line work harmonizing perfectly with the light roman type face.

The Dance of Death was a theme that haunted the medieval mind. And well it might, for the vision of sudden and inevitable death was a vivid and terrible reality in the later Middle Ages. There had been plagues in Europe before, but in 1348 the Black Death or bubonic plague swept through the whole of Europe in successive epidemics with an overwhelming loss of life. It is estimated that in England over half the population lost their lives; in Venice two-fifths of the people died; in certain districts of France only one-tenth of the population survived. There were two reactions possible toward this catastrophe: one licentious, "eat, drink and be merry, for tomorrow we die," and the other ascetic, "memento mori." Both attitudes had their reflection in the art of the time, though the austere attitude predominated. An example of the first attitude is Boccaccio's *Decameron*, which as every one knows were the tales told to pass the time away by a group of people who had retired to escape the plague. (This work is here represented by illustra-

32

tion 3, from the Venice edition of 1492.) The *Danse Macabre*, a typical expression of the more austere attitude, was immensely popular for several centuries to come. Not only was it literally performed as a Dance of Death, a sort of Mystery Play, but the sequence was painted on the walls of churches, cemeteries, and covered bridges, and appeared in innumerable prints and books. Perhaps the idea of death as the great leveler, before whom all ranks and privileges were abolished, unconsciously nourished certain democratic notions that were growing at the time. Typical of the earlier *Danses Macabres*, and indeed based upon the lost frescoes in the cemetery of Les Innocents at Paris, is the *Danse Macabre des Hommes* which Pierre le Rouge printed for Guyot Marchant in 1485 (illustration 34). Here the Doctor and the Lover are confronted with their dead selves in the shape of grinning corpses and skeletons. The series is completed by representatives of all walks and ranks of men, and was followed later by the equivalent panorama for women. In Holbein's woodcut series of the Dance of Death (illustration 31) first published by Trechsel at Lyon in 1538, the obvious dance form has been discarded in favor of a more subtle and imaginative juxtaposition of death and victim. The illustrations, dramatic in conception, masterly in drawing, and beautifully executed in wood by Hans Lützelberger, are justly famous in the annals of printmaking. It was perhaps the last great sequence of the Dance of Death and was copied many times. Other artists have touched upon the theme, but usually in single examples rather than in a connected series.

As an example of the woodcut in relation to science, a cut from Bartholomaeus Anglicus' book, *El Libro de Proprietatibus Rerum en Romance*, printed in Spanish at Toulouse in 1494 is reproduced (illustration 27). Although the work is perhaps not as important as the Mainz *Gart der Gesuntheit*, the Mainz *Hortus Sanitatis*, and other herbals and compendiums of natural history, nevertheless it reflects accurately enough the unscientific state of science at the time, and its illustrations with their naive and decorative stylizations, have a charm that transcends their scientific interest. They were probably designed by a Spanish artist. Another example of a book printed in Spain, representing King Jaime I of Aragon and the Cortes of Leida (illustration 17) was taken from the

33

book *Usatges de Barcelona e Constitucións de Cataluña*, printed in Barcelona in 1495. The print, of striking decorative character, was undoubtedly printed from metal instead of wood, and cut in the dotted or *manière criblée*. Spanish art, essentially aristocratic in character, never took kindly to such democratic forms as books and prints, and little of interest was produced in Spain until Goya's time.

One further example of the relation of prints to science is a woodcut map (illustration 179) taken from Hartmann Schedel's *Weltchronik*, familiarly known as the *Nuremberg Chronicle* of 1493. Its significance in relation to voyages and explorations will be discussed later; it is here cited in relation to the book as a whole. The work was a ponderous and popular encyclopedia of world history and geography, profusely illustrated with 1809 cuts of decidedly mediocre quality, few of them being distinguished either in design, in cutting, or in the arrangement on the page. Sydney Cockerell has analyzed the woodcuts, and discovered that there are in reality only 645, the other 1164 being repeats, doing service for portraits and city views without much regard for historical or scientific accuracy. The whole was designed to impress rather by its quantity than its quality. It sold bound for two Rhenish florins and is an early example of mass production made possible by the fact that the printer Koberger had agents in Paris, Lyon, and Toulouse for the sale of his books. A transition was taking place between the printer or the craftsman who sold books at his printing-shop and possibly at some of the local and more important distant fairs, and the publisher with a regular selling organization and international affiliations. The capitalist nature of Koberger's undertaking is further emphasized by the fact that two rich men of Nuremberg, Sebald Schreyer and Sebastian Cammermeister, advanced money to be used in publishing enterprises including the *Nuremberg Chronicle*. Koberger at one time employed twenty-four presses and over one hundred workmen. Koberger's was far from being an isolated example of capitalistic enterprise, since similar ventures have been recorded in Italy, Basel, and elsewhere.

We must now return to an earlier period and trace the origin and development of the second great class of reproductive technique, line engraving on metal. The most important of those artists who, possibly

34

inspired by the successful example of reduplication through woodcuts, first thought of engraving on copper for the purpose of multiplying his designs on paper, was an unknown whom scholarship has designated as the Master of the Playing Cards, so called from one of his outstanding works. That he was an artist of some power and sensibility is evident from such engravings as the *Handkerchief of Veronica*, the *Virgin and the Serpent*, and the set of playing cards one of which, the Cyclamen Queen, is reproduced as illustration 124. According to Geisberg he was active in the neighborhood of Basel from 1430 to 1445. His work stands out from a large group of rather mediocre work which has been associated by modern scholarship with such nebulous personalities as the Master of the Nuremberg Passion, the Master of Balaam (who engraved a fine portrait of St. Bernardino of Sienna and a quaint St. Eligus, patron saint of goldsmiths, seated in a goldsmith's workshop), the Master of the Gardens of Love (from two prints of Gardens of Love interesting for their reflection of the manners of the Burgundian court), Master of the Banderolles and the like. A print by one of these, the Master of the Power of Women, is reproduced as illustration 137, not so much for its artistic merit, for it is the creation of a derivative artist who copied much from the Master of the Playing Cards and other sources, but because it is typical of a genre which had a vogue at all times in popular art—satire. The print is a satire on the power of woman. The obvious symbolism is confirmed by the verse that is flaunted on a banderolle: "A donkey I ride when I choose; a cuckoo is my pet; with it I catch many fools and monkeys." Another variant of the theme is the feminine *Fight for the Trousers*, which has a strangely modern sound, yet which can be traced in prints from the fifteenth century down to the *imagerie populaire* of the early nineteenth century. Still another theme is the antithesis of love and gold: old man and young girl, youth and old woman. Four-fifths of the engraving of the fifteenth century, however, had religious subjects.

The next important personality in engraving is Master E. S., who is supposed to have flourished from about 1440 to 1467 in the neighborhood of the Lake of Constance. Three hundred and seventeen different prints by this goldsmith engraver have come down to us. In spite of the fact that we have never been able to discover his name (the E. S. being a monogram found on some of his prints) a definite personality speaks through his work. His types of men and especially women have an easily discernible style, a mingling of sweetness and naiveté. One feels, somehow, the presence of a real human being, albeit vague and shadowy, behind these rare engravings, the figure of a man with likes and dislikes, a certain ideal of womanly beauty, some quiet touches of humor, a simple religious feeling combined with quite a sensuous appreciation of the lusts of the flesh (there are extant a half dozen rather free subjects engraved by him). He composed a whole alphabet of grotesque figures, a procession of saints, knights, ladies, gross-looking monks, grotesque animals, and the like. One of them, the letter Q, made up of mounted knights and villains, is reproduced as illustration 143. It is doubtful whether he realized the significance that might be read into the positions of the men of such different stations of life. An important and typical example of his religious work is the large *Madonna of Einsiedeln* of 1466 (illustration 130). At the Swiss monastery of Einsiedeln was a famous shrine of the Virgin much visited by pilgrims. "Pilgrimages," as Douglas Percy Bliss has charmingly put it, "were a form of medieval holidaying, combining spiritual benefits with enjoyment. With the sweet showers of April, says the most famous of all pilgrims, Wives of Bath, Prioresses, and Millers all get restive—'Than longen folk to goon on pilgrimages.' And just as Chaucer's Pardoner, who had been at Rome, bore a pewter vernicle upon his hat and when he had got to Canterbury would pin an ampulla beside it, so if you went to a shrine or convent in Germany at a later date, you would buy a print or even, at some places, a block-book." On the print the Virgin and Child are seen enthroned between an angel and St. Meinrad, and in front are kneeling a male and female pilgrim with their staffs and hats and robes. Above, as if by a personal appearance from a balcony, are revealed the Trinity and the whole heavenly host. Altogether a most delightful picture. Other charming prints are the *Hortus Conclusus*, the *Virgin with Child Bathing*, and the *Nativity*, in which last the artist has suggested psychological reverberations in the characters of Joseph and Mary, simi-

36

lar in mood to the famous *Cherry Tree Carol*. Dürer later used a similar theme in his woodcut of the *Holy Family with the Three Hares*.

The technique of Master E. S. is typical of the goldsmith's approach, based entirely on line, and showing a loving preoccupation with ornament. His work is among the earliest bearing a signature or monogram. It has been suggested that this monogram might be more in the nature of a hallmark (following the practice of goldsmiths), a guaranty of honest and masterly workmanship rather than a signature in the modern sense of the word. It may thus represent a transition stage between the complete anonymity of the Middle Ages or of oriental countries like India, and the thorough capitalization of the individual artist's personality beginning with the Renaissance in Western art. In the medieval, and to a large extent in the oriental conception of art, the artist's personality was completely submerged in his work; whereas in Western art, with the growth of capitalist society and the development of the artist as a trader, the artist's name became a valuable asset, and his work, issued under his trademark, became almost a special brand of merchandise. Under such a scheme questions of forgery and plagiarism become important, in the Middle Ages they were not. Artists copied and recopied each other's work without feeling that they were committing a crime; there were certain traditional ways of depicting things which were transmitted from artist to artist and generation to generation. Van Meckenem as we shall see, acquired many of the coppers of Master E. S., retouched them, and put his own mark on some of them.

Only a few of the prints of Master E. S. were signed, and those late in his life; every one of the 115 engravings by Martin Schongauer, of the third generation of early German engravers, was signed with a monogram and distinctive mark. He was born around 1445 at Colmar. The son of a well-to-do goldsmith, he matriculated at the University of Leipzig in 1465. He must have given up scholarly pursuits to follow the career of artist. Although he was a painter, he still worked largely in the goldsmith tradition, and is better known for his engravings than his paintings. He was famous in his day: the young Dürer came to study in his workshop, only to find that he had come too late, for Schongauer died in 1491. Later, Vasari cites a number of his engravings and concludes as follows: "In another he did St. Anthony beaten by devils and carried into the air by a swarm of them, of the most curious forms imaginable, a sheet which so pleased Michelangelo when young that he began to color it." But he is still essentially the medieval artist, occasionally depicting devils and fantastic monsters like the *Griffin* (illustration 145). In complicated compositions such as the *Death of the Virgin,* or *Christ Carrying the Cross,* he is not quite so successful, since he lacks the dramatic sense to subordinate detail for the sake of pictorial emphasis; he still has the goldsmith's conception of a flat linear pattern. He is at his best in the simpler compositions such as *Christ and the Magdalen,* the *Virgin and Child in the Courtyard, St. Michael* and other Saints and Madonnas, where his innate delicacy and refinement find untrammeled expression. In this class, too, falls his lovely *Nativity* (illustration 128), carried out in an exalted mood of adoration and beauty. It has all the grace, the enchanting unworldliness of a fairy story.

It was more or less traditional to conceive of the Nativity in terms of fantasy and imagination. It was likewise more or less customary to treat the Birth of the Virgin realistically with a wealth of literal detail. A typical example by Israhel van Meckenem is reproduced as illustration 129. The theme was similarly treated by Dürer in his woodcut series of the *Life of the Virgin.* We see the newly born infant about to be bathed by a neighborly housewife who is testing the temperature of the water with her foot; we see roast chicken and drink being offered to the exhausted mother; we see the cradle and other utensils at hand —an interesting glimpse into the daily life of the fifteenth century. Van Meckenem is one of the most baffling artists in the history of engraving, as well as the most prolific of the fifteenth century, about 570 examples having been ascribed to his hand. He produced some of the most banal and mediocre engravings ever made, yet at times he was capable of work of considerable merit. We know what manner of man he was, since he has left a striking portrait of himself and his wife (illustration 134), not a particularly spiritual face, but a cheerful industrious type with a sense of humor and a keen eye for business. He must have been one of the earliest commercially professional engravers. He copied works by E. S., Schongauer, Master of the Amsterdam Cabinet, Wenzel von

38

Olmütz, Hans Holbein the Elder, and Dürer. He acquired the original plates of Master E. S. on his death in 1467 (he had been his pupil in 1466 and 1467) and a number by the Netherlands Master F. V. B.; he retouched them and did a thriving business selling prints. He is one of the first engravers whose work shows any great variation in the number of states—a fact which has endeared him to many modern collectors. He was born some time before 1450 and lived most of his life at Bocholt in Flanders. He died there in 1503. Among the best of his work, interesting chiefly as reflections of the life of the time, may be counted the large *Dance at the Court of Herod*, the *Death of Lucretia*, a series of genre subjects such as *A Woman Spinning and a Visitor* and the *Enraged Wife*, and a group of engravings of ornament.

Engravings of ornament were in the fifteenth century, and continued to be for several centuries to come, an important class of non-religious engravings. These engravings of ornament were designs to be followed, or models to be copied, by fellow artists and craftsmen, such as woodcarvers and carpenters, masons and stonecarvers, goldsmiths and metal workers, embroiderers, weavers, and other textile workers, decorative painters and the like. Master E. S., Schongauer, and many other fifteenth century artists made ornament prints. Two representative examples of Gothic ornament are reproduced. The first a pattern with figures on the theme of the *Fight for the Trousers* by Master E. S. (illustration 141). The second a model for a Baldachin or shrine (illustration 140), by that unknown but highly individual artist, Master I. A. M. with the Weaver's Shuttle, who flourished at Zwolle in Holland about 1485 and who engraved a most moving *Lamentation over the Body of Christ* and a striking *Adoration of the Magi*.

Two more examples complete the survey of Gothic engravings. Both are by artists who were not in any broad sense professional engravers, but rather painters or sculptors who made a few plates. Thus they may be said to inaugurate a long and interesting line of graphic productions in which their authors brought to their task a freshness and breadth of view often lacking in the pure craftsman's approach. The first is the charming *Madonna with the Apple* (illustration 125) by the famous Nuremberg sculptor, Veit Stoss (1439?-1523). The

39

second is by an artist about whom little is known, and who is variously designated as the Master of the Amsterdam Cabinet (where some eighty of his total eighty-nine engravings are conserved, many of them in unique impressions) or as the *Meister des Hausbuchs* from a book containing some of his drawings at Wolfegg. He probably was active somewhere in the Middle Rhine from about 1475 to 1490. Little else is known about this personality who speaks so charmingly and attractively from his prints. He can hardly be classed as a professional engraver, since, owing to the extreme scarcity of his prints (many existing in only one impression), it is evident that he made comparatively little effort to multiply and sell his designs. Furthermore his technique was not that of the regular goldsmith engraver: it was more like a drypoint line (scratched into the metal) which would not hold up under many impressions. His approach is rather that of a painter having an eye for the figure as a whole and the interplay of light and color. But especially attractive are the freshness of his conception and the lovely lyric spirit that pervades his work. Seldom has the enchantment of love, the sweet and quiet delight of lovers in each other's company, been more charmingly depicted than in his print (illustration 127). Equally outstanding in their way are his *Death and the Young Man*, the *Three Knights Confronted with Their Dead Selves*, the *Crucifixion*, *Two Men Talking*, and a delightfully realistic picture of a dog scratching himself, one of the first in that genre of prints. Altogether, the work of the Master of the Amsterdam Cabinet is one of the dewy and fragrant pages in the history of the graphic arts.

Henry Adams wrote:

The Gothic is singular in this: one seems easily at home in the Renaissance; one is not too strange in the Byzantine; as for the Roman, it is ourselves; and we could walk blindfolded through every chink and cranny of the Greek mind; all these styles seem modern, when we come close to them; but the Gothic gets away. No two men think alike about it, and no woman agrees with either man. The Church itself never agreed about it, and the architects agree even less than the priests. To most minds it casts too many shadows; it wraps itself in mystery; and when people talk of mystery, they commonly mean fear.

It is true that the Gothic era seems more alien to our modern temper than most of the other periods. To be sure the Gothic as reflected in the graphic arts represented the latest period, its decadence so to speak. The great glory of the Gothic was the Cathedral and the painting and sculpture that went into it. It was an age of faith and a Universal Church —which our age emphatically is not. It is difficult for us, brought up as we are from earliest childhood with the notion of a rational physical universe, to accept such impossible contradictions as simultaneous existence in two places, miraculous changes without natural causes, anachronisms based upon ignorance of historical development and the like. The Gothic was a credulous age of beautiful legend and little science, of touching faith and macabre humor, of unworldliness and chivalry and starving serfs, of uncertain life and violent death. The medieval artist sought to express an idea, not to imitate nature. As St. Thomas Aquinas said: "Art imitates nature [not in its form but] in its processes, *ars naturem imitat in sua operatione.*" It was symbolic in form, and lacking in sensuous and realistic elements. When Worringer spoke of "the ceaseless melody of Northern line," he was referring particularly to architecture, but the phrase also has a certain aptness in regard to engraving. The Gothic line is calligraphic, that is to say it has a rhythm and melody of its own. The folds of drapery for example, as depicted in a print or drawing, may not be at all naturalistic or revealing of the figure beneath; they may be arbitrary and abstract; but they have intrinsic beauty and vitality nevertheless. After all, graphic art, which expresses everything, color, form, atmosphere, largely by black and white lines, is in itself an abstract and arbitrary art.

In conclusion it might be well to summarize the conditions which brought about the development of the graphic arts. In the first place there was the desire for religious images inculcated by organized religion. At the end of the Middle Ages the worship of a multitude of saints and above all of the Virgin Mary, reached its fullest development. Religion had been humanized. Every occupation and profession had its patron saint who was endowed with special virtues (as we have seen for example in St. Christopher). A canonized saint was a comforter in tribulation and a mediator between a sinner and a remote Godhead.

Thus the saints and their attributes figured largely in the thoughts and feelings of the people. In a sense they personified them, as the feeling of tenderness and sweetness and mother love is personified in the Virgin and Child, as sorrow and affliction are personified in the drama of the Passion, as fear and terror are personified in the *Danse Macabre* and the Vision of the Last Judgment. Thus were the desire and the need for images provided, while economic conditions—a larger and larger number of people coming to enjoy a slight margin above a subsistence level—provided the means to satisfy the desire. Organized religion has at almost all times furnished a stimulus to the practice of the arts. It was likewise so, as we shall see in another chapter, when the spread of Mahayana Buddhism in China produced the demand for religious images and charms which had magical properties, and thus brought about the perfection of woodcutting and printing throughout the Chinese Empire as early as the eighth century. In addition to the religious stimulus, the graphic arts had other organic roots in the lives of the people. There were playing cards and prints of gallantry that ministered to the play instinct. There were prints of satire and caricature, those lightning rods that channeled the fury and resentment of the oppressed. Portraiture, a deep-seated desire in man, made a halting beginning in the fifteenth century, but was destined later to be one of the chief functions of prints. There were prints illustrating science and exploration. And finally there were prints of ornament, the trade secrets which the artists circulated among themselves. All these prints were purposive; there was no thought as yet of art for art's sake.

3. The Renaissance

THE dramatic transition from Gothic to Renaissance can be personified in the life and works of one man—Albrecht Dürer. He began in the Gothic tradition and died a painter and engraver of the Renaissance, acclaimed in Germany, Flanders, and even in Italy, the home of the Renaissance. Distinguished as he is as an artist, he is even greater as a dramatic figure, as a man in whom the tremendous forces of his age had their play and interplay, all the more so because he has left such a voluminous documentation of his thoughts and feelings. Many of the qualities which we particularly associate with the Renaissance—intellectual interests, passion for the antique, self-conscious interest in fame, pride in individual achievement, proficiency in diverse professions ("the man of virtu"), devotion to science as well as to art, a preoccupation with proportion and perspective—found their expression in his many-sided personality.

He was born in Nuremberg in 1471, the son of a goldsmith. Of himself Dürer wrote:

And my father took special pleasure in me, because he saw that I was diligent to learn. So he sent me to school, and when I had learned to read and write he took me away from it, and taught me the goldsmith's craft. But when I could work neatly, my liking drew me rather to painting than to goldsmith's work, so I laid it before my father; but he was not well pleased, regretting the time lost while I had been learning to be a goldsmith. Still he let it be as I wished, and in 1486 on St. Andrew's Day my father bound me apprentice to Michael Wolgemut, to serve him three years long. During that time God gave me diligence, so that I learned well, but I had much to suffer from his lads.

Having served his term with Wolgemut (who had supplied designs to Koberger for the *Schatzbehalter* and the *Nuremberg Chronicle*) and thus become steeped in the Gothic tradition not only from him but from his goldsmith father, he spent four years wandering about as a journeyman. It is not known what places he visited, but it is reasonably certain that he spent some time at Basle designing woodcuts for the publishers, notably two series of illustrations for the *Ritter vom Thurn* and for Sebastian Brant's *Ship of Fools*, both satiric commentaries on the foibles of mankind. One of these about the fool who miscalculates his costs in building a house and finds his workmen walking out on the job, is reproduced herewith (illustration 24). There is little to distinguish these works from a number of Gothic illustrations except possibly a certain competence of drawing and gusto of observation. It is generally assumed that from the fall of 1494 to the spring of 1495 he made a trip to Venice. Before this, while still in Nuremberg, he had seen (interesting side-light on the international trade in prints) and copied in pen and ink two engravings by Mantegna and one by a North Italian engraver of the *Death of Orpheus*. At any rate from about this time a new note came into his work, a stronger painter-like feeling (thinking in terms of color, and painting in watercolors), a preoccupation with tactile form instead of the calligraphic line characteristic of the Gothic North. And in the woodcuts and the copper engravings (in which he seems to be largely self-taught) he gradually began to perfect the style associated with his name. In the series of fifteen large woodcut illustrations of the *Apocalypse*, issued in 1498, this style may already be seen in its completeness. When a print like the *Four Riders of the Apocalypse* (illustration 25) is compared with a similar subject from, say, the Cologne Bible, the measure of his achievement is obvious. The print is conceived as a complete picture with the bounds of a rectangle, the figures and the details are disposed within that space with the most telling dramatic effect. There is a sense of movement and of color; the figures are drawn in the round with some regard for realistic tactile values. Dürer managed to perfect a system of representation, a combination of the calligraphic and ideographic elements of Gothic art and the more painter-like pictorial qualities of the Renaissance, which became the prevailing idiom in Germany and the Netherlands for a century to come. Of course in comparison with the work of Parmigiano or Rembrandt, Dürer's style

44

as a whole seems Gothic. Nevertheless it will always remain an exemplar of a striking and effective mode of graphic expression.

About 1500 he met in Nuremberg the painter Jacopo de' Barbari (illustration 131) and wrote of him thus:

I can find no one who hath written aught about how to form a canon of human proportions, save one man, Jacopo by name, born at Venice, and a charming painter. He showed me the figures of a man and woman, which he had drawn according to a canon of proportions; and now I would rather be shown what he meant than behold a new kingdom. If I had this canon, I would put it into print in his honor, for the use of all men. Then, however, I was still young and had not heard of such things before. Howbeit I was very fond of art, so I set myself to discover how such a canon might be wrought out. For this aforesaid Jacopo, as I clearly saw, would not explain to me the principles upon which he went. Accordingly I set to work on my own idea and read Vitruvius, who writes somewhat about the human figure. Thus it was from, or out of, these two men aforesaid that I took my start, and thence, from day to day, have I followed up my search according to my own notions.

From that time on indeed he gathered, with more zeal perhaps than style, the notes, measurements, and researches, that eventually were published in his book *On Human Proportions*. Meanwhile in 1504, making use of his studies in the ideal figure, he engraved his famous *Adam and Eve* (illustration 147), which he proudly signed "Albert Dürer of Nuremberg made this 1504." In it he expressed his dream of an ideal Adam and Eve, prototype of Man and Woman, and his nostalgia for the antique, Apollo and Venus transformed into the First Pair—the Adam indeed is based upon the Apollo Belvedere. This print typifies the emancipation of the North from a medieval contempt for the flesh, a sensuous interest and a freedom in the handling of the nude, characteristic of Renaissance artists. A half century before such a picture would have been unthinkable, except in Italy, which had the advantage of a more or less unbroken tradition from the antique. Not only were the medieval artists restricted in depicting the nude and semi-nude to such subjects as the Last Judgment, Adam and Eve, the Crucifixion, a few saints like St. Sebastian, and biblical stories like David and Bathsheba,

45

but there was also little opportunity to draw from the nude. Professional models were unknown. For male models the artists often used themselves or their apprentices, for female models their wives and mistresses and occasionally prostitutes and the attendants in the public baths (which had none too respectable a reputation even as late as Casanova's time). Drawings exist by Pisanello, Dürer, Dirick Vellert, and others, of bath attendants, and Dürer made a woodcut of a Men's Bath. Professional models first came into use in Carracci's Academy. During the Renaissance there was a general feeling that the male body was superior in beauty and proportion to the female. Michelangelo used male models for a number of his Sibyls. And Dürer in his engraving worked with more *esprit* on his Adam than on his Eve. He, however, retained an interest in the nude of both sexes till the end. In 1520 he was at Antwerp and witnessed the triumphal entry of Charles V.

He afterwards described to Melanchthon the splendid spectacles he had beheld, and how, in what were mythological groups, the most beautiful maidens figured almost naked, and covered only with a thin transparent veil. The young Emperor did not honor them with a single glance, but Dürer himself was very glad to get near, not less for the purpose of seeing the tableaux, than to have the opportunity of observing closely the perfect figures of the young girls. As he said, "Being a painter, I looked about me a little more boldly."

Meanwhile he led in Nuremberg a busy and industrious existence, doing portrait commissions, engraving sacred and profane subjects, Madonna pictures and the like. One of the most beautiful and charming of these is the *Virgin and Child with the Monkey* of about 1498 (illustration 148) with its lovely landscape background of the Weierhaus, which was copied by Giulio Campagnola in his engraving of Ganymede. Dürer's fame had spread far into Italy; many of his prints were sold and copied there. So much so that he was moved to make a second journey to Venice to protest against the wholesale forgery of his prints by Marcantonio Raimondi (no less than seventy-eight in all).

Marcantonio [wrote Vasari] began by imitating the things of Albert, studying all the prints which he had bought, which for their novelty and

46

beauty, were sought by everyone. Having engraved on copper, all the Passion and Life of Christ in thirty-six sheets, with the A.D. with which Albert signed his works, Marcantonio succeeded in making them so like that no one could tell the difference, who did not know; and they were sold and bought as Albert's works. On being informed of this, one of the counterfeits being sent to Flanders [Vasari was vague about geography outside of Italy], Albert flew into such a rage that he left Flanders and came to Venice, and complained of Marcantonio to the Signoria. But all he obtained was that Marcantonio should no longer use his signature.

Dürer's letters to his friend Pirkheimer give a picture of his life in Italy. He exerted himself (perhaps in vain) to show that he was a great painter as well as a great draughtsman and engraver. He encountered the jealousy of the Italian painters; Bellini alone wished him well. He found everything expensive. Yet he wrote, "How I shall freeze after this sun! Here I am a gentleman, at home only a parasite." He made a pilgrimage to Mantua to visit Andrea Mantegna whom he greatly admired. "But," as Camerarius wrote, "before he could reach Mantua Andrea was dead, and Dürer used to say that this was the saddest event in all his life." An interesting side-light on Dürer's relations with Raphael is given on a Raphael drawing which has the following inscription in Dürer's handwriting: "Rafahel de' Urbin, who is held in such high esteem by the Pope, he made these naked figures and sent them to Albrecht Dürer at Nuremberg to show him his hand." Raphael had, we are told by Lodovico Dolce, drawings, engravings, and woodcuts of Dürer's hanging in his studio; and Vasari quoted Raphael as saying, "If Dürer had been acquainted with the antique he would have surpassed us all."

There is not space to recount all of Dürer's contacts with the writers and humanists, Erasmus, Melanchthon, Luther, Hans Sachs, Conrad Celtes, Stabius, Camerarius; with the great merchants, the Imhofs and Fuggers and Paumgartners; with the Court of the Emperor Maximilian. Dürer's portrait of Pirkheimer, patrician, humanist, and councilor of Nuremberg, and his life-long friend, will have to typify his contacts with the learned world. Pirkheimer was a ponderous, pompous, irascible individual—what we would today call a stuffed shirt—and the engraving

47

(illustration 151) does give a suggestion of this, though it lacks any sense of style. The textures are built up in a rather dull and literal way, and Dürer indulges in the somewhat flashy trick of showing the reflection of a window in the subject's eyes. But Dürer was no flatterer. The Gothic North has a fairly honorable reputation in this regard, being on the whole more interested in "character" than in elegance. Later, Titian, Van Dyck, and the French portrait engravers marked the beginning of the elegant style which eventually developed into the official or fashionable portrait, an art of flattery pure and simple. Dürer's engraved portrait of Erasmus was no likeness at all. Erasmus when he saw it, politely excused its deficiency by saying that no doubt he had changed somewhat in the years since the drawing was made. The truth of the matter, however, probably was that the artist engraved the portrait some five or six years after he had made the preliminary drawings and he had simply "gone cold" on the subject. He had hoped to compensate for this by over-elaborating all the accessories. Whether Pirkheimer liked his portrait or not is not known. He had the plate in his possession and no doubt had proofs printed as one would of a photograph today. It later passed into the hands of the Imhof family (Pirkheimer's daughter married an Imhof), and was sold by Hans Imhof in 1636 to the Earl of Arundel for forty Reichsthaler.

Dürer designed or engraved several great series besides the *Apocalypse*, such as the Large Woodcut Passion (12 blocks), the Little Woodcut Passion (37 blocks) (illustration 26), the *Life of the Virgin* (20 blocks), all three published by Dürer himself in 1511 (though some of the individual blocks were completed before that), and the Copper Plate Passion (16 plates). These and a number of single blocks and plates proved a considerable source of income to him. When he made his journey to the Netherlands in 1520, he took a large quantity of prints with him which he sold, exchanged, or gave away, as we learn from his detailed diary. He even sold to a dealer at wholesale prices:

Sebald Fischer bought of me at Antwerp sixteen small Passions [woodcut] for four florins [about $2.50 per set], thirty-two of the large books [sets of the Apocalypse and Large Passion] for eight florins [about $2.50

per set], also six engraved Passions [on copper] for three florins [about $5.00 per set].

He exchanged prints with other artists: "I gave eight florins' worth of my prints for a whole set of Lucas' [van Leyden's] engravings." Again: "I gave to Tommaso of Bologna a whole set of prints to send for me to Rome to another painter, who will send me Raphael's work [engraved by Marcantonio] in return." Occasionally he jotted down retail prices: "I sold a woodcut Passion for twelve stivers [about $5.00], besides an Adam and Eve [copper engraving] for four stivers [about $1.65].

One of the most famous of the later engravings is the *Melancholia* (illustration 150), more or less uniform with two other famous engravings, the *St. Jerome in his Cell*, and the *Knight, Death, and the Devil*. It is possible that Dürer intended to illustrate in a series the various temperaments of man such as the phlegmatic, choleric, and melancholic. The idea of melancholy is capable of extended and diverse elaboration as readers of Burton's *Anatomy of Melancholy* well know. Much has been written about the significance of Dürer's strange plate, but nobody has succeeded in producing a complete and satisfying interpretation. Dr. Panofsky has come as close as any one:

Dürer was, or thought he was, a melancholic . . . He was also an artist-geometrician who suffered from the very limitations of the discipline he loved. In his younger days, when he prepared the *Adam and Eve*, he had hoped to capture absolute beauty by means of a ruler and compass. Shortly before he composed the *Melancolia* he was forced to admit: "But what absolute beauty is, I know not. Nobody knows it but God". . . . Thus Dürer's most perplexing engraving is the objective statement of a general philosophy and the subjective confession of an individual man. It fuses two great representational and literary traditions, that of Melancholy as one of the Four Humors and that of Geometry as one of the Seven Liberal Arts. It typifies the artist of the Renaissance . . . who feels "inspired" by celestial influences and eternal ideas, but suffers all the more from his human frailty and intellectual finiteness. But in doing all this it is in a sense a spiritual self-portrait of Albrecht Dürer.

In the early sixteenth century a new technique was developed for engraving on metal. It was called etching and was probably derived from the armorer's craft. One of the first to use the new craft was Daniel Hopfer; few, however, of his works bear a date on the plate (illustration 157). The first etching with a date is the *Woman Bathing Her Feet* by Urs Graf, 1513. Dürer tried his hand at the new technique, and made in all, six etchings, two of which, the *Christ on the Mount of Olives* of 1515 and the *Cannon* of 1518, are reproduced herewith (illustrations 149 and 156). These early etchings were made on iron with red lead as a ground, and the lines were all of one uniform thickness in the biting. The *Christ on the Mount of Olives* is one of the noblest of Dürer's works. The storm-tossed tree mirrors the psychological drama of Christ's Agony, and the whole is conceived and executed with a fury and spontaneity rare in his work. The *Cannon* represents a showpiece called the Nuremberg Serpent, popular at the moment, and was made in etching as a quick means of supplying a transient demand. The Turks for whom, as pictured, the cannon was a warning and a threat, were the great bugaboo of the time. The first siege of Vienna by the Turks occurred in 1529. The landscape in the background is quite charming in spite of its lack of subtlety, and the print is prized not only because it is one of the earliest etchings but also because it is one of the earliest examples of the growing interest in landscape.

Augustin Hirschvogel made a number of etchings of pure landscape, that is to say, without any figure interest (illustration 155). They are notable because they show a variation in the quality of line accomplished, possibly by more than one biting of the plate, but more likely by the use of needles of varying thickness. Other early etchings of pure landscape were made by Albrecht Altdorfer and Hans Sebald Lautensack. The full development of the landscape print, however, was to come with the Dutch etchers of the seventeenth century, and with Bruegel and Rubens in engraving and Titian in woodcut.

Dürer died in Nuremberg in 1528 after a life of unremitting application to his craft. He was a great draughtsman and technician. If we sometimes miss in his work the fire of a great emotion, we nevertheless must be impressed by his insatiable pre-occupation with the representation of all natural objects. It may be questioned whether his scientific

50

interests, the canon of proportion, the mathematics and mensuration, the military engineering, all the things he wrote about in his books, did not affect his art adversely. Leonardo's scientific interests were even greater than Dürer's, and they may have affected the quantity but certainly not the quality of his art. The matter goes deeper: Dürer pinned his faith too much on externals. "To paint," he wrote, "is to be able to portray upon a flat surface any visible thing what so ever that may be chosen." He was, par excellence, the extrovert artist. The world was too much with him. His power of description and analysis stood in the way of a vitalizing synthesis. He attempted to storm Heaven with a pedlar's pack of literal details. That he searched all his life for some elusive secret of art is in itself revealing. Yet withal he is a most engaging figure, in Melanchthon's words, "a wise man, whose genius as a painter, were it ever so brilliant, would be the least of his gifts." His pride and his humility, his wisdom of life, his childlike delight in all natural objects, his systematizing capacity and technical skill, and his recording instinct make him one of the most fascinating men of art that the world has ever known.

One of the most famous of Dürer's friends was Lucas van Leyden, born at Leyden in 1494. Dürer exchanged prints with him and drew his portrait during his visit to the Netherlands. Lucas was a precocious artist, having engraved his first plate, *Mahomet and Sergius*, at the age of fourteen. He engraved many religious subjects, but like Schongauer and Dürer, also executed several genre scenes or illustrations of popular life. One of the most delightful of these is *The Milkmaid* of 1510 (illustration 158). He also designed a number of distinguished woodcuts. One of his masterpieces is the portrait of the Emperor Maximilian of 1520 (illustration 154). In addition to its masterly characterization and draughtsmanship, the plate has a technical interest. It is one of the earliest examples of a combination of etching and engraving. The earliest etchings had been made on iron which could be engraved with difficulty. By using copper instead of iron, it was possible to combine etching and engraving on the same plate. Lucas van Leyden's plate inaugurated that technical procedure of etching the preliminary work and finishing up with the graver, that reached its culmination in the engravings of the

51

eighteenth and early nineteenth centuries. In his later work Lucas assimilated the technique of Marcantonio, and with it gave up Dutch raciness for a rather empty Renaissance allegorical style. He died at the early age of thirty-nine. Another Flemish artist whom Dürer mentions in his diary is Dirick Vellert, painter, glass-worker, engraver. He made about nineteen engravings and etchings, many of them small in size. One of the most charming of these, the *Faun on a Wine Barrel*, 1522, is reproduced as illustration 172.

The Emperor Maximilian, "the last of the Knights," was a great patron of the arts. Inspired perhaps by the *Chevalier Delibéré*, he commissioned a number of elaborately illustrated works designed to glorify his person and his exploits, often imaginary—*Genealogy*, the *Theuerdank*, the *Weisskunig*, the *Freydal*, the *Triumphal Arch*, and the *Triumphal Procession*. Dürer, Burgkmair, Altdorfer, Springinklee, Schäufelein, and others were employed on these works. Most of it is pedantic and heraldic, interesting chiefly to the historian; some of it indeed was left unpublished at the death of Maximilian. Most of the figures of the *Triumphal Procession* were mythological and allegorical, but toward its end are a group of figures at one time attributed to Burgkmair which have a touch of reality. The scene might easily represent a highway of the time with its rumbling wagons, horsemen, and straggling foot passengers. Hans Burgkmair (illustration 38), was a typical court painter, witty, elegant, courtly, competent to undertake any subject upon request. He did a series of 135 prints representing the triumphs of the Emperor. After the death of Maximilian he went back again to work for the Augsburg book publishers.

Lucas Cranach was also a court painter (he entered the service of the Elector of Saxony about 1505). His later work suffers from the dilution so often attendant upon official renditions, but at its best it is charming, sensuous, elegant, and saturated with real feeling for nature. Through his residence in Wittenberg he came in close contact with Luther and other leaders of the Reformation. He designed woodcuts for the first edition of Luther's German Bible in 1522, and also engraved on copper the vivid portrait of 1521 (illustration 152), which fixes for eternity the warm, fanatic, yet human personality of the miner's son who defied Rome and established the written form of the German vernacular.

The sixteenth century was a warlike one. According to Sombart there were only twenty-five years which did not witness a war somewhere in Europe. Soldiers were everywhere, including a new kind of soldier, the mercenary. Erasmus wrote that the German disorders were "partly due to the natural fierceness of the race, partly to the division into so many separate States, and partly to the tendency of the people to serve as mercenaries." The insolent swaggering type and his female counterpart have been pictured by many German artists: Dürer, Virgil Solis, Burgkmair, Huber, Nicholas Manuel, Beham, Holbein, and Cranach (illustration 37). But most typical of all were the woodcuts of Urs Graf, who was himself a Landsknecht and fought in the murderous battle of Marignano. He led a violent and undisciplined life, was repeatedly brought before the authorities "because of his licentious life that he openly and shamelessly leads with strumpets," and once was made to promise that "he would no longer push, beat, crush, or pinch his lawfully wedded wife, the daughter of an honorable tanner, who married against the will of her parents." Much of this wild and wayward energy, of this bluster and swagger, of this excess of animal spirits, is carried over into his prints, *The Soldiers and Death* (illustration 36) and the *Standard Bearer of the Arms of Unterwalden* of 1521 (illustration 51). This last is a wood engraving, conceived as a white line engraving, and is an interesting anticipation of the method which Bewick later made famous.

Hans Holbein is famous as the painter of the court of Henry VIII, but he is equally outstanding for his work for the Basel publishers, Froben and others, for the drawings illustrating his friend Erasmus' *Praise of Folly*, and for his woodcut designs for the Bible and the *Dance of Death* both of 1538 (illustrations 32 and 31). In these last he carried the method of Dürer to its classic perfection, the completest expression of the German Renaissance.

In strong contrast to his classic feeling of balance and restraint, is the demonic energy of Hans Baldung, surnamed Grien. Comparatively little is known of his life. He was born in 1476 near Strassburg; he was

53

a friend and possibly a pupil of Dürer; he later fell under the spell of that strange genius Grünewald, he probably died at Strassburg around 1540. His fame has suffered strange mutations. In his lifetime he achieved considerable acclaim and reputation; Baldung's prints were the only ones outside of his own that Dürer took with him for trade on his Netherlands journey. But in the seventeenth and eighteenth centuries his name and work were practically forgotten. In the early nineteenth century his name was again discovered, and at one time even Grünewald's masterpiece, the *Isenheimer Altar*, was ascribed to him. The twentieth century has resurrected his works and accorded them high praise. Indeed in such works as *Adam and Eve*, the *Fall of Man*, the *Conversion of St. Paul*, the *Ascension of Christ*, the *Nativity*, the *Lamentation*, the *Witches*, the *Horses*, and the *Groom Bewitched*, there is an emotional intensity of conception, an originality and appropriateness of composition, a passionate and sensuous expression, and above all a wild and haunting power that are peculiarly appealing to the modern temper. Consider for example that most vivid drama of the flesh—the color and sensuousness of it—in the *Fall of Man* (illustration 54); the magic unearthly beauty of the *Nativity* (illustration 52); the breath-taking power of the composition, the tenderness of feeling—Christ not triumphant but crushed, utterly crushed, by the evil forces of this world, carried to the pitying arms of God the Father—in the woodcut of the *Ascension* (illustration 53). Or the demonic overtones, the bold recession of planes, in the *Groom Bewitched* (illustration 55); the swirling lines of force in the *Witches* (illustration 169); or the wild and elemental energy of the *Horses in the Wood* (illustration 40). And finally the dynamic balance of forces, the thrusts and parallelisms of the lines in that dramatic illustration of the Fifth Commandment, *Thou Shalt Not Kill* (illustration 35). Baldung was a fiery partisan of the Reformation but he also seems to have been one of a circle, with Brunfels, Indagine, and Johannes Has, interested in chiromancy, astrology, and magic. He made several woodcuts and drawings of witches, notably the famous chiaroscuro already mentioned. The belief in witches which had been growing for centuries was crystallized and officially encouraged by the growth in power of the Inquisition and the publication of the *Malleus Malificarum*,

54

or *Inquisitor's Manual* in 1489. The belief in and punishment for witchcraft continued through the seventeenth century.

There was another group of artists most of whom had had some contact with Dürer either as pupil or as indirect influence. From the small size of most of their prints, they are generally called the Little Masters. Three of them, Georg Pencz and the two brothers, Barthel and Hans Sebald Beham, got themselves in trouble for atheistic utterances and sympathies for the Peasant Revolt, and were banished from Nuremberg. An interesting reflection of this is seen in H. S. Beham's *Drummer and Standard Bearer* with an inscription "In the Peasant War 1525" (illustration 173). Barthel Beham's print, the *Bookplate of Baumgartner* (illustration 175) is not perhaps typical of his work (he was by far the more pictorially creative of the two brothers) but it is interesting as an early example of a class of print which has continued its popularity to the present day. The Little Masters were very much interested in applied art of all kinds, and much of their work consists of prints of ornament, models for other arts, such as goldsmith's work, costume, etcetera. Heinrich Aldegrever was one of the most talented of them, and produced some of the best Renaissance ornament in Germany, as well as some elegant costume studies of patricians, wedding dancers, and the like. The engraving, *Ornament with Lettering* (illustration 177) has been chosen to represent his work because it touches upon a field which had great interest especially during the sixteenth century. It was the period when the forms of letters were being established and new variations were being experimented with. First there were the theoreticians on the shaping of Roman letters, Fra Luca Pacioli in 1509, Sigismondo de' Fanti in 1514, Dürer in his *Treatise on Mensuration*, 1525, Tory in his *Champfleury*, 1529. The growth of the trade and culture of the middle class produced a demand for correct models for various types of script, legal, notarial, chancellary, documentary, ornate, as used in various countries and languages. The first practical book of this kind was by Ludovico Vicentino, the official scribe at the Papal Court, in Rome, 1522 (illustration 61). Similar books were produced in Italy, France, Spain, Holland, Germany, and England during the sixteenth, seventeenth, and eighteenth centuries, by Tagliente, Palatino,

55

Yciar, van de Velde, and many others. Another interesting phase of applied art were the costume books and the model books for lace and embroidery. The *Corona delle Nobili et Virtuose Donne*, published at Venice in 1592 (illustration 63), may serve as representative of the pattern books published by Gastel, Sibmacher, Quentel, Pellegrino, Vavassore, Pagan, Osthaus, Vinciolo, Parasole, Franco, and others. The *Corona* was issued by Cesare Vecellio, a cousin of Titian, and he also published in 1590 a famous work on costume, the first indeed with any pretense to historical or scientific accuracy, though similar works had been issued previously by Vico, de Bruyn, Boissard, Weigel, and Amman. Venice occupied during the sixteenth century, as Max von Boehn points out, a position as an emporium of luxury and fashionable amusement similar to that of Paris during the eighteenth and nineteenth centuries.

Another aspect of applied art is treated in the model for a highly ornamented bed, 1533 (illustration 62), by the Swiss German wood-carver, architect, and woodcutter, Peter Flöttner. He designed, and undoubtedly cut with his own hand (as evidenced by the woodcutting tools which he introduced in many of his pictures as his trade mark) a considerable number of woodcuts of architectural ornament and models for intarsia or inlay work. He also designed a set of playing cards one of which is reproduced as illustration 58. Many books of herbals were issued to satisfy popular demand. One of the most noteworthy was the *Herbarum Vivae Eicones* by Otto von Brunfels (whose portrait Hans Baldung cut in wood, illustration 46) published at Strassburg in 1530. The woodcuts of the plants, the most accurate of their time, were designed by Hans Weiditz (illustration 57). The works of this master, whose name and personality were rediscovered only in recent times, are among the most appealing and charming in the history of prints. He illustrated several popular moralizing works compiled from Petrarch and Cicero, extolling all the good old bourgeois virtues of thrift, prudence, moderation, piety, and the like. He was a born story-teller, and he illustrated these dull books with such zest and charm, above all with such a wealth of observation, that they have become a treasure-house of the manners and customs of the Augsburg of his day. He had what the

56

historian loves above all else—a talent for the obvious. He rarely shows any great gift for design, but he more than makes up for this lack by his talent as a narrator and observer. Two characteristic woodcuts are reproduced herewith, one from a popular story *The Tragedy of Calixtus and Melibea*, Augsburg, 1520 (illustration 42), and the other from Petrarch's *Consolation in Fortune and Misfortune*, Augsburg, 1532 (illustration 43), illustrating the story of the man who was so proud of his wife's unadorned beauty that he showed her off to a friend. Incidentally it reveals the norm of female beauty that was prevalent in Augsburg at the time.

One more of the Little Masters still remains to be considered, the most important of the group—Albrecht Altdorfer, who flourished at Regensburg on the Danube as a painter, engraver, architect, and city councilor, from about 1505 till his death in 1538. There is something very personal and appealing in his style, filled with homely feeling and endowed with a simple love of nature. There is something a bit amateurish about his engravings, as if he did them for his own pleasure: his draughtsmanship at times leaves something to be desired. In 1515 he executed (for it is believed that he cut many of his own blocks) a series of forty small woodcuts of the Passion which have truly the distinction of being *multum in parvo*. They display an imagination, a dramatic power, and a depth of feeling that have been seldom surpassed. In the example here reproduced, the *Death of the Virgin* (illustration 33), consider how the weight of the composition presses down upon the dying woman. The lovely and serene *Holy Family at the Fountain* of 1520 is also reproduced (illustration 41). Notable among his copper engravings are the *Crucifixion*, the *Virgin and Child in a Landscape*. As an example of his burin work in a sweet and tender vein the *Virgin and Child at the Cradle* is reproduced as illustration 171.

With the consideration of Altdorfer the survey of German graphic art of the Renaissance now comes to a close. At its best it was of brief duration: by the middle of the century there were no important German artists. Thereafter German art merits no serious consideration for several centuries to come. Some critics, among them William Morris, have ascribed this to the injurious influence of the Italian Renaissance upon so alien a culture as that of the Gothic North. Although it is true that the Renaissance, and likewise the Reformation, produced first a quickening and later a depressing effect on German art, there were nevertheless other factors which contributed strongly to its downfall. The political, social, and economic conditions in Germany at the middle and end of the century were not conducive to the cultivation of art. The country was in a state of anarchy, torn by the religious factionalism of Catholic against Protestant which culminated in the disastrous Thirty Years War of the seventeenth century, broken up into a multitude of avaricious, cruel and warlike principalities, checked by practically no central authority. Travel was unsafe. The trade which had flourished so auspiciously in the previous century had been impaired by two events of far-reaching importance: the Portuguese development of a sea trade route around Africa to India, and the closing of the overland caravan routes by the conquests of the Suliman Turks which ruined the Venetian monopoly of oriental trade. With the decline of the Venetian trade and the rise of Dutch naval commerce, the Hansa merchants and the Free Cities along the overland German trade route suffered a disastrous decline. In addition, the vast influx of silver and gold from the Spanish colonies caused a serious depreciation in the value of the precious metal mined in Germany. From these considerations it is easy to see that art suffered a blight which took centuries to overcome.

II

The Italians, set in the midst of natural loveliness and among the ruins of ancient art, had never wholly lost the sense of beauty; they may have paid but slight attention to what was about them, but they lived lifelong in the daily sight of fair scenes and beautiful forms, which impressed their senses and molded their nature, so that, when with the revival of letters they felt the native impulse of humanity toward the higher life stirring once more in their hearts, they found themselves endued with powers of perception and appreciation beyond any other people in the world. These powers were not the peculiar possession of a well-born class; the centuries had bred them unobserved into the nature of the race, into the physical constitution of the people. The artisan, no less than the prince, took delight in the dawn of art, and welcomed it with equal worship. Nor was this artistic instinct the only common acquisition; the enthusiasm for letters was likewise widely shared so that some of the best manuscripts of the classics have come down to modern times from the hands of humble Florentine workmen. Italy, indeed, was the first country where democratic civilization had place; here the contempt of the Northern lord for the peasant and the mechanic had never been widespread, partly because mercantile life was early held to be honorable, and partly because of peculiar social conditions. The long, uninterrupted intercourse with the remains of Roman civilization in the unbarbarized East, the contact with Saracenic civilization in the South, the culture of the court of the Two Sicilies, and the invariably leveling influence of commerce, had made Italy the most cosmopolitan of European countries; the sharp and warlike rivalry of small but intensely patriotic states, and the necessity they lay under of utilizing for their own preservation whatever individual energy might arise among them, perhaps most of all the powerful example of the omnipresent Church in which the son of a swineherd might take the Papal Throne, had contributed to make it comparatively easy to pass from lower to higher social ranks; the aristocratic structure remained but the distinction of classes was obscured, and the excellence of the individual's faculties, the energy and scope of his powers, were recognized as the real dignities which were worthy of respect. In this recognition of the individual, and this common taste for art and letters, lay the conditions of new and vigorous intellectual life; they resulted in the great age of Italy. It was this in the main that made possible the popular fervor for the things of the mind in the Italian Renaissance, to which nothing else in the world's history is comparable but the popular enthusiasm of the modern Revolution for liberty. Dante gave his country a native language, the Humanists gave it the literature of Rome, the Hellenists the literature of Greece; poets sang and artists painted with a loftiness and dignity of imagination, a sweetness and delicacy of sentiment, and energy and reach of thought, a music of verse and harmony of line and color, still unsurpassed. The gifts which these men brought were not for a few, but for the many who shared in this mastering, absorbing interest in the things of the mind, in beauty and wisdom, which was the vital spirit of the Italian Renaissance.

Thus did George Edward Woodberry summarize the background of the Italian Renaissance, from which sprang, about the middle of the fifteenth century, the art of engraving apparently quite independently of Germany. Just as in the northern countries, its development was bound up with the goldsmith. Modern scholarship has distinguished two schools or workshops of goldsmiths in Florence where the new art probably had its origin. The first workshop, traditionally associated with the name of Maso Finiguerra (to whom indeed Vasari mistakenly attributes the invention of engraving), produced prints in the "Fine Manner." The distinguishing characteristic of this technique was a system of crosshatching by fine lines giving somewhat the effect of a wash drawing. One of the outstanding works of this school is a series of *The Planets* with their attributes and influences on daily life. The *Planet Mercury*, patron of commerce and art (illustration 122) presents a delightful picture of the flourishing state of the arts in Florence. In the foreground a sculptor is carving a portrait bust. To the left is a goldsmith's shop with an artist making an engraving, and a customer bargaining for a handsome goblet. Above on a scaffolding an artist is painting a fresco while his assistant is grinding colors. In the background is an astrologer with an astrolabe. To the right scholarly pursuits are illustrated. In the foreground a richly dressed youth is feasting in the company of the innkeeper. Truly a paradise for artists and scholars. Similar in technique is a class of goldsmiths' work, known as nielli. These were small plates, usually of silver, in which a decorative design had been engraved and filled with a kind of enamel of contrasting color. The artist sometimes kept a record of his design by inking the plate and making a proof on paper or other material; from this—another transition step in the art of printmaking—he got the idea of making plates for the specific purpose of printing off designs. Two later tiny ornament prints, in the style of nielli, by Peregrino da Cesena are reproduced as illustrations 138 and 139. Another charming group in the Fine Manner are the so-called Otto Prints, from the name of an early owner (illustration 144). They were round ornamental engravings and were perhaps designed for decorative purposes just as we might paste designs on a candy box.

The second large group of Florentine engravings are in the "Broad Manner." They are differentiated from the Fine Manner engravings by the use of parallel lines of shading, giving somewhat the effect of a pen and ink drawing. Two examples of the Broad Manner are shown in the *Libyan Sibyl* from the series of the *Prophets and Sibyls* (illustration 120) and the *Assumption of the Virgin* (illustration 123). The latter, one of the finest and also largest of the early Italian engravings, was undoubtedly based upon a design by Botticelli. The composition is noble and distinguished, and the engraving manages to translate some of the linear movement, rugged characterization, and lyric beauty that is associated with Botticelli in his last period.

One of the most important productions of the North Italian School is the set of so-called *Tarocchi Cards* of Mantegna which, as Hind points out, are neither cards nor Tarocchi nor by Mantegna. They are a series of fifty instructive prints divided into five series classified as *Ranks and Conditions of Men, Apollo and the Muses, Arts and Sciences, Genii and Virtues,* and *Planets and Spheres.* The *Primum Mobile,* or *Angel of the Ninth Sphere,* of the last-named series is reproduced as illustration 121. The engravings were probably made at Ferrara around 1465. Dürer made a copy of this print on his first journey to Italy; the drawing is preserved in the British Museum. The greatest artist of the North Italian School, however, was Andrea Mantegna. He was born of humble parentage near Padua about 1430. He studied at the studio of Squarcione, a mediocre painter and dealer in antiquities, whose shop was the meeting place of the scholars and humanists of Padua. It was in this atmosphere that he developed the admiration for the works and culture of Roman civilization which became the ruling passion of his life. In Vasari's words, "Andrea always maintained that the good antique statues were more perfect and beautiful than anything in nature." He lived in an ideal world of his own imagination, the world of Rome in which moved figures of incomparable nobility, dignity, and grandeur. And he set out to embody his dreams with all the tactile feeling, the sculpturesque power, the knowledge of nature and of representation, all the resources of a supremely creative temperament. His engravings, so seemingly dry and austere, are in truth loaded with emotion: every line is saturated with feeling. Never has tenderness and brooding protection been more superbly expressed than in the *Virgin and Child* (illustration 136a). For breath-taking grandeur *The Risen Christ be-*

tween St. Andrew and Longinus has never been surpassed; for the expression of sorrow and lofty sense of tragedy, his three *Entombments* (illustration 126). Consider also those re-creations of the antique, the *Battle of the Sea Gods,* and the *Bacchanal with Silenus* and the *Bacchanal with a Wine Press* (illustration 118); with what solidity and tactile reality these types are rendered concrete. There they are—brought into being by Mantegna to live forever like the figures on Keats' urn—types of revelry, types of tenderness, types of grandeur, types of sorrow and tribulation. The concrete embodiment of types is creation of a high order, much higher in fact than realistic representation of natural objects, because it requires a much greater concentration of mental and emotional faculties. So, in spite of the smallness of his *œuvre,* seven engravings in all and the score that are associated as engravings of his school, Mantegna ranks as one of the supremely great artists in the history of prints.

Mantegna established a reputation with some twenty prints, but Pollaiuolo became famous for only one, the *Battle of the Naked Men* (illustration 119). Antonio del Pollaiuolo was born in Florence about 1432 and was one of the most famous goldsmiths, sculptors, and painters of his time. "Antonio's treatment of the nude," says Vasari, "is more modern than that of any of the masters who preceded him, and he dissected many bodies to examine their anatomy, being the first to represent the proper action of the muscles." Berenson's famous appreciation of this engraving, one of the world's greatest masterpieces, is well known:

What is it that makes us return to this sheet with ever renewed, ever increased pleasure? Surely it is not the hideous faces of most of the figures and their scarcely less hideous bodies. Nor is it the pattern as decorative design, which is of great beauty indeed, but not at all in proportion to the spell exerted upon us. Least of all is it—for most of us—an interest in the technique or history of engraving. No, the pleasure we take in these savagely battling forms arises from their power to directly communicate life, to immensely heighten our sense of vitality. Look at the combatant prostrate on the ground and his assailant bending over, each intent on stabbing the other. See how the prostrate man plants his foot on the thigh of his enemy, and note the tremendous energy he exerts to keep off the foe, who, turning

62

as upon a pivot, with his grip on the other's head, exerts no less force to keep the advantage gained. The significance of all these muscular strains and pressures is so rendered that we cannot help realizing them; we imagine ourselves imitating all the movements, and exerting the force required for them—and all without the least effort on our side. If all this without moving a muscle, what should we feel if we too had exerted ourselves! And thus while under the spell of this illusion—this hyperaesthesia not bought with drugs, and not paid for with cheques drawn on our vitality—we feel as if the elixir of life, not our own sluggish blood, were coursing through our veins.

There is a charming profile *Portrait of a Lady* (illustration 135) of a style made famous by the paintings of Domenico Veneziano, Verrocchio, Pollaiuolo, and others. This engraving was formerly classified among the early anonymous prints in the Fine Manner, but Hind in his recent big *Catalogue of Early Italian Engravings* attributes it to the School of Pollaiuolo. In any case, with its emphasis on ornament and linear values, it is the work of a goldsmith rather than a painter. There is another profile *Portrait of a Lady* (illustration 136) which is sometimes ascribed to Leonardo da Vinci. That the great experimenter might have tried his hand at a new art technique is not improbable; and the slipped stroke on the forehead, as Hind points out, might be evidence of an unpracticed hand. Other critics, however, have felt that the engraving was much too professional for a one and only plate.

Some of the charm and enchantment of the School of Giorgione are carried over in the engravings of Giulio Campagnola, born at Padua about 1482. The son of the writer, Girolamo Campagnola, Giulio was precocious and many-sided in his development: painter, engraver, poet, musician, scholar, and designer of type. About 1507 he went to Venice and may have had some direct contact with Giorgione. He died after 1515. Of the sixteen plates which he engraved, some are quite banal, being copies after Dürer and others; but there are about a half dozen that are among the most exquisite prints of the period, the *Shepherds in a Landscape*, the *Stag at Rest*, the *Astrologer*, the *Young Shepherd*, the *St. John the Baptist*, and *Christ and the Woman of Samaria*. It is hard to analyze wherein the magic of an engraving like the *Christ and the Woman of*

63

Samaria (illustration 160) lies, but it is equally obvious that the enchantment exists. Perhaps it lies in the perfect identification of matter and form (in Walter Pater's words) or in the mood of serene and pure beauty that it so elusively suggests. The *St. John the Baptist* (illustration 137a)—the landscape Giorgionesque, the figure deriving its nobility from Mantegna—likewise manages to convey a definite emotion in purely pictorial terms. Campagnola's work is distinguished not for intensity or strength but for sensibility and grace. Some of his works like the *Young Shepherd*, the *Stag at Rest*, or the *St. John*, are executed with an exquisite placement of every detail, including the lettering of the name. In this embodiment of sensibility and good taste as a creative principle, Campagnola is the exemplar of a long line of artists reaching to the present day. His technique is noteworthy also for its use of dots and flick-work combined with more or less amounts of regular graver work to blend and soften his effects. It is an interesting anticipation of stipple engraving, not so much in its method as in its final result.

The allegories and mythological conceits dear to the Renaissance and Humanist temperament were depicted by a number of secondary yet charming engravers such as Robetta (illustration 137b), Master I. B. with the Bird, Nicoletto da Modena, Jacopo Francia, Benedetto Montagna, and others. The man who was destined to make engraving into a professional system was Marcantonio Raimondi. He was born in Bologna about 1480 and studied with the goldsmith-painter, Francesco Francia. In due course he left his native city to seek his fortune in the big world. He was a facile engraver and had a great talent for assimilation. In Venice, most cosmopolitan of cities, he discovered the work of Dürer and as we have already heard, copied much of it. "Arrived at Rome," in Vasari's words, "he made a beautiful copper engraving of a drawing of Raphael, representing Lucretia killing herself, executed with such beauty and diligence that, when it was shown to Raphael, the artist was disposed to issue some prints himself from his own designs." This was the beginning of a long and fruitful partnership between artist and engraver in the dissemination of designs, which had enormous influence on art for centuries to come. It established a practice of reproductive engraving which was to last until the perfection of photographic reproductions. It was in the form of reproductive engraving that a large portion of art was made accessible to other practicing artists. Not only did Marcantonio, in collaboration with Raphael establish the practice but he also, through his pupils, laid down a system of technique. As Ivins points out, "Marcantonio combined the German linear scheme for representation of textures and rotundity with the Italian feeling for volumes, and in so doing gave engraving its pictorial enfranchisement." Two of the greatest examples of these two artists' collaboration are the *Judgment of Paris* and the *Massacre of the Innocents* (illustrations 161 and 162). They are marvels of space composition, rhythmic movement and balance, linear design and felicitous handling of the figure. The engraving of *Two Fauns* (illustration 146), based upon the antique, shows the extent to which Renaissance decoration deviated from medieval ornament. After the death of Raphael, Marcantonio's work suffered a strong deterioration, and this decline was completed by his financial ruin in the sack of Rome in 1527. He fled to Bologna and died a broken man.

Another engraver who collaborated with Raphael in still another form of reproductive engraving was Ugo da Carpi. Vasari credits da Carpi with the invention of chiaroscuro wood engraving or the use of several blocks in color for the reproduction of drawings. It has been discovered, however, that the Germans, Burgkmair, 1508, Cranach, 1509 (illustration 170), Baldung Grien (illustration 169), Altdorfer, Wechtlin, and others had perfected the process either previously or contemporaneously with the Italian. The methods of the two schools were nevertheless slightly different. The Germans in general worked up the black and white key block to its completion so that it could function as a woodcut independently (see illustration 44) and then added color blocks to heighten the effect. Whereas the Italians conceived the whole in terms of color and made less use of detailed black and white accents. In the *Miraculous Draught of Fishes* by da Carpi after the drawing by Raphael (illustration 168) the details are treated so broadly and so completely in terms of color, that the key block would have no meaning independently of the other blocks. Another example, the *Saturn*, by da Carpi after Parmigiano, is reproduced as illustration 167. Other prac-

65

titioners of the art in Italy were Andreani, Vicentino, and Antonio da Trento.

Mention of the woodcut leads us back half a century to trace the development of the art in Italy. Single woodcuts of the fifteenth century were not so frequent in Italy as in Germany, though woodcut playing cards are mentioned as a flourishing industry at Venice as early as 1441. The illustrated book, however, soon developed into one of the most important achievements of the Renaissance in Italy. The first illustrated book in Italy was the *Meditations of Cardinal Turrecremata* printed in Rome in 1467 (illustration 1). The cuts were probably made by a German craftsman, but the interesting thing about them was the printed statement that they were reproductions of frescoes appearing in the Church of Marie de Minerva in Rome, and thus the earliest extant example of the use of engraving for reproducing artists' paintings and designs, the practice which Raphael and Marcantonio first put on a successful business basis.

The second illustrated book in Italy was Valturius, *De Re Militari*, printed at Verona in 1472. The designs of this early and important book on military engineering have been attributed to the medallist, Matteo de Pastis or to Valturius himself (illustration 2). As an example of the pictorial treatment of another of the arts, the *Organist* from Gafurius, *Theorica Musicae*, printed in Milan in 1492, is reproduced as illustration 13. In Ferrara in 1497 was published an illustrated book with the same title though not with the same contents as the Ulm *De Claris Mulieribus* of 1473. The picture, which serves as a portrait of both Paula Gonzaga and of Marcella Romana (illustration 9), is in striking contrast to the earlier *Sappho*, and shows how divergent were Gothic and Renaissance ideals.

The two great centers of book production in Italy were Venice and Florence. The illustrators of Venice perfected a kind of engraving in outline not only intrinsically charming and graceful but also perfectly in keeping with the roman type face. The *Decameron* of 1492 has already been mentioned (illustration 3). One of the most distinguished examples of Venetian illustration is Ketham's *Fascicolo di Medicina* of 1493 (illustration 14). This noble and dignified work gives us a glimpse

66

of the medical practice of the time: we see the doctor visiting the patient ill with the plague, being careful not to come too close for fear of infection. Perhaps the most famous Venetian book was the *Hypnerotomachia Poliphili*, or the *Strife of Love in a Dreame*, as an Elizabethan translated it. It was printed by Aldus in 1499 at the expense of Leonardus Crassus (illustration 4). The text by Colonna is a mélange of humanist and classical conceits, and the book is now remembered only for the beauty of its woodcuts and the harmony of its type and illustrations. The work has been a model to many subsequent illustrators, notably Ricketts and Maillol in modern times.

In Florence, among other things, were published a large group of illustrated books which bear the same relation to the Renaissance, in their perfection of a popular art, that the French Books of Hours bear to the Gothic spirit: the essence of the Renaissance is distilled in their pages. These woodcuts, like the cuts of the *Horae*, possess a distinctive and easily recognizable style. And curiously enough, the period of their greatest production coincided almost exactly with that of the French books, that is to say the ten years before and the thirty years after the beginning of the sixteenth century. Like them, too, the names of the artists or engravers are not known. Many of the Florentine cuts appeared in little booklets, manifestations of popular art, *Rappresentazione* or sacred mystery plays, sermons, poems, little novels—an enormous range of subject matter. The daily life of Florence is re-created before our eyes. Hundreds of scenes, the facts, the gestures, the characters of everyday life are transformed into decorative pictures of lasting charm. We see a group singing before an image in church, we see the swain bringing his sweetheart a flower (illustration 48), we see the citizen at the shoemaker's shop or at the fishmonger buying fish during Lent (illustration 11), we see young bucks carousing. We see dramatic incidents from the lives of the saints, we see Savonarola preaching in church (illustration 10), nay we almost hear him as he holds his audience spellbound by his eloquence:

Women, you rejoice in being beautiful. Be beautiful, it is woman's greatest delight. But tell me in what does beauty consist? In colors? No. In contours? No. It is in the harmony between them. And how is that harmony revealed? By light. Beauty is light. You see happy spirits; their beauty consists in light. You know, God is light: He is beauty also. The more truly that creatures participate in the beauty of God and approach it, the more beautiful they become. . . .

We see illustrations to poems, Dante's *Divina Commedia* (illustration 49), Pulci's *Morganti Maggiore*, Boccaccio's *Ninfale Fiesolano* (illustration 12), a charming pastoral bit. And this whole panorama is depicted with such charming decorative effect, such color and vivacity, such zest and *joie de vivre*, such unerring balance between particular and universal, that they have never been surpassed in the history of prints.

Single sheet woodcuts were not made in great quantities in the sixteenth century in Italy except for a few in Venice. Here Titian was the dominant influence. The five sheets of the *Triumph of Faith*, dated 1508, and the twelve sheets of *Pharaoh's Army Submerged in the Red Sea*, of 1549, are epoch-making works, grand both in size and significance. These works are too huge for reduction on a small scale, and two other works by Titian (illustrations 45 and 39) have been chosen for reproduction, one cut by Nicolo Boldrini, the *Venus and Amor*, and the *Landscape with the Woman Milking a Cow*. They are faithful translations into wood of the characteristics of Titian's drawing, and one of them shows Titian's pastoral interest and method of treating pure landscape, which probably influenced Bruegel and Rubens when they came to take up the same theme. Titian's portraits were famous for their penetration of character, their decorative fullness and nobility of style. Typical of these is Titian's portrait of his friend, the great poet, Ariosto, cut in wood by Francesco de Nanto and published in an edition of his *Orlando Furioso*, Ferrara, 1532 (illustration 47). Incidentally Ariosto mentions Titian in his poem. The great Venetian died in 1576 at the age of ninety-nine, rich in honors and achievement, one of the first professional artists in the modern sense of the word.

A distinguished portrait of Titian was engraved by Agostino Carracci (illustration 153), one of three brothers who founded the Eclectic School of Bologna, and who also were among the first to introduce the Academy system of teaching to replace the older master-apprentice

68

method. The Carracci, dominant in the second half of the sixteenth century, represented the eclectic and somewhat decadent tendency which followed the great outburst of the Renaissance. Two other painters whose work anticipated and led up to some of the qualities associated with Baroque art were Parmigiano and Baroccio. Francesco Mazzuoli, called Parmigiano, was the first Italian who practiced etching. His etchings, dating from about 1520 onwards, have the spontaneity and charm, the refinement and feminine grace of his drawings (illustration 166). He was one of the first of the Mannerists. Federigo Baroccio (1528–1612) made about four etchings, notably the large *Annunciation* (illustration 165). This plate is rather theatrical in style but executed with considerable subtlety of biting. Baroccio was to have considerable influence on the religious painting of Boucher and other artists of the eighteenth century.

The early illustrated books had been decorated with woodcuts. But at the end of the sixteenth century woodcut illustrations were being replaced by intaglio or copperplate engravings. There were several reasons for this. Copper engraving became more fashionable than woodcuts. But there also was a growing differentiation in the purpose of the book: between the book as a cheap popular work and the book as an object of luxury. In the fifteenth century the differentiation had been between the cheap printed book and the sumptuous illuminated manuscript. Now, the differentiation was made between the cheap woodcut book and the expensive copperplate book. There was no doubt that the copperplate book was more expensive to produce: it required more than one printing, the plates took longer to print and could not yield as many impressions as a woodblock. Thus the illustrated book became intaglio in character and luxurious and expensive in production. The woodcut went underground, as it were, and continued an unbroken tradition from the fifteenth century to the nineteenth century in the chapbooks, broadsheets, *images populaires*, and fugitive prints of the people. Of course in certain kinds of scientific work such as maps or architectural illustrations, where the greater precision of copper engraving was desirable, there were reasons other than economic for the change. By the middle of the sixteenth century the technical difficulties in the way of using intaglio illustrations had been more or less overcome. Three books may be used to typify the new tendency. The first, catering to an aristocratic luxurious class, is Gualterotti's *Description of the Royal Fête at the Marriage of Christina of Lorraine with Don Ferdinando de' Medici, Grand Duke of Tuscany*, published at Florence in 1589. It was a sort of souvenir book of the ceremonies describing all the pageants, mimic battles, balls, triumphal arches, allegories, etcetera, that were part of the festivities. There were sixty-seven paintings made of the various incidents by a number of court painters, and for the book they were etched with great zest and vigor by some unknown hand. The illustration chosen (182) apparently represents the actual wedding ceremony, and was painted by Giovanni Balducci, called Cosci. The etching is carried out with a breadth and power, an incisive line and flair for style that is truly a delight to the eye. It contains a trace of mannerism but there is still a lot of sap in the manner. Incidentally, at this same wedding a number of musical *intermezzi*, precursors of opera, were produced. One of them, *The Harmony of the Spheres*, was composed by Emilio del Cavaliere, who later produced the first oratorio.

The second example is midway between the scientific and the sumptuous book: *Della Trasportazione dell' Obelisco Vaticano*, published at Rome in 1589 (illustration 178). This work, written by Domenico Fontana, the well-known architect of Pope Sixtus V, describes the engineering feat of transporting the obelisk to its present location in the Piazza of St. Pietro, and is illustrated with a number of engravings by Natalis Bonifaccio after Fontana's designs. The plates were executed with gusto and a fine balance between scientific and pictorial interest. The artistic treatment of scaffolding, building construction, "the wonder of work," has been generally assumed to be of modern origin. Although the scientific aspect is stressed, it is probable that it was considered more as a sumptuous gift book given out by the Pope and his friends. The third example is more specifically of scientific interest, a page from the great Atlas of Ortelius, the *Map of America* of 1589 (illustration 180), printed by the famous Antwerp printer, Plantin, of whom we shall hear further in connection with Rubens. It is interesting to contrast this map with the Nuremberg map of the

70

world in 1493 and trace the growth of man's geographical knowledge. In 1492 Columbus discovered America; in 1497 Cabot discovered New-foundland; in 1498 Vasco de Gama sailed to India around Africa; in 1499 Amerigo Vespucci discovered Venezuela; in 1513 Balboa discovered the Pacific at Panama; in 1514 the Portuguese were in China and in 1542 in Japan; in 1520 Magellan sailed around the world; from 1539 to 1577 the explorations of de Soto, Coronado, Cartier, Frobisher, and Drake took place. Ortelius was one of the first cartographers to issue maps that were based on actual scientific observations. Yet withal the map is beautifully designed, with a fine sense of placement of the decorative cartouches and other accessories. The ship in the Pacific represents Magellan sailing around the world. Ortelius drew at a time when the truth about geography was still beautiful. Later on it was to become strictly utilitarian.

About this time in Antwerp and later at Brussels there lived a man who was one of the world's greatest artists, Peter Bruegel. He was born about 1525 and studied with Pieter Koeck van Aeist, whose daughter he afterwards married. He undoubtedly derived inspiration in his macabre aspects from Hieronymus Bosch. In 1551 he was enrolled in the artists' Guild of St. Luke at Antwerp, and was furnishing designs to the print publisher, Jerome Cock. Most of our knowledge of his life comes from the almost contemporary account of Karel van Mander.

With [his friend and patron] Franckert, Bruegel often went on trips among the peasants, to their weddings and fairs [illustration 186]. The two dressed like peasants, brought presents like the other guests, and acted as if they belonged to the families or acquaintances of the bride or groom. Here Bruegel delighted in observing the manners of the peasants in eating, drinking, dancing, jumping, making love, and engaging in various drolleries, all of which he knew how to copy very comically and skillfully. . . . He was astonishingly sure of his composition and drew most ably and beauti-fully with the pen. . . . Bruegel was a quiet man who did not talk much, but was jovial in company, and he loved to frighten people, often his own pupils with all kinds of ghostly sounds and pranks that he played. . . . He painted a *Massacre of the Innocents,* in which there is much to see that is done true to life—a whole family, for instance, begging for the life of a peasant child whom a murderous soldier has seized in order to kill it; the grief and the swooning of the mother and other events appear realistic. . . . Many of Bruegel's strange compositions and comical subjects one may see in his copper engravings. But he has made many skillful and beautiful drawings; he supplied them with inscriptions which, at the time, were too biting and too sharp, and which he had burned by his wife during his last illness, because of remorse, or fear that the most disagreeble consequences might grow out of them. In his will he left his wife a picture of a Magpie on a Gallows. By the magpie he meant the gossips whom he delivered to the gallows. In addition, he had painted a picture in which Truth triumphs. According to his own statement, this was the best thing painted by him.

Bruegel had a deep and abiding love for humanity, for the peasant and common man, for life in its essentials. But it was not a patronizing attitude, something he could exploit cynically or commercially for his own ends. It grew out of his innate sympathy for all the manifestations of life, high and low, the eternal verities of man and woman. He also had a great love for nature, its trees and rocks, its rivers and mountains, its fertile plains, as his many landscapes show (illustration 183). But he was also a great intellect, one of the world's greatest pictorial designers in line and color in space; like Bach, whom he resembled in many respects, a master of noble and intricate contrapuntal effects. Above all he was a philosopher who meditated on first and last things, who was capable of those profound syntheses of human experience which he clothed in archetypes of the most convincing realism. He gave his allegiance to no faction but to humanity as a whole. He pursued his way serenely in troublous times with an enduring faith in Truth and Man. And parlous times they were: the presence of sudden and cruel death, bitter religious strife, rapine and wanton destruction, the horrible oppression of the Spanish rulers and soldiery. That he felt all these things is evident from the inscriptions he destroyed and from the nostalgia that permeates his *Luilekkerland* (illustration 185), the "Land of Cocaigne," the "Rock-Candy Mountains," that land of milk and honey where sorrow and effort and care are banished. But he also faced the facts with unflinching realism in the *Massacre of the Innocents* or in that magnificent synthesis of *Justice* (illustration 184) where are

72

assembled all the tortures of the Inquisition. He never took sides in the narrow sense. Is this the role of the artist? At any rate it is one solution of the artist's problem. It must be remembered that the issues were not as clear at the time as they are to us in perspective; even the oppressed were disorganized and torn with opposing factions, and he died before the Spanish Fury had reached its climax. He never took sides, but he always believed that his greatest painting was the *Triumph of Truth*.

France contributed relatively little to the history of prints during the sixteenth century. The chief school of the first half of the century was the School of Fontainebleau, largely an importation from Italy, and in the second half-century France was rent with civil strife. The etching by Sebastiano Serlio, the distinguished Italian architect of the palace of Fontainebleau, of a measured drawing of a capital from the Colosseum in Rome (illustration 181) indicates how printmaking served as a valuable tool to the builder by recording existing architectural monuments. The *Diana* (illustration 181a) by Master L. D. after Primaticcio is characteristic of the work of the School of Fontainebleau. One strange and mysterious figure stands out, however, among the early engravers of France—Jean Duvet. This goldsmith-engraver was born about 1485, probably at Dijon, and died after 1561 at Langres. He executed some goldsmith's work as a present from the town of Langres to Francis I, and was honored with the title of Goldsmith to the King. He made some sixty engravings including a series of the *Apocalypse* and the *History of the Unicorn,* an allegory bearing some relation to the amours of Henri II and Diane de Poitiers. But this summary recital of his life and work give no hint of the particular quality of his genius. He was a mystic, one of those extraordinary figures whose prints are moving not by what they say but by what they imply. As with many mystics his expression is often turgid and confused, often his very language and forms are derivative—mystics are indifferent to such matters, since mundane expression bears the same relation to the inner light as a candle does to the sun. But through these naive and clumsy engravings shine breath-taking illumination and fiery emotion. His conception is so much greater than his execution that he sometimes leaves his plates unfinished in despair. His plates of the *Apocalypse* (illustration 164) with their swirling forms and phantasmagoric appearances, seem more akin to the

73

spirit of that great mystical document than Dürer's somewhat more prosaic version, from which many of the details are borrowed. In a serener, more joyous vein is the *Marriage of Adam and Eve* (illustration 163). It is interesting to compare this with Dürer's *Adam and Eve* for a further contrast between the mystic and the man of the world.

Jean Cousin, painter, sculptor, engraver, architect, glass-worker, mathematician, and writer, made a small number of engravings, notably an *Entombment* (illustration 159) distinguished for its moving arrangement of figures against a background of classical landscape. His *Book of Perspective* of 1560 with its charming and precise woodcuts bears witness to the great interest that existed in that branch of science. But the first French work, indeed the first printed work on perspective in any language, was issued at Toul in 1505 by Jean Pélerin. Pélerin, or Viator, was Canon of the Cathedral, had been in the service of the historian Philippe de Commines, and wrote books on Ptolemy as well as on devotional subjects. It is not known how he achieved the miracle of working out to perfection the complete system of perspective, but he did and illustrated it with a series of woodcut diagrams of a room (illustration 59), bridges, a courtyard, Notre Dame Cathedral, etcetera. The book was popular and went through several editions, and was pirated in a Nuremberg edition of 1509. The work was dedicated to artists and in the dedication he mentions some that he considered worthy in his day. They are, as far as they can be identified, as follows: Mantegna, Leonardo, Raphael, Michelangelo, Perugino, Bellini, Lucas van Leyden, Cranach, Dürer, Baldung Grien, Hugo van der Goes, Schäufelein, and Fouquet.

This concludes the survey of the Renaissance as expressed in prints. The astonishing thing about the Italian Renaissance was the extent to which all the people participated in it. There are always a few cultivated and creative people in every age, but when these qualities are spread among all the people, it becomes a great period. Artists and craftsmen of great talent sprang up on every hand; but there were also a great demand and encouragement for their work. Time and time again one comes across passages in Vasari like this: "Agnolo Doni was then in Florence, and though sparing in other things, spent willingly upon

74

paintings and sculpture, of which he was very fond." Or the following: "All of which brought Marcantonio such fame that his things were more valued than those of the Flemings for their good design, and the merchants found them very profitable." It was in Italy that the print-seller-publisher first developed. There were Il Baviera (Raphael's agent), Nicolo Nelli, Antonio Salamanca, Antoine Lafrery, C. Duchetti, Jerome Cock of Antwerp, and others. Even the commonest books and pamphlets were beautiful. But in the mutations of man's fate, this widespread cultivation of the beautiful did not last for long. We marvel at the calmness and casualness with which Vasari mentions the sack of Rome in 1527. Italy had been broken up into many rival cities and principalities, and the Hapsburg vied with the rulers of France for their domination and control. Italy was undoubtedly the most civilized country of Europe, civilized not only in the sense of culture and refinement but also in the sense of commerce and manufacture. Italy gave much to Germany and Flanders and especially to France through the encouragement of its rulers from Francis I to Catherine de' Medici. With the development of these countries, Italy's prestige and its trade gradually declined. The dominant power in the second half of the sixteenth century was Spain with all the wealth of the Americas at its command (illustration 206), and its policy was reactionary and monarchical, definitely opposed to the relatively democratic cultures of Italy, England, and Flanders.

4. Seventeenth Century

THE seventeenth century has sometimes been called the century of the Baroque. And although an art period or style cannot be precisely delimited by centuries, many of the artists of the time display qualities that are associated with this style. The Baroque developed from the Renaissance and to a certain extent was a reaction against it. It was the age of the counter-Reformation, a re-affirmation of faith and dogma, initiated largely by the Jesuits against the individualist interpretations of the Protestant Reformation. It has been claimed that the Baroque had a relation to the Gothic in its stress upon emotional elements. It is true that both Gothic and Baroque were ages of faith; but in the one case it was naive faith, a primary and creative impulse, in the second case it was a faith in established dogma, a secondary or derivative impulse. The Baroque would have been impossible without the Renaissance. A definite convention, a dogma had been firmly established—a convention that embraced not only religious but also social and artistic forms, absolute monarchy, forms of building and painting, forms of social life—and the Baroque was the individual's reaction to this. The dogmas were not challenged: they were taken for granted; and with that foundation they were either expanded into a swelling system as with Rubens, or embroidered with grotesque themes as with Callot. The Baroque was a product of leisure and luxury, a slackening of the terrific outburst of energy of the Renaissance. The fires had died down; what remained were the flickerings of fantasy. The artists of the Renaissance expressed their ideas in attitudes and gestures energetically and beautifully appropriate to the occasion, the natural outgrowth of the action expressed. In the Baroque the gesture became important for its own sake; the artists played with it, they heightened it or exaggerated it, played variations on it, till it became largely devoid

76

of logical meaning. The gesture became a mannerism, a form often employed purely for compositional effect. They were bored with austere or tragic effects; they craved novelty and ingenious invention. The positive, the affirming, the best side of the Baroque was expressed by Rubens.

Peter Paul Rubens, the Prince of Painters, lived and breathed in the grand manner. His work is one grand *largesse;* which was not with him a mannered attitude only: out of his fecundity, his incomparable zest, he endowed his forms with swelling pulsating life. He was a man of action: he painted pictures as a general would direct an army or a prince would rule a principality. He had vast organizing skill: he organized his pictures into masterly compositions, he organized his pupils and assistants to execute them; on both his instrument and his creation he put his own impress. He did not innovate, he summed up. He did not create new forms, he used the material at hand, he worked in the spirit of the age. He lived as Fromentin said, *"en plein lumière,"* in full light—never a shadow of scepticism or doubt. Born in 1577, he started his career as a court page; he died in 1640 the most renowned painter of his time. He studied with three masters and went to Italy to complete his education. At thirty-three he was a successful man with a beloved wife and children and an imposing house filled with art treasures. He became a diplomat, working consistently to maintain peace between Protestant Holland and Catholic Belgium. He was the courteous friend of Philip II of Spain, the companion of the art-loving Charles I, the painter of the *Triumphs of Marie de' Medici,* the confidant and trusted agent of the Infanta Isabella of Belgium. He engaged in vast correspondence in Latin, Spanish, Italian, and Flemish on many matters of diplomacy, business, antiquities, collecting, but never any speculation on art. We have a contemporary account of his daily life by the Dane, Otto Sperling:

We paid a visit to the very celebrated and eminent painter, Rubens, whom we found at work, and, while he went on with his painting, listening to a reading from Tacitus and dictating a letter. We kept silent for fear of disturbing him; but he spoke to us without stopping his work or the reading or the dictation, and answered our questions as if to give us proof of his powerful faculties. Then he ordered a servant to conduct us round his magnificent palace and show us his antiquities and the Greek and Roman statues of which he owns a great quantity.

It is natural that such an expansive and practical nature should, like Raphael, see the advantage of publishing engravings of his work under his own auspices. He set about to train and employ a school of engravers of whom Soutman, Vorsterman, Pontius, and the two Bolswerts were the most famous. In the Bibliothèque Nationale in Paris, there exist proofs of their engravings containing corrections and emendations in Rubens' hand. It is doubtful whether he ever himself handled the burin. One etching, however, is ascribed to him with considerable certainty— the superb *St. Catherine* with its monumental swelling forms (illustration 222). The more than eight hundred engravings that were made after his works did much to spread Rubens' fame throughout Europe. As an example of landscape with genre interest the *Village Dance* engraved by Bolswert is reproduced as illustration 204. As an example of a religious subject, *The Temptation of Christ* from the plafond of the Jesuit Church in Antwerp, cut in wood by Christophel Jegher, is reproduced as illustration 64. In the archives of Plantin-Moretus museum in Antwerp is preserved Moretus' account referring to the printing of this very woodcut on September 2 and 8, 1633, "*item, doibt pour l'impression de 2000 images de bois avec le papier etc. Florins 72*" (item, to printing 2000 proofs of woodcut with paper 72 florins).

Anthony van Dyck was Rubens' most talented pupil. Before he settled permanently in England as court painter to Charles I in 1632, he began an ambitious undertaking known as the *Iconography* or collection of one hundred portraits of the famous men of his day. He executed eighteen of these in etching, of which five remained unchanged (*Peter Bruegel the Younger, Erasmus, Snellinx, Suttermans* and *Josse de Momper* [illustration 201]), six others were later supplied with engraved backgrounds (*Jan Bruegel, Franken, van Noort, Pontius, Vorsterman,* and *de Wael*) and the balance completely reworked by professional engravers. He initiated a new style of portraiture, the freely etched portrait, concentrating on certain features of the face with open lines and dots, and leaving the body and background lightly sketched in. But the prevailing taste of his day was for the more formal portrait and the balance of the *Iconography* was executed by the engravers of the Rubens school after his own drawings. It was not until several centuries later that the etchings themselves were appreciated. Van Dyck perfected a method for setting down the external features of a sitter without prying too deep into his essential character, which made him the eminently successful and fashionable portrait painter that he was. Even in his early days before the formula had mastered him completely, and when he was portraying his friends and fellow-painters, he could not resist endowing them all with a flattering dignity and nobility. It is known that van Dyck painted Charles I forty times and his Queen Henrietta thirty times. After the Countess Sophie of the Palatinate had been presented to the Queen and her attendants she recorded her naive astonishment at the discrepancy between fact and fiction: she had had such a different impression of the court from van Dyck's portraits.

Van Dyck died in 1641 just before the Great Rebellion in England. Another foreign etcher, Wenzel Hollar, allied himself with the Cavalier cause and fought in some of its battles. He was born in Prague in 1607 and studied with Mathias Merian. In 1637 he came to England under the patronage of the Earl of Arundel who employed him to reproduce treasures in his collection. Born in a noble family which had lost everything in the Bohemian wars, Hollar took up etching as his life profession: he made about 2700 plates, characterized by sobriety, precision, and great technical skill. He married a lady-in-waiting at the Court and was very much interested in depicting costume, as for instance in the famous series of the *Theatrum Mulierum* of 1643. Characteristic is the *Winter* (illustration 220) of the set of the *Seasons*. The background shows a view of Cornhill and the Old Exchange in London. Underneath are four lines of verse in the spirit of the court of Charles:

> "The cold, not cruelty makes her weare
> In Winter, furrs and Wild beasts haire
> For a smoother skinn at night.
> Embraceth her with more delight."

After the Restoration he fell into poverty and worked for the book and print publishers at twelve pence per hour. According to his friend,

Francis Place, "he had a method of working not common. He did all by the hour, in which he was very exact, for if anybody came in, and kept him from his business, he always laid the hourglass on one side, till they were gone." He died in extreme poverty in 1677.

As a foil to the almost feminine daintiness of Hollar one might put forward the masculine exuberance of Hendrick Goltzius. Born in 1558 of a long line of artists, he early developed an artistic temperament, and many stories are told of his pranks, of his posing as a cheese merchant before the engraver, Sadeler, of making engravings in the style of Dürer and Lucas van Leyden which fooled many would-be connoisseurs, of making his servant pose as the master while he in the role of servant listened to unguarded comments about the master. In his engraving he perfected the system of the swelling line, or minute variations in the thickness of each engraved line, which enabled him to render surface textures and color with more facility. This carried engraving further in the direction of a purely reproductive or copying technique in contrast to the systems of Dürer and Marcantonio which were more in the nature of translations of one medium into the conventions of another. Nevertheless his technical proficiency brought him great fame, and he was specially invited to Paris to do the portrait of Henri IV (illustration 236). He was one of the few seventeenth century artists who also made chiaroscuros and woodcuts, of which the *Landscape* (illustration 65) is a charming example. In his figure work he carried the Baroque tendency of mannered gesture, of swelling out and puffing up forms to the limit, as may be seen in the typical engraving of the *Statue of Hercules in the Farnese Palace in Rome* (illustration 219). With its glimpse of the visitors gazing in admiration at the statue, it affords a delightful suggestion of the *tourisme* of the time. John Evelyn in his diary thus records his visit in 1644:

In the first place, our sights-man (for so they name certain persons here who get their living by leading strangers about to see the city) went to the Palace Farnese, a magnificent square structure built by Michael Angelo. . . . Descending into the court, we with astonishment contemplated those two incomparable statues of Hercules and Flora, so much celebrated by Pliny.

80

Italy and its many art treasures were still the goal of artists and cultured tourists. The names of two great French etchers of the early seventeenth century were intimately associated with Italy: Callot and Claude Gellée of Lorraine.

Callot [wrote Meaume] when a child of thirteen ran away from his home at Nancy, meaning to journey to Rome and study art. It was in the spring of 1606 the young fugitive departed on foot, almost without money, and quite without influence, relying entirely on his face and his good luck. He was soon obliged to join a troupe of gypsies who were going to Florence. There he was recognized by merchants from Nancy and was taken home to his parents. He ran away a second time and was again brought home, this time by his brother. In 1608 Callot's parents finally permitted him to go to Rome where he studied under Thomassin.

In 1611 he left Rome for Florence (according to legend on account of a gallant adventure with his master's wife) and entered the service of Cosmo II de' Medici. Eleven years later he returned to his native Lorraine where he remained with brief outside excursions till his death in 1635. Callot was a great etcher and perfected the technique of repeated bitings to secure effects of great delicacy and subtlety. He was also a great Baroque artist in his predilection for the grotesque (the *Temptation of St. Anthony* and the series of *Gobbi*), for masks and pageants (in *Florence* and *Nancy*), for mannered religious engravings (the series of *The Saints, The Passion,* and *The Prodigal Son*) and in his research in the characters of the *Commedia dell'Arte*. Faithful reflections, too, of the movements of his time were his numerous war pictures, the *Military Exercises,* the three huge *Sieges of Breda,* the *Island of Ré,* and *La Rochelle,* and the larger and smaller *Disasters of War*. It is said that after the invasion of Lorraine in 1633, Louis XIII asked him to commemorate the siege of Nancy in another huge battle piece, but Callot refused to "do anything against the honor of my prince and my country." At any rate he had seen enough of the horrors of war during the French invasion in 1632 and 1633 to execute his two bitter series of *Les Misères de la Guerre* while his memory was still vivid. They are the first of a series of terrific indictments of war that have been drawn up by artists. No greater contrast could be imagined than between the brutality of the subject and the exquisite delicacy of the treatment (illustrations 210 and 211). Not only were the savage lusts of murder and plunder depicted but also the equally devastating starvation and poverty. The social system of the age was rich in contrasts, and Callot has faithfully recorded its full range, from the *Garden at Nancy* (illustration 209) and the *Costumes of the Nobility* to the studies of *Beggars* (illustration 208), card sharpers, and wandering gypsy life (illustration 212). But in no respect was he so much a child of his age as in his picturing of the *Commedia dell'Arte* (illustration 217). The *Commedia* was the quintessence of the Baroque: it was improvised, often extravagant and satiric, anti-intellectual and anti-rational, stressing emotional values, raising the caprice to an art form, playing variations on an accepted theme, a comedy of attitudes and gestures. In the *Commedia dell'Arte* certain types (Harlequin, Columbine, Isabelle, Scaramouche, Pulcinella, Pantaloon, Brighella, Mezzetino, Scapin, Sganarelle, Cantarina, Inamorata, Soubrette, Pierrot, El Capitan, The Doctor) with attributes known to everyone played their parts in dramatic situations which again were familiar to all. The dialogue was not written down or fixed, but was improvised by the actors following patterns that were well established. Thus the emphasis and charm of the art form lay not in the significance or meaning of the drama, but in its expression, in the gestures and pantomime of the actors, and in the wit, the satire, the *double entendre* of their speech. The *Commedia* flourished chiefly in the Latin countries during the seventeenth and eighteenth centuries.

According to legend Callot's contemporary, Claude, was a pastry cook's apprentice who longed for Arcadia and found it. Claude Gellée, called Lorrain, was born in the Vosges in 1600. Left an orphan at twelve he wandered about Italy, Germany, Switzerland, and Lorraine, pursued by many adventures and misadventures, falling sick, being several times robbed, and picking up here and there a knowledge of the technique of art. In 1627 he settled down in Rome where he lived a quiet and uneventful life. He did not associate with the French academicians in Rome, or perhaps they would not associate with him, though he occasionally went on painting excursions with Poussin; he was no courtier,

82

said Sandrart, and he had but few intimates like Swanevelt, Bombaccio, Andries Both, and Sandrart. He never married; all his passion went into his work, the task of rendering visible his dream of Arcadia, where all is peace and beauty and order. Sandrart wrote:

He applied himself with great earnestness and industry to perfect himself in his art and learn the secrets of nature. Day after day he would spend in the Campagna, from sunrise till long after nightfall, noting the tints of the dawn and the splendor of the setting sun. . . . As a master of aerial perspective, he well knew how to blend the sharp division of colors to make them appear like nature's. And at his studio he would sit long hours in reverie till there came to him those grand conceptions which grew in his mind so saturated with images of life and nature.

Claude made about twenty-seven etchings. He was no great technician and some of his plates suffer from foul biting and poor printing. But the best of them are among the masterpieces of the art. Claude was the first great impressionist in etching. He knew how to suggest the play of light on objects, and shimmering quivering atmosphere. His plates are sometimes heroically composed like the *Sunrise*, the *Seaport with Tower*, the *Herd in a Storm*, or the *Rape of Europa* (illustration 203) or touched with soft arcadian charm like the *Bouvier*, the *Dance under the Trees*, the *Dance by the Waterside* (illustration 205). The etching of *The Brigands* strikes an unpleasantly realistic note unusual in his work, yet even this is infused with so soft and pastoral an atmosphere as to make it seem like an illustration of Daphnis and Chloe. Fortunately success came to him later in life (he never could have carved it out for himself) and he died in peace at the age of eighty-two—a simple, naive, unlettered man who dreamed a sweet and beautiful dream.

There was another foreign artist living in Rome whose works display creative power and imagination but whose life ended tragically at thirty-two after years in a debtor's prison—the German painter, Adam Elsheimer. Both Rubens and Rembrandt admired his work. His small paintings of religious and mythological subjects have a strange and moving quality, which has been successfully carried over into black and white by his friend, the amateur engraver, Count Goudt, who also seems to have suffered a mysterious and tragic fate. Goudt engraved seven plates, all after Elsheimer, among them the large *Tobit and the Angel* with its lovely sky, the *Aurora* with an equally lovely sky, the mysterious *Mocking of Ceres*, the *Flight into Egypt* copied by Seghers, and finally the *Philemon and Baucis* (illustration 198). This last engraving, so beautiful in composition and magical in its chiaroscuro, illustrates the legend of Philemon and Baucis as told in the eighth book of Ovid's *Metamorphoses*. It is one of the most beautiful stories of hospitality ever told. Jupiter and Mercury disguised as travelers wandered into a Phrygian village. Asking for hospitality they were turned away at every door until at last they came to the humble dwelling of Philemon and Baucis. Here they were received with genuine hospitality by the aged couple. They bustled about to minister to their comfort and set before the weary travelers what provisions they could muster from their slender store. During the repast the old folks were astonished to see that the wine, as fast as it was poured out, renewed itself in the pitcher. Struck with terror, they recognized their heavenly guests and implored forgiveness for their poor entertainment. And they replied, "We are gods; this inhospitable village shall pay the penalty of its impiety; you alone shall go unpunished." They destroyed the village and transformed the humble dwelling into a beautiful temple, and Jove in a benignant mood asked the mortals what boon they might wish of him. And, counseling with Baucis, Philemon replied, "Grant us to be priests and guardians of this your temple; and since here we have passed our lives in love and concord, we wish that one and the same hour may take us both from life, that I may not live to see her grave, nor be laid in my own by her." And their prayer was granted.

Another great personality in print history with an equally tragic maladjustment to his surroundings was the Dutchman, Hercules Seghers. He was born about 1590 and died about 1640 as the result, it is said, of an accident while trying to drown his sorrows in drink. "He approached his art," related his contemporary, van Hoogstraaten, "with incomparable zeal." The outstanding mark of his work is its emotional quality, its intensive identification with nature. Like a Chinese mystic he became one with rocks and brooks in forbidding Alpine valleys

84

(illustration 195), with moss-laden firs, with crumbling ruins, with sunny fertile plains, with tiny ships battling alone on a desperate sea. Nature became the *mise-en-scène* for the tortured drama of his soul. There was something in him that was akin to his countryman van Gogh, something of his passionate absorption, something of his rhythmic vibrant manner of drawing. He was no doubt a bit unbalanced: he felt too keenly, he went too deeply into things. The baffled public would have none of his work; they did not know what it was all about. At that moment they preferred realism to imagination, with the result that his life was one continuous struggle against poverty and despair. Today we look at the little that has been preserved of his work with more favorable eyes. Take for example that masterpiece, *The Three Books* (illustration 196), existing only in two impressions, both printed with brownish black ink on yellow colored linen with the background painted black; how simple it is, how beautiful in composition, with what emotional overtones of brooding and mystery. Seghers was a great experimenter; he apparently conceived many of his etchings in terms of color. He worked with various colored inks on various colored papers and even on linen, and often colored the prints still further by hand. He was one of the first of the Dutch artists to take up etching and especially to fall under the spell of wild mountain scenery. Some sixty etchings have come down to us, many of them existing only in one or two impressions. But we value him today not so much for his technical experiments as for his spirit, for the imagination and the emotional *timbre* with which his work is so richly endowed. And we couple his name—not in equality but in kinship—with that of Rembrandt, who admired his work and owned some of his pictures.

Rembrandt was the greatest etcher who ever lived. No one had a greater range and greater mastery within that range than he. Religious subjects, portraits, landscapes, nude studies, still life—in all of these he created masterpieces. In the field of genre alone he did not produce much, unless we consider his studies of beggars, the *Hog*, and his *Jews in the Synagogue*, as genre pictures. We learn little from him of the externals of life as lived in Amsterdam, but we learn much about humanity, the essentials of life which do not change from age to age. He

85

was the visionary, the man apart, who moved above or below contemporary life. To the Holland of the seventeenth century he was an enigma; it took the world several centuries to catch up with him. Rembrandt Harmenz van Ryn, the miller's son, was born in Leyden in 1606. His parents were ambitious that he become a scholar, and he entered the University of Leyden in 1620. But he had no call for letters and he left within a year to enter a painter's studio. After studying with three different masters, he set up for himself, and in 1628 he received his first pupil, Gerard Dou. In 1631 he moved to Amsterdam. Three years later he married Saskia van Ulenburch, a woman of some wealth and position. He was successful; he sold his pictures and obtained portrait commissions; his studio was crowded with pupils. He bought a house and filled it with treasures, jewels and rich robes for his Saskia, with sculpture and oriental carpets, Dutch and Italian paintings, engravings by Lucas van Leyden and others. This period of prosperity was checked by two events, the death of his wife and the debacle of the *Night Watch* in 1642. Thereupon his material affairs went into a decline which culminated in his bankruptcy in 1656. He always had been generous and impractical, he always had been a passionate and extravagant collector of art works. But this would not account for all the debts and money spent. It may easily be, as Carrington suggests, that after the death of Saskia, he got into the clutches of a female gold-digger who worked him for all he was worth. This part of his life is exceedingly obscure. His last years were solaced by the affection and care of his serving maid, Hendrickje Stoffels (to the scandal of pious folk!). Forgotten or ignored by the burghers of Amsterdam, he was driven more and more to himself. Hendrickje died in 1664 and his son Titus in 1668. In 1669 Rembrandt himself died, possessing, as the formal inventory records: *"alleenlijck sijne cleederen van linnen en wollen en 't schildergereetschap"*—only certain linen and woolen garments and his painting materials.

Rembrandt's first etchings are dated 1628. His early work, with a few notable exceptions, is not especially distinguished. He was learning his metier, his language. Rembrandt had great capacity for self-development; he could profit by his mistakes in art, however badly he managed in practical life. The process went slowly, for he was building up an independent art form: he raised etching into a major art. It was he who gave to etching the significance and direction it was subsequently to take. The following are but a few of the artists (quoted by Lumsden) who show his influence: Bauer, Bone, Bracquemond, Cameron, Forain, Geddes, Goya, Haden, Jacque, John, Jongkind, Legros, McBey, Ostade, Potter, Tiepolo, and Whistler. He explored the medium and showed the way. He gave to etching the freedom and spontaneity and subtlety of drawing; and because his drawing was distinguished, dramatic, and noble he proved that an etching could be as lofty a work of art as a painting or statue. Most prints before Rembrandt had been translations as it were from another medium; he composed directly in the language of etching itself. In him we see the beginning of the modern attitude.

His early work consisted largely of studies of single figures: beggars (illustration 207), portraits of his father and mother (illustration 188), studies of "picturesque" types, expression studies, mostly of himself, in every attitude, grimace, and costume. Many of these were obviously experimental, for the sake of his own training or for teaching purposes. There were also some compositions that were fumbling and petty, without the grandeur of his later work. The *Self-Portrait Leaning on a Stone Sill* (illustration 187) perhaps inspired by Raphael's portrait of Castiglione, and made in the height of his prosperity in 1639, shows that he could beat van Dyck at his own game. But Rembrandt went on to make the supremely self-revealing *Self-Portrait Drawing at a Window* in 1648, which van Dyck never could have done. With the skill and freedom of expression acquired in these early experiments, fortified by the development of his inner nature, he went on to execute the great portraits where the inner character, the breathing essence of the sitter, is revealed in the outward form, the *Jan Sylvius* of 1646, the *Clement de Jonghe* of 1651, the *Older and the Younger Haaring* of 1655, the *Tholinx and Lutma* of 1656.

The illness and death of Saskia apparently turned his interest temporarily in the direction of nature. He had already made a few landscapes, inspired possibly by the example of his friend Seghers: the

87

View of Amsterdam, the *Cottage with Hay Barn,* and the *Mill.* And in 1643 he etched the *Three Trees* (illustration 192). If, as Ivins penetratingly remarks, Bruegel is the Bach of landscape, then Rembrandt is its Beethoven. Rembrandt in these and his other etched landscapes, *Six's Bridge, Landscape with Square Tower, Goldweighers' Field,* and *Landscape with Sportsman,* displays the emotional power and the transmutation of natural forms into perfect artistic expression that is characteristic only of genius. How marvelously the freshness of the passing shower has been suggested in the *Three Trees;* how enchantingly the pattern of light and dark and rhythmic line is arranged in the *Landscape with Farm Buildings and Tower* (illustration 191). Most landscape prints before Rembrandt were composed or heroic landscapes; he took the intimate themes familiar to all and turned them into songs of lasting beauty.

Like most emotionally creative types, Rembrandt had a strong dramatic sense, and this was the quality that vitalized his mythological and religious pictures. Take the *Dr. Faustus,* for example (illustration 189), in his study gazing at the magic disk, the intensity and suspense, the way the painter emphasizes, dramatizes by means of line, by means of light. His approach to the religious picture is unique and personal; he serves no religious dogma. He retells the sacred story in human terms. He makes the characters live with incomparable art and dramatic effect: with tenderness in the *Rest on the Flight, lightly etched,* or in the *Holy Family with Cat* (note the reminiscence of Mantegna in the Virgin and Child); with humor in *Abraham Entertaining the Angels,* and *Christ among the Doctors;* with pathos in the *Blindness of Tobit,* the *Christ Carried to the Tomb,* the *Entombment in the Vaulted Chamber,* and the *Descent from the Cross by Torchlight;* with splendor in the *Presentation in the Temple;* with epic monumentality in the *Three Crosses, Christ Healing the Sick,* and *Abraham's Sacrifice.* One of the most satisfying and completely realized of his religious works is the *Christ Preaching* (illustration 194). The composition is exceptionally beautiful, and the range of characters delineated is almost as great as that of the *Hundred Guilder Print,* and expressed in more purely linear terms. The vista into the courtyard beyond, shows what Rembrandt could do in rendering buildings. In all these representations there is no touch of the theater: all is pure drama, the perfect fusion of stirring theme and expressive form.

There has been much difference of opinion about Rembrandt's nudes. To many they are inexpressibly ugly and realistic. But in such early plates as the *Naked Woman on a Mound* (the Adam and Eve is, I am convinced, just a parody), Rembrandt was not interested in drawing a so-called pretty figure; he wanted to learn how to etch flesh, and he took what models he could find. It was not always easy to find handsome models, as Raphael records in 1515 in a letter to Baldessare Castiglione (who evidently had made some complimentary remarks about the model for the *Galatea*):

As far as the Galatea is concerned I would consider myself a great master if only half of the things you said about it were true. I recognize in your words the high regard you have for me. However I must tell you that whenever I have to paint a beautiful woman, it is necessary that I see a number of beauties (with the stipulation that you be present to choose the most beautiful!). Since, however, there is a dearth of such accomplished connoisseurs of women, as well as of beautiful women themselves, I depend upon a certain ideal and idea that I have in my mind. If this be an artistic advantage I know not, nevertheless I strive to attain it.

The question of the esthetic qualities of nudes, especially of the female sex, is a very complex one; when people say that a particular nude drawing is not artistic they often mean something else. It is questionable whether Rembrandt ever intended to emphasize the sexual attractiveness of a nude (as for example Zorn did) although the painting of *Danaë* in the Hermitage is quite as sensuous as Goya's *Maja*. In his later etchings of the nude, the *Woman beside the Stove*, the *Woman Bathing with a Hat beside Her*, the *Woman with the Arrow* (illustration 190), he aimed to present just Woman, the wholeness of a human being in an intimate pose. In these later etchings he came closer to that fusion of universal (Raphael's idea and ideal) and particular (convincing detail) which is the mark of great art.

Rembrandt's influence on succeeding generations has not been in

89

every respect beneficial. His early etchings of picturesque types were the starting point of a flood of mediocre and sentimental and patronizing exploitations of the theme. His many experimental sketches, probably made with no thought of wide publication, became the excuse for countless trivialities by subsequent artists. In his endeavor to make etching an important and independent mode of creative expression, he sometimes forced the medium far beyond the limits of appropriateness, as in the *Portrait of Jan Six,* the various night pieces and even the *Hundred Guilder Print.* It is to be regretted that he was not familiar with the technique of mezzotint and lithograph. Nevertheless he was one of the titans of art, a visionary who lived most truly in the world of his imagination. Fortune smiled on him for a while and then turned her back to him. It would have been better perhaps if she had not noticed him at all. He posed as a man of the world, yet he never was, and the world soon found him out. Like Claude he was no courtier; he consorted with humble folk and beggars and doctors and preachers. His influence on his immediate contemporaries was negligible. Amsterdam in the seventeenth century was a tough place to live for one not of this world. Like his friends, Roghman and Seghers, and like his contemporary, Spinoza, whom he never met, Rembrandt died neglected and in want.

Now that we have sketched some of the outstanding personalities of the seventeenth century we shall take up the broader aspects of its schools and tendencies. The most flourishing and homogeneous movement of the first half of the seventeenth century was the Dutch School. The Dutch had emerged victorious from their desperate struggle against the domination of Spain. Their independence had intensified their national consciousness. They were vigorous, industrious, and enterprising. They became a great trading nation and entered upon a period of unparalleled prosperity. They were practically supreme on the sea. They had vast colonial possessions; they carried the world's goods in their vessels. Their cities were the commodity markets of Europe; they were the first to institute the practice of auction sales. They took the lead in the development of the banking system which originated in the seventeenth century: through the extension of bills of exchange and the practice of leaving money and gold on deposit with the goldsmiths for safe keeping and carrying on commercial transactions by means of checks and credit, they became the bankers of the world. All of which is by way of saying that they became rich and prosperous. And so they bought art. John Evelyn relates in his diary for 1641:

We arrived late at Rotterdam, where was their annual mart or fair, so furnished with pictures (especially landscapes and drolleries, as they call those clownish representations), that I was amazed. Some of these I bought and sent to England. The reason of this store of pictures, and their cheapness, proceeds from their want of land to employ their stock, so that it is an ordinary thing to find a common farmer to lay out two or three thousand pounds in this commodity. Their houses are full of them, and they vend them at their fairs to very great gains.

There was monetary inflation and so they invested their money in art. It was a special kind of art. As they acquired and rejoiced in tangible possessions, so they demanded of art that it be a representation of tangible objects, familiar scenes in daily life or landscape. No doubt other factors beside the economic entered into this predilection. It was a secular and not a religious art, because the tradition of religious art had been broken, not only by iconoclasm and the destruction of Catholic art during the wars, but also by the Protestant-Puritan attitude toward religious art in general. The general tone was bourgeois and middle-class because there was no outstanding court to set the fashion. It was realistic, literal, and factual; it was technically accomplished, but not inspired by any tremendous depths of feeling. It is easy now to see why Seghers and Rembrandt did not fit into the scheme. Nevertheless within its limits it was an art of great distinction and charm, and the world is richer for the picture it gives of the Holland of the seventeenth century.

The work as a whole can be classified into several general groups. The first is the picture of daily life, the genre scene, which the Dutch may be said to have invented. One of the outstanding artists in this field was the painter and etcher, Adriaen van Ostade (1610–1685). He etched fifty plates, not all equal in merit, but at their best displaying fine draughtsmanship and compositional effect and considerable feeling. Two characteristic examples are reproduced, the *Family* of 1647 (illustration 199) and the *Fisherman* (illustration 228). His tradition was carried on by Dusart and Bega (illustration 213). Contrasting with Ostade's and Teniers' representations of peasants and artisans (illustration 214) is Willem Buytewech's etching of the patrician *Lovers* (illustration 200) executed in an elegant, stylized, almost caricatured manner. The next group are the landscape etchers, Pieter Molyn, Roelant Roghman, A. Waterloo (illustration 225), A. van Everdingen, the painters Jan van Goyen and Jacob van Ruysdael (illustration 226) important in the landscape tradition. Jan van de Velde's etchings (illustration 228a), though executed in a dry formalized technique, have a charm of textural variation and inventive composition. The van de Veldes were precursors of Rembrandt in the molding of a pure landscape tradition. There were some etchers who specialized in pictures of the sea, and of these Renier Nooms, called Zeeman (so much admired by Meryon), and Ludolph Backhuysen were outstanding. Zeeman (illustration 228c) could portray marine effects with great skill, and Backhuysen in his *Distant View of Amsterdam* (illustration 228d) has admirably rendered a breezy day and a choppy sea. Then there were the etchers of animals and pastoral life, Claes Berchem, Karel du Jardin, and above all Paul Potter (illustration 228b). Another and slightly overlapping group are the Italianizers like Breenbergh, Jan Both (illustration 227), and Swanevelt, who had been to Italy and sought to impose the arcadian tradition of Claude upon the realism of Holland.

The journeyings of these later Dutchmen bring us back to Italy again. Italian art of the seicento lacked the force of the preceding centuries. There is undoubted sweetness and charm in the etchings of Guido Reni and his pupil Cantarini (illustration 223) and Giovanni Barbieri, called Guercino (illustration 221). But they represent the gradual ebbing away of the religious tradition. Castiglione in his etchings was influenced by both van Dyck and Rembrandt. The Venetian, Carpioni, did a few charming plates. José Ribera, Lo Spagnoletto, Spanish born, but living in Naples, represented the naturalistic school of Caravaggio, in his few but very accomplished etchings (illustration 197). Salvator Rosa, also of Naples, had a wild and adventurous enough life. Poet, painter, musician, he took part in the insurrection of Masaniello against the Spanish rule, and lived for a while with bandits. His etchings (illustration 224) have the mannerism and show of force of the Baroque style but in their delineation of wild and rugged scenery they anticipate to a certain extent a favorite theme of the Romantic School.

In France during the first half of the seventeenth century, the foundation was laid for the reign of Louis XIV, which for its patronage of arts and letters Voltaire called "the most enlightened age the world has ever seen." The build-up was favored by the policies of the Queen Mother Marie de' Medici, Cardinal Richelieu, founder of the French Academy, and Cardinal Mazarin, patron of art, music, and the theater. It was firmly established by Louis XIV and his minister Colbert upon his accession in 1661. Colbert believed "that it was by the standard of monuments that one measured kings." The Academy of Painters was founded; artists and craftsmen were encouraged with pensions and given lodging in the apartments of the Louvre and the Gobelins. The Gobelins, a state institution, was the center not only of the finest tapestry manufactured in Europe but also of the manufacture of furniture, metal work, and jewelry. It was also a training school for artists, and in this way a high standard of craftsmanship was maintained. An interesting glimpse of its activities is given in Le Clerc's engraving (illustration 234) where Colbert is seen inspecting some new tapestries. The seventeenth century witnessed a vast extension of luxury which found its reflection in ornament prints, models for jewelry (illustrations 229 and 230), lace, leather work, metal work (illustration 232), vases, furniture, and wall decoration (illustration 233). Formal gardens, with grottoes, etc. (illustrations 235 and 209) were laid out in greater and greater numbers. Ornament itself, in keeping with the Baroque style, tended to become exaggerated, grotesque, bursting with swelling bands and fantastic cartouches (illustration 231). All these exuberant elements were organized and somewhat restrained into a standardized and coherent system of great taste and decorative value by the artists and craftsmen under Louis XIV.

For a faithful picture of comfortable French life during the Regency and early part of the reign of Louis XIV, one must turn to the etchings of Abraham Bosse. He was typically the artist of the upper middle class, and he depicted their manners and customs with peculiar fidelity, sobriety, and vividness (illustrations 215 and 216). The upper middle class are in general the backbone of the culture of a nation. It is they, through their opportunities for higher education, who supply the learned professions, law, medicine, and theology. They stand midway between the frivolousness of the court and the indigence of the proletariat. It is they who buy books and pictures, who patronize the theater, who cultivate music. A charming picture of a musical gathering is given in Bosse's engraving, *Hearing*, from the series of the *Five Senses*. In the sixteenth and seventeenth centuries music was still a language familiar to many cultivated amateurs. Many of the charming compositions of the contrapuntal schools, part songs, madrigals, motets and the like, were performed in company with accomplished musicianship. The century also witnessed the development of stringed instruments (Stradivarius, etcetera), and also a form of dramatic music which eventually became opera. Another picture of the time is given in the contrast between the two accouchement scenes portrayed by Bosse and by Callot in his *Gypsies*. Bosse made about 1400 engravings and is also famous for his text book on the art of etching and engraving. Bosse and Hollar have much in common.

The portrait of Molière in the role of Sganarelle in his own play *L'Ecole des Maris* (illustration 218) is a reminder of the great development of the drama in the seventeenth century, not only in France with Corneille, Racine, and Molière, but also in England with Shakespeare and the other Elizabethan dramatists, and in Spain with Calderon and Lope de Vega.

The portrait received great impetus in the seventeenth century, and in France there grew up a school of portrait engraving that has never been surpassed. The earliest practitioner was Claude Mellan who developed Goltzius' linear system into an instrument of great power, as may be seen in the portrait of Fabri de Peiresc (illustration 202), Rubens' great friend. Jean Morin (illustration 237b) engraved some colorful portraits. But Robert Nanteuil was the chief glory of the school. He was quartered in the Gobelins, and Louis XIV also granted in his favor the famous Edict of St. Jean-de-Luz which declared that engraving henceforth was to rank as a liberal and not as a mechanical art. He

94

engraved over two hundred portraits, including eleven of "*le Grand Monarque*" (illustration 238), and a host of great men of the time, Richelieu, Mazarin, Cardinal de Retz, Jacques Amelot, Colbert, Fouquet, Loret (illustration 238a), Gassendi, John Evelyn, etcetera. He usually received about 2000 livres per plate (about $400). He set the style of portraiture which was followed by his pupils and associates, Masson, Edelinck, Poilly, Pitau, van Schuppen, and others. He perfected the frame which gave the portrait its formal decorative quality. A consummate draughtsman, he concentrated, as Thomas points out, on the expression of character by the head. There is nothing spontaneous about these portrait engravings: every detail is studied and calculated. It is the opposite extreme of the candid camera shot: it is the "set portrait," where the sitter looks and appears as he would like to be, noble, dignified, in the grand manner. Mlle. de Scudéry wrote a quatrain which sums it up:

> "Nanteuil en faisant son image
> A de son art divin signalé le pouvoir.
> Je hais mes traits dans mon miroir,
> Je les aime dans son ouvrage."

(Nanteuil in his pictures has shown the power of his divine art. I hate my features in the mirror, I love them in his work.) Pepys in his *Diary* for January 1668-69 records: "My wife showed me many excellent prints of Nantueill's and others, which W. Batelier hath, at my desire, brought me out of France, to my great content." As the prevailing taste changed from the sober delineation of character to a greater ostentation and display, so the portrait changed from the head to the full-length figure in gorgeous array of silks and satins. Drevet's *Bossuet* or Bervic's *Louis XVI* are characteristic of this tendency. However, Drevet's portrait of the architect, *Robert de Cotte*, is reproduced (illustration 239) because (as Kimball points out) he, though not the inventor, was a figurehead in the invention of the Rococo style. As a companion, there is Wille's portrait of the *Marquis de Marigny*, the brother of La Pompadour, who played a similar role in the spread of the "Classical" style of the later eighteenth century (illustration 239a). The French School of portrait engraving was the most distinguished in Europe; it drew many foreign artists, notably the Fleming Edelinck, to Paris. Comparatively little portraiture of merit was made during the century outside of the engraved portraits of Paris or the etched portraits of Rembrandt and van Dyck. An exception must be recorded, however, in the charming portrait engravings of Ottavio Leoni of Rome. The portrait of the astronomer Galileo, who got in trouble with the Inquisition, is reproduced in illustration 237. The portrait of the Duke of Olivares, often ascribed to Velasquez, is probably by Leoni.

The seventeenth century witnessed a further widening of the breach between rich and poor. The extensive wars of this and the preceding centuries contributed greatly to the spread of capitalism by nourishing that one great form of luxury, the army. Not only was a military career a direct avenue to riches through the opportunities for plunder and exaction of indemnities (Wallenstein when he was assassinated was worth nine million gulden) but the army encouraged lucrative capitalist enterprises through the contract system and large-scale production of food, clothing, guns, and ammunition. Wealth was becoming more and more concentrated in the hands of a few, while the great mass of the people were being ground down in abject poverty. Holland was the exception to this rule, but there it was the middle class which was acquiring wealth. Elsewhere the Court, the Church and the rich were the chief supporters of art. Rubens' chief patrons were the Church, the extravagant Charles I and his favorites, and Philip of Spain whose income came from the gold of America. The seventeenth century saw the emergence of the collector of prints on a vast scale. To be sure there had been collectors in previous centuries, the Fuggers, Imhoffs, Welser (Dürer and van Leyden complete), Paul Praum, 1548-1616 (Dürer and Italian masters); and prints were included among the contents of the countless *Wunderkammern*, or Chambers of Curios, along with shells, insects, minerals, stuffed animals, cameos, etcetera. (Evelyn as late as 1651 notes: "I went to see the collection of one Monsieur Poignant which for variety of agates, crystals, onyxes, porcelain, medals, statues, relievos, paintings, taille-douces [prints], and antiquities, might compare with the Italian virtuosos.") And artists such as Dürer and Rubens, as

96

we have seen, and Rembrandt who at one time owned over one hundred paintings and a huge collection of prints by Mantegna and many other artists, were passionate collectors. But the first real print collector was Claude Maugis, Abbé de St. Ambroise, 1600–1658, who spent forty years amassing a collection which eventually passed into the hands of Michel Marolles. Michel Marolles, Abbé de Villeloin, who had been given a fat living by Mazarin, was one of the world's great print collectors. No sooner had he disposed of his first huge collection, than he started all over again. As he wrote:

God has given me grace to devote myself to pictures without superstition, and I have been able to acquire a collection numbering more than 70,000 engravings of all subjects. I began it in 1644, and have continued it with so much zeal, and with such an expense for one not wealthy, that I can claim to possess some of the work of all the known masters. . . . I have found that collecting such things was more suited to my purse than collecting paintings, and more serviceable to the building up of a library. Had we in France a dozen such collectors among the nobility, there would not be enough prints to satisfy them all, and the works of Dürer, Lucas, and Marcantonio for which we now pay four and five hundred écus when in perfect condition would be worth three times that amount.

In 1666 his collection had grown to 123,400 prints and drawings by over 6000 artists. The entire collection was bought by Colbert for the King and became the foundation of that huge public collection numbering over 4,000,000 prints now housed in the Bibliothèque Nationale. In England there were collectors like Lord Pembroke and the Earl of Arundel (Hollar's patron), but it was in Paris that Marolles' suggestion was really followed. In 1673 there were eighty-five large collections of prints, often in connection with libraries; towards the end of the century there were one hundred and thirty. It became so much the fashion that La Bruyère took note of it in his "Characters":

You wish to see my prints, says Democenes, and he forthwith brings them out and sets them before you. You see one that is neither dark nor clear nor completely drawn, and better fit to decorate on a holiday the walls of the Petit Pont or the Rue Neuve than be treasured in a famous collection. He admits that it is engraved badly and drawn worse, but hastens to inform you that it is the work of an Italian artist who produced very little, and that the plate had hardly any printing; that, moreover, it is the only one of its kind in France; that he paid much for it, and would not exchange it for something far better. I am, he adds, in such serious trouble that it will prevent any further collecting. I have all of Callot but one print, which is not only not one of his best plates, but actually one of his worst; nevertheless it would complete my Callot. I have been looking for it for twenty years, and, despairing of success, I find life very hard indeed.

5. Eighteenth Century

THE history of eighteenth century prints may be summed up as a year in Paris, a month in London, and a week-end in Italy. France was the artistic center of Europe, and France meant Paris. No city was ever so documented by its artists as Paris. It was, however, essentially an urban culture, highly civilized and highly artificial. Paris was the apex of the pyramid which rested on the broad base of the peasants of France. The flowers that grew in the hothouse at the apex had no strong roots in the free soil of the country. Nevertheless they were in many respects beautiful flowers, among the most extraordinary the world has ever seen. The documentation of Paris may be said to have proceeded on four separate levels. At the top, the most artificial and the most completely documented, was the life of the court. Below was the life of the middle class, sober, industrious, and urbane, untainted by the excesses of the court. The third was the life of the artists themselves, another aspect of the middle class. Below all these, the most meager in detail, yet represented in the *Cries of Paris*, the representations of the lower artisan class and the *imagerie populaire*, was the level of the workers.

At the beginning of the century there lived and dreamed and painted a rare artist, Antoine Watteau. His work may be said to symbolize, in its most ideal and beautiful aspects, the spirit of Louis XV. He was born in Valenciennes of Flemish ancestry in 1684. He died of consumption at the early age of twenty-seven. He was supported by wealthy patrons like M. de Julienne; he had access, through his friend the great collector Crozat, to drawings and paintings by Rubens, Titian, Giorgione, and Campagnola. Out of the leisure which good fortune brought him and out of the contacts with the great art of the world, and impelled by the heart-breaking nostalgia of the consumptive, he proceeded to make con-

99

crete one more dream of an ideal world. It was the world of the *fête galante,* the *Embarkation for the Isle of Cythère* (Love), exquisite glimpses of picnics in beautiful gardens, of couples in amorous conversation, of music and dancing and the theater in the open. He made a few unimportant etchings: he poured himself out in his drawings and paintings. It was his lifelong friend, M. de Julienne, who undertook at his expense to have his work engraved by the best engravers of the time and published in four huge volumes in 1734 at a price of five hundred livres. It is from this magnificent *Recueil* that our three reproductions are drawn (illustrations 243 and 244 and 271). Never has the spirit of play, of cultivated pastime, the *otium cum dignitate* of the ancients, been clothed in more enchanting dress. This escape from reality, this flight to a carefree island of love and beauty, strikes a responsive chord in every one of us at some time in our lives. It is Watteau's great achievement that he made the dream so tangible and so beautiful. All his contemporaries, Gersaint, De Caylus, testify to the unhappiness of his personal life. He was melancholy, irritable, and diffident. It was only when he was actually painting or drawing, said De Caylus, that he was the Watteau of his own pictures. It may be, as Wilenski suggests, that this unhappiness was due not only to the inroads of his malady, but also to his dilemma as a creative artist. He had every reason to be grateful to his rich patrons who had rescued him from a life of hack work (he had started as a painter outside the pale of the all-powerful Academy) and to his dealers Sirois and Gersaint (illustration 271) for their affectionate and continued assistance, but they were all men of the world and did not look at a picture in the way he looked at it, nor see what he saw in it. He lived in the apartments which Crozat provided for him in his palace, but after a year he ran away. The world was not fashioned according to his heart's desire, and he was driven to his dreams. Yet, curiously enough, in this instance, the world, that is to say the court of Louis XV, tried to imitate his dream. Such a utopia as Watteau's Isle of Cythère can exist only in the world of art or imagination. When its happy irresponsible existence was translated into reality, it predicated the support of countless servants or slaves. Its grace and sensibility, its tender note of ideal love became tainted with wanton extravagance and display, sordid intrigue and unbridled licentiousness. And so it was, as history tells us, at the court of Louis XV. Yet comparatively little of the sordid side is carried over into the pictorial record by the artists of the time. The obverse of the shield we discover from other sources and from the fact that suddenly the whole system collapsed. The artists set out to glorify the reign of Louis XV as they had that of the Grand Monarch, and they did a magnificent job. They did it in two ways: by embellishing the setting and by recording it.

First of all there were the decorators, Boucher for example. François Boucher (1703–1770) was one of the most accomplished artists in France, director of the schools of the Academy and of the tapestry manufactory of Beauvais and the Gobelins, painter of murals for the king and for Mme de Pompadour. We know his features from the striking portrait by Roslin, an unassuming, somewhat cynical man of the world with able hands and piercing eyes. He is represented by the decorative composition engraved by Demarteau, *Venus Desarmée par les Amours* (illustration 241), and the color print, *Femme à la Rose*, engraved by Bonnet (illustration 265). We all remember Renoir's estimate of Boucher as recorded by Vollard:

As if being a decorator made any difference! Why Boucher is one of the painters who best understood the female body. What fresh youthful buttocks he painted, with the most enchanting dimples. It's odd that people are never willing to give a man credit for what he can do. They say they like Titian better. Good Lord so do I! But that has nothing to do with the fact that Boucher painted lovely women superbly. A painter who has the feel for breasts and buttocks is saved!

The second decorator, Jean Honoré Fragonard (1732-1806), was typical of the more frivolous spirit toward the end of the century. Pupil of Chardin, protégé of Boucher, influenced by Rembrandt and Tiepolo, he painted decorations for Du Barry and other fashionable women, and made countless drawings and paintings. He made among others a series of four etchings of *Bacchanals* (illustration 240) of great spirit and charm in a form probably suggested by the *Caprices* of Tiepolo. Some delightful engravings were made from his paintings, including the *Chiffre*

d'Amour, *La Bonne Mère*, and *The Happy Accidents of the Swing*
(illustration 246), frivolous yet charming, and filled with a certain gallant suggestiveness.

The setting was embellished in many ways. The enormous impetus
given to architecture and the applied arts had its repercussion in ornament prints. The earlier academic tradition is represented in the *Rape
of Europa* after Le Moyne (illustration 245). The gestures have become very elegant and rococo; it is interesting to contrast this with
Claude's treatment of the same subject. There were two trends of ornament in the eighteenth century: one, the Rococo, was a development
of the Baroque, carrying its mannerism and eccentricity to even greater
limits, and the other a reaction against it in favor of the antique (stimulated perhaps by the excavations at Herculaneum and also by Adam and
Piranesi) which culminated in the severely classic style of the Direc-
toire and Empire. In flower arrangement and design there was a range
from the seventeenth century Monnoyer (illustration 287) through the
early eighteenth century van Huysum (illustration 298) to the late eighteenth century Ranson. Characteristic Rococo ornament was supplied
by Meissonier, Oppenordt, Gillot, Watteau, Oudry, Huet, Huquier,
Nilsen, Habermann, and notably in the delightful inventions of Pillemont (illustration 66). Chinoiserie and other exotic notes were fashionable. Among the notable furniture designers in France were Oppenordt,
Toro, Pineau, and Cornille; in England Heppelwhite, Sheraton, Chippendale (illustration 284), Ince and Mayhew, and Robert Adam. The classic
style in France was developed by Neufforge, Delafosse, Forty, Babel,
and Lalonde (illustration 67). One field was specially cultivated, under
the patronage of the Regent Philippe d'Orleans and of Madame de Pompadour both of whom dabbled in design, by the luxury-loving age—
the illustrated book. Sumptuous and expensive editions were published,
illustrated with engravings and vignettes by the best artists of the time:
Molière's Works illustrated by Boucher, the *Fermiers Généraux* edition
of La Fontaine (an allusion to the source of its financing) illustrated by
Eisen and others, Corneille's *Works* illustrated by Gravelot (illustrations 263, 291a, 291b), Marmontel's *Contes Moraux* illustrated by
Gravelot, 1765, the *Metamorphoses* of Ovid illustrated by Boucher.

Eisen, Gravelot, Moreau, and Choffard, 1767–1771, *Les Baisers* illustrated by Eisen, 1770, the *Choix de Chansons* de M. de la Borde illustrated by Moreau-le-Jeune, 1773 (illustration 288), one of the most beautiful books ever made, and finally Rousseau's *Works*, 1774–1783, also illustrated by Moreau-le-Jeune. And so "Monsieur" and "Madame" were provided with books to look at (though perhaps not to read), furniture, wall decorations, jewelry, costumes, china, gardens, coaches, and rooms to live in, designed and executed by the greatest talent in France.

How they looked and acted amid these luxurious surroundings we discover from *Les Estampes Galantes, Estampes de la Mode*, and *Gravures des Mœurs*. There is a close resemblance between these engravings and Dutch seventeenth century prints. There is the same factual literal representation of a contemporary scene. There is to be sure a greater perfection of execution, a more magnificent sense of style, a more effective feeling for the dramatic aspect, in the French engravings, but the ultimate aim is the same—it is "giving the customers what they want." In spite of certain notable exceptions there is a spiritual poverty about both, a lack of creative conviction or passion on the part of the artists that prevents the work from being classed with the world's greatest art. It was a faithful, impersonal, and business-like reflection of the age, and since the milieu was hardly a spiritual one, the art never rose above it, as the works of the greatest artists and thinkers always do. Incidentally Dutch genre pictures of the seventeenth century were assiduously collected by French amateurs of the eighteenth century. Both groups catered definitely to a certain class, the Dutch seventeenth century prints to a rising middle class; the French *éstampes galantes* to the nobility and the underlying strata which imitated them. Who was it that bought these French prints? Certainly not the impoverished peasants and workers, for they had no money, nor even the lower middle class. Nor was it in general the principal personages of the court; there was no reason why they should buy pictures of the scenes they saw every day. It was rather that class which had a slight or indirect contact with the court and had grown rich through it, that sought these prints in order perhaps that their wives and daughters might see the latest fashions. Or it was the roué who bought the *sujets grivois*, the suggestive subjects, to add piquancy to his relations with his mistress in the sumptuous apartment where he maintained her. Or it was the rich amateur with a taste for art and nothing to do who succumbed to the collecting mania.

French eighteenth century prints have been the subject of much argument pro and con. Even in their day, they and the paintings from which they were often derived, were savagely attacked by Diderot as a symbol of a society of which he disapproved. Diderot incidentally was one of the first of the professional art critics. It was in the eighteenth century (1699 to be exact) that official exhibitions of paintings and drawings by many artists were inaugurated by the Academy (Gabriel de St. Aubin made a delightful etching of the "Salon" of the Academy held at the Louvre in the year 1753). Of course pictures had been exhibited, as we have seen, at the fairs and markets in Germany, Italy, and Holland, and also at the Foire de St. Germain in Paris, but these had no official recognition. Therefore when society was confronted with several hundred pictures at a Salon which it was *de rigeur* to attend, the writers stepped in, as has been said, to tell it what to talk about, and thus art criticism or rather art journalism began. Unquestionably, the tone of society, pampered and protected as it was from reality, was highly artificial and frivolous. In Chamfort's words: " 'A genuine sentiment is so rare,' said M. de V——, 'that when I leave Versailles I sometimes stand still to see a dog gnaw a bone.' " French eighteenth century prints, on the other hand, have had apologists who maintain that their licentious and irresponsible tone has been exaggerated, and point to the number of prints which extol the virtues of happy family life (illustration 252). Even those subjects which are rather free are never gross: they tell their story as a *double entendre*, with subtlety and a proper regard for the conventions. It is quite likely that the moral degradation of the age has been exaggerated, that it was confined to a few sensational and destructive examples at the court, and that the main body of the people went on in their accustomed ways. After all, even in our day financiers have kept mistresses and squandered fortunes without having overthrown the structure of society. A case can be made out on both sides. In either case the prints themselves build up a complete picture

104

of a mode of life that is elegant, refined, and luxurious. It is only when we go beyond the picture to examine its implications that we are compelled to exercise moral judgment. Incidentally it is interesting to discover that nearly all the engravers welcomed the Revolution and some took an active part in it.

After this rather philosophic preamble let us visit Paris and with the artist to give us entrée, let us visit the court and participate in its functions. First, having been introduced to Augustin de St. Aubin and his charming wife paying each other compliments in *Au Moins Soyez Discrets* and *Comptez sur mes Serments* we accompany him to the *Concert* or to the court ball, *Le Bal Paré*, following an invitation engraved by Choffard. With the Swede Lavreince we might visit two other functions *chez* le Duc de Luynes, the *Assemblée au Salon* and *Assemblée au Concert*, or listen to Beaumarchais reading extracts from his *Figaro* in *Le Mercure de France*, or explore with him such crises of sentiment as *Consolation de l'Absence*, *L'Heureux Moment*, *L'Indiscretion*, or *L'Aveu Difficile*, or, entering the more formal salon, hear *Qu'en dit l'Abbé* or see the furtive passing of the *Billet Doux* (illustration 249). Walking through the park with Baudouin, we might glimpse a charming tête-à-tête in *La Soirée des Tuileries* (illustration 247) and witness in the boudoir an intimacy close to the border line in *Le Danger du Tête-à-tête* and especially in *Le Carquois Épuisé* (*The Empty Quiver*) with its double meaning (illustration 248) or participate in the dramatic scenes, *Le Couché de la Mariée* or *L'Enlevement Nocturne*. We might see and purchase the latest portraits of the king and queen, or Pompadour (illustration 264) or Du Barry, or as a novelty that of Mr. Franklin, the new Philosopher from America who made such a hit at court and among the savants (illustration 267). We might with Carmontelle patronize the concert of a new infant prodigy of music, the seven-year-old Mozart (illustration 260). With the Swiss artist Freudeberg we might trace the round of daily life in luxury: *Le Lever*, *Le Bain*, the charmingly domestic *Le Petit Jour*, and *Le Coucher*. For a taste of gallantry there are Baudouin's *Marchez Tout Doux*, and *L'Épouse Indiscrète*, Fragonard's *Le Verrou*, Boilly's *L'Amant Favorisé*, Boucher's *La Cour-*

tisane Amoureuse, Debucourt's *L'Escalade*, or Lavreince's *La Comparaison*.

Jean Michel Moreau-le-Jeune was perhaps, all things considered, the finest and most accomplished designer and engraver of French manners. He was born in 1741 and studied engraving with jolly old Le Bas. In 1760 he married the daughter of Pineau the furniture designer. In 1770 he was appointed *Dessinateur des Menus-Plaisirs du Roi* and in 1781 he was made an associate of the Academy. His engravings, the *Coronation of Louis XVI* in 1776, the *Festin Royal*, the *Bal Masqué*, the *Feu d'Artifice* (the last three are in the Chalcographie du Louvre), and his engravings of *Le Couché de la Mariée* and *Le Modèle Honnête* after Baudouin are well known, but his chief title to fame rests on his book illustrations and the great *Monument du Costume* of 1776 and 1783. Confronted with the problem of designing a series of costume plates, he composed them as scenes from daily life with such perfection of draughtsmanship and incomparable dramatic power that the twenty-four plates may almost be said to sum up a complete age and mode of society. Certainly the society of Louis XVI has never been displayed in a better light. The young king and queen were weak and mildly benevolent characters; they believed in a happy family life and asked nothing better than to play at being shepherds and shepherdesses in an irresponsible pastoral life. They merely reaped the whirlwind that was sown by the grandfather. Thus, true happiness, *Le Vrai Bonheur*, is visualized in the *Monument* as a happy farmer surrounded by his family and his pet animals. No more charming picture of domestic felicity has been made than the *Délices de la Maternité* (illustration 252). Has there ever been a more charming dinner party than *Le Souper Fin* (illustration 254)? The grace and glamor, the polished and distinguished manners of an aristocratic court will live forever in such plates as *Les Adieux*, or *La Sortie de l'Opera* (illustrations 255 and 253). They seem like concrete embodiments of the maxims of one who was perhaps the most eloquent apologist of the courtly manner, Lord Chesterfield:

Courts are the best keys to character; there every passion is busy, every art exerted, every character analyzed; jealousy, ever watchful, not only discovers, but exposes, the mysteries of the trade, so that even bystanders, *y apprennent à déviner*. There, too, the great art of pleasing is practiced, taught, and learned, with all its graces and delicacies. It is the first thing needful there; it is the absolutely necessary harbinger of merit and talents, let them be ever so great. There is no advancing a step without it. Let misanthropes and would-be philosophers declaim as much as they please against the vices, the simulation, and dissimulation of Courts; those invectives are always the result of ignorance, ill-humor, or envy. Let them show me a cottage, where there are not the same vices of which they accuse the Courts; with this difference only, that in a cottage they appear in their native deformity, and that in Courts, manners and good breeding make them less shocking, and blunt their edge. No, be convinced that good breeding, the *tournure, la douceur dans les manières,* which alone are to be acquired at Courts, are not the showish trifles only, which some people call or think them; they are a solid good; they prevent a good deal of mischief; they create, adorn, and strengthen friendships; they keep hatred within bounds; they promote good-humor and good-will in families, where the want of good breeding and gentleness of manners is commonly the original cause of discord.

From the court to the middle class—from Moreau to Chardin. Jean Baptiste Siméon Chardin was born in Paris in 1699 and died there in 1779. He was a simple kindly man who loved the city and its ways—especially the middle-class life that he lived and knew. He poured into his simple genre pieces and still lifes such a wealth of feeling, such love and tenderness, such consummate craftsmanship and perfection of design and placement that they seem to come to life before our eyes. He had much in common with Vermeer of Delft. About fifty engravings were made after his paintings, which had considerable vogue in his day. Among the best known are *Le Bénédicité, Le Dessinateur, L'Écureuse, L'Étude de Dessin, La Mère Laborieuse, La Pourvoieuse, La Bonne Éducation,* and *L'Instant de la Meditation.* All of them have an intangible quality, a certain inwardness that haunts the imagination. We identify ourselves with the characters, and experience in a magic moment the simplicity and charm they so beautifully express. Two of the most charming are reproduced here, *La Gouvernante* and *Le Négligé* (illustrations 251 and 250). When the painting of *Le Négligé* was exhibited

107

in the Salon of 1741, Chamarande reviewed it as follows: "No woman of the third estate of the Realm stands before one of Chardin's canvases without discerning a reflection of her own morals, manners, and daily avocations, of the ways of her children, of her household gods and wardrobe." Furthermore there is a story that "when Le Bas [the engraver of this picture] was asked what instructions the painter had given him for the interpretation of his colors, he, knowing very well that for the complete harmony of a picture there can be no fixed rule, replied: to use sentiment."

Chardin, sure of himself, pursued his own quiet way, and, though an academician through the influence of Largillière, seldom exhibited with them and had little sympathy with their historical grand manner. There was one other, a profoundly original artist and a rare personality, who did not fit into the academic mold—Gabriel de St. Aubin (1724–1780). He had a brother, Augustin de St. Aubin, who was a man of the world and became *Graveur du Roi* and an artist of influence (illustration 267). But Gabriel, after competing unsuccessfully for the Prix de Rome, renounced academic ambitions and was content to remain an obscure professor of drawing at Blondel's School of Architecture.

He drew [recounts his brother] at all times and in all places. If he was taking a walk his crayon would be taking note of the passers-by. The lectures of the Academy were for him but a moving tableau for his sketches. One holiday, having placed himself in the nave of Notre Dame to hear a celebrated preacher, he drew out his sketchbook from habit and started to draw the orator. People nearby watched him as he worked; those in front of him turned around, those behind raised themselves in their chairs. Finally the attention of the listeners was so completely distracted that the preacher, interrupting his discourse, said, "When the eyes have been satisfied, I hope you will lend me your ears." This passion, joined to the desire to see everything and know everything, made him extremely negligent of his person and his health. He died completely worn out at the age of fifty-five. He was singular, bizarre: often before going out, he would rub white chalk from his crayons either on his hair to powder it or on his stockings to whiten them. He left a great number of curious drawings. We have several prints engraved after his designs and some etchings which display his genius.

108

He was in truth a singular and profoundly original artist. In an age and country where line engraving was supreme he gave his preference to etching and made some fifty plates, probably largely for his own pleasure and amusement. At a time when all expression was keyed up to the grand manner he came out with modest little etchings singularly free from pretense, each one a masterpiece of mood and atmosphere. His work strikes a very modern note: he is concerned only with entering into the spirit of a scene and reflecting with rare art his personal impression of it. Since he was an artist of great feeling and sensibility, his "impressions" have great charm for us. Take for example the *Spectacle de Tuileries* (illustration 256); with what subtlety and penetration he has invoked the spirit of the scene, the summer night under the swaying trees, the cool fragrance, the buzz of the conversation, the play of shadows and half-lights. On one proof of this etching St. Aubin wrote the following quatrain:

"Le faste se repose en ces jardins charmants;
Les cercles sont formés autour de chaque belle.
Nonchalamment assis, mille couple d'amants
S'y jurent à leur age un flame éternelle."

How simply and effectively he has re-created an eighteenth-century Coffeehouse in *Les Nouvellistes* (illustration 257). "There are," wrote the traveler Nemeitz in 1727, "an infinite number of coffeehouses in Paris, often ten or twelve on the same street. . . . There are still others where one finds *Les Nouvellistes* (news mongers) who discuss the news and the latest affairs of the state. Since there are a number of idlers in Paris, some of them do nothing else all day but frequent the cafés to hear the latest bit of news or gossip." Daumier later took up the same theme in his *Coffeehouse Politicians*. Two contemporary theatrical representations form an instructive contrast: Moreau-le-Jeune's *The Crowning of the Bust of Voltaire* (illustration 272) and St. Aubin's *Théâtre Italien* (illustration 261). The first is brilliant and polished, a showy panorama of stage and audience with Voltaire in a box bowing to the applause; the other is simple and unpretentious and enters into the very spirit of Harlequin and Columbine. St. Aubin's picture reminds one of Degas' studies of the essential gesture, the "magic moment" in his pictures of ballet dancers. In fact in many of St. Aubin's works we find anticipations of the modern point of view.

Another charming little etching is the *Académie Particulier* (illustration 268) a glimpse of the artist drawing from a model. There were many delightful pictures made of artists' life in the eighteenth century, such as for example, the *Cabinet d'un Peintre* (illustration 269) by the Polish engraver Chodowiecki living in Berlin. The engravers generally lived uneventful lives concerned with apprenticeship, technique, commissions, etcetera, and were more or less conscious of their middle-class station. The younger Cochin in his memoirs, when recounting a dispute with Comte de Caylus, said, "I was met by that contempt which, I know only too well, is felt by men of birth, in spite of their fine seeming politeness, for all who are, like artists, but of the bourgeoisie." The diary of J. G. Wille abounds in illuminating passages relating to contemporary life. He was an uninspired, rather mannered, but highly successful reproductive engraver (illustration 239a) but he was a delightful social historian. He tells of his contacts with patrons and dealers, of the immense speculation in art at the time, how long it took to engrave a plate (two years and four months on the *Family Concert*) and the prices he received for his work (six livres or about $1.20 for the same print). Like many of the engravers, such as Cochin, Tardieu, Poilly, Chereau, and others, he was his own dealer, that is to say he also sold prints from his engraving studio. Pierre François Basan, a glimpse of whose shop is given in Choffard's engraving (illustration 270), was more a dealer than engraver. He was the first to establish the practice of printing a large number of "proofs before letters" to supply the vast demand on the part of amateurs for such "rarities." He acquired a number of the coppers by Rembrandt and other Dutch etchers which he published in collected form. He organized and managed auction sales, printing for them illustrated auction catalogues in the modern manner, of such important collections as those of Bouchardon, van Loo, Marigny, and Wille. But the most important sale of all under Basan's management was that of the tremendous private collection of Pierre Jean Mariette in 1775 and 1776. The three generations of the Mariette family, the grandfather Pierre, the father Jean (illustration 291c), and Pierre Jean, were among the great print-dealers of the world. They had dealings with Marolles, Charles I, Crozat, and the genial Prince Eugene of Savoy whose own enormous collection of prints was eventually housed in the Imperial Library at Vienna under the curatorship of Adam von Bartsch (illustration 291d) and formed the basis of Bartsch's monumental catalogue of prints still in use today. Another important engraver, publisher, and dealer was Gabriel Huquier, whose shop was the center for the ornament prints of France. Still another dealer, C. F. Joullain, in his *Reflexions sur la Peinture et la Gravure accompagnées d'une courte dissertation sur la commerce de la curiosité et les ventes en général*, offers further sidelights on the traffic in prints, the psychology of collecting, the excitements of auction, and a complete description of how unscrupulous dealers formed a ring to control prices at an auction. In the eighteenth century picture-selling had become the business that it is today.

In the eighteenth century several discoveries in printmaking technique were made which resulted in a widening of the range of its expression. Chief of these was the invention of aquatint by Jean Baptiste Le Prince about 1768 (illustration 242). This process allowed for a wider use of tonal effects in intaglio printing and also made possible one form of color printing which was developed and perfected by Janinet (illustration 289), Descourtis, Alix, Jazet, and Sergent-Marceau. The most original of these perhaps was P. L. Debucourt (1755-1842) who engraved much after his own designs. He seems to have had no strong political convictions since he issued plates that found favor with the *Ancien Régime*, the Revolution, Napoleon, and the Restoration. Perhaps he had a contempt for the whole human race, and political convictions did not matter, since much of his work has a strong satiric tendency. He spent his last years raising rabbits, pigeons, and chickens which he allowed to run wild and never would kill. Among his most famous plates are *Les Deux Baisers*, *Le Menuet de la Mariée* and *La Noce au Château*, *La Matinée du Jour de l'An*, and *La Promenade de la Galerie du Palais Royal*. But his greatest print undoubtedly is the *Promenade Publique* of 1792 (illustration 291), a vivid panorama of society in the picturesque and stirring days of the National Convention.

III

It is probable that Debucourt received the impulse to make his picture from Rowlandson's equally famous color print, *Vauxhall* (illustration 290). Still another technique developed in the eighteenth century was the stipple and crayon process. The crayon manner was developed by François and Demarteau (illustration 241) to reproduce the effect of crayon drawings, and by Marin and Bonnet (illustration 265) to reproduce the quality of a pastel drawing. The most famous practitioner of the stipple technique was Francesco Bartolozzi (illustration 299) an Italian who settled in London in 1764. Indeed stipple engraving was popular chiefly in England where it was used to reproduce the sweet and sentimental works of Cipriani, Cosway, Angelica Kauffmann, and others.

Still another technical discovery was the invention of the Physionotrace about 1768 by the court musician Gilles Louis Chrétien. The machine is really an adaptation of the pantograph idea to the making of outline silhouettes of the head. By this means the foundation of a good workman-like likeness can be made in a sitting of less than five minutes. This tiny drawing could then be worked up on a copper plate with roulette work and etching into a complete portrait from which any number of prints could be taken. The speed of its production and its consequent cheapness ensured to the process an immediate success, especially with the rising middle class. Hitherto portraiture had been necessarily confined to distinguished people or to those few who could afford to commission an artist for a regular portrait. With the new process people of moderate means could afford to have portraits made of themselves (illustration 285). In addition to Chrétien there were other practitioners of the art, Quenedey and the émigré Favret de St. Memin, who came to America and made about eight hundred portraits (illustration 286). St. Memin charged thirty-three dollars for the original drawing, the copper plate, and twelve impressions.

Meanwhile, side by side with all these activities of the *haute monde*, flowed the daily life of the people. Some reflection of this—patronizing to be sure—was given in several series of *Cries of Paris* or pictures of various crafts and professions by Boucher and Bouchardon, and in such genre pictures as *La Place des Halles* and *La Place Maubert* by Jeaurat.

These were prints of the people but not for them. Such prints as they had were the rude woodcuts from chapbooks, in direct tradition from the fifteenth century through generations of obscure craftsmen, such as the *Robinson Crusoe* (illustration 68) or the *Notre Dame de Bonne Deliverance* (illustration 69) of which 500,000 proofs had been printed by 1766. Or they were the peep-show prints exhibited by wandering showmen like the *View of Lammerk* (illustration 274) or crude engravings of famous events like the *Boston Massacre* by Paul Revere (illustration 275) or the woodcut image, *View of the Place de Grève on the Day of the Fall of the Bastille* (illustration 72). Or else they were slightly satiric prints like the *World Upside Down* (illustration 71), which indirectly suggested that perhaps the world could be made a better place to live in, and which had their small share in the factors bringing about that experiment of direct action known as the Revolution. Yet there was relatively little use of pictures as propaganda. This form of persuasion and conversion was to receive a much wider development in the nineteenth century.

In 1789 began the debacle of the *Ancien Régime*. Very many of the artists and engravers such as Moreau, Choffard, Debucourt, Ponce, welcomed the ideas of the Revolution; some of them like Sergent took an active part in it; but trained as they had been in the faithful delineation of an old order, they were unable to transfer their new convictions to their art. In spite of the eloquent appeal to artists of Minister Benezech on the ninth Floreal of the Year IV ("Liberty invites you to retrace its triumphs. . . . You should acquire a national character in order that succeeding generations can not reproach you with not having been French in the most remarkable epoch of our history"), most of the work was cold and uninspired. New forms were required for a new conception of society, and the academic, Roman classicism of David or Regnault was not adequate. Prud'hon, in many ways perhaps the most characteristic painter of the Revolutionary period, is here represented by an allegory on *Liberty* engraved by Copia (illustration 293). There was a great deal of documentation of the Revolution, much of it interesting to the historian rather than to the art-lover. *The Interior of a Revolutionary Committee under the Terror*, engraved by Berthault after the younger

Fragonard (illustration 273), does manage to dramatize some of the emotional currents of the Revolution—members of the nobility, often innocently suffering for the sins of their class, on the defensive before a group of "roughnecks" of the Terror. Such minor tragedies are enacted in every revolution. One of the most vivid pictures of those stirring times is Sergent-Marceau's color print, the *People Running through the Streets with Torches* (illustration 292). The tenseness of passions unloosed, the uncertainties of alarms and excursions have been admirably suggested. Antoine François Sergent, called Sergent-Marceau (for he added his wife's name to his own), was a fiery and picturesque character. He married the sister of General Marceau, Maria Marceau, to whom he paid the tribute of the ardent devotion of a lifetime. On her death at the age of eighty he published a pamphlet giving a detailed description of her mental and physical charms. When the Revolution broke, he threw himself into the thick of it, was one of the deputies who voted for the death of the king, celebrated at Chartres Cathedral the Festival of Reason, was instrumental in preventing the destruction or mutilation of many works of art during the Terror. After the reaction of the ninth Thermidor he fled to Switzerland; he returned later and was again exiled after the eighteenth Brumaire, and lived in Italy for the rest of his life. Eight days before his death in 1847, totally blind and ninety-six years of age, he declared to Carnot that "far from repenting his revolutionary activity, he considered it, on the contrary, as his chief title to fame."

We have had little to say about printmaking in England during the centuries. The country had been backward as far as the visual arts were concerned; its genius was expressed in other ways, in literature and science, in empire-building, in commerce and manufacture. Whatever production of art there had been, was through foreign talent such as Holbein, Hollar, Sir Anthony van Dyck, Sir Peter Lely, and Sir Godfrey Kneller. But in the late seventeenth century and in the eighteenth century there was perfected a new printmaking medium eminently suited to the English taste—mezzotint—and native artists quickly sprang up to develop its possibilities. The process was invented by Ludwig von Siegen (1609–1676) and the first dated mezzotint was a portrait of the

Landgravin of Hesse (illustration 237a). The secret of the process was communicated to Prince Rupert, to whom Evelyn in his "Sculptura" gives the credit for its invention by what appears to have been a willful juggling with the facts. A. Blooteling (illustration 213a) perfected the technique by inventing the rocker for laying uniform and rich tone areas. The romantic Prince Rupert executed several plates, and though he did not invent the art, he encouraged its development in England with the result that in due course of time mezzotint was practiced chiefly in England, and labeled as "the English manner" everywhere on the Continent. The mezzotint process, based upon gradations of tone, was particularly suited to reproduce paintings. Since the English were interested chiefly in portrait painting, the great bulk of mezzotints are portraits.

In Holland [wrote Hogarth] selfishness is the ruling passion; in England vanity is united with it. Portrait painting therefore ever has, and ever will succeed better in this country than in any other; the demand will be as constant as new faces arise. . . . Upon the whole, it must be acknowledged that the artists and the age are fitted for each other. If hereafter the times alter, the arts, like water, will find their level.

And Horace Walpole wrote to Sir Horace Mann:

Another rage is for prints of English portraits: I have been collecting them above thirty years, and originally never gave for a mezzotint above one or two shillings. The lowest are now a crown; most, from half a guinea to a guinea. . . . In short, we are at the height of extravagance and improvements, for we do improve rapidly in taste as well as in the former. I cannot say as much for our genius. Poetry is gone to bed, or into our prose; we are like the Romans in that too. If we have the arts of the Antonines— we have the fustian also.

England had become a prosperous nation, that is to say there were many noblemen owning much of the land who had grown rich through the enclosing of communal lands for sheep raising and through the improvements in agriculture during the seventeenth and eighteenth centuries, and there were many merchants who had grown rich in commerce. Manufacture, chiefly of woolen cloth, had made great strides in the seventeenth century and had been aided materially by the influx of great numbers of skilled artisans possessing considerable capital, the Dutch and Flemish weavers who fled from the Spanish invasion, and the Huguenots, the pick of France's industrial population, who were expelled from France by Louis XIV. The beginning of the eighteenth century witnessed the naval and commercial supremacy of the English over the Dutch and Spanish; henceforth Britannia ruled the waves. In the conflict between the French and the English over India, England emerged victorious with the whole of India in her possession, an enormous source of wealth procured at very little cost. Furthermore in 1769 James Watt took out his patent for a steam engine; and further inventions by Hargreaves, Arkwright, and Crompton benefited the spinning and weaving industries and brought about the Industrial Revolution, the full effects of which were not felt until the nineteenth century. All of these factors, however, combined to make England the richest nation in Europe. And how did the English spend their money? The merchants invested theirs for further profits, but many of the noblemen, with the Grand Tour in Italy as a traditional part of their education, posed as collectors, dilettantes of the arts, connoisseurs or virtuosi as they were called. Unfortunately they purchased chiefly Italian pictures since there was little native art which had any prestige. The only native art which they patronized was portrait painting, and the fact that they patronized this one branch was largely due to the achievement and personality of one man, Sir Joshua Reynolds:

Sir Joshua, shrewd man of the world, suave member of Dr. Johnson's circle, dignified first President of the Royal Academy, continued the aristocratic tradition of van Dyck. As a portrait painter he substituted for elegance the glamor of the Grand Manner. He evolved an eclectic style based upon the achievements of the Venetian and Flemish Schools, believing that genius was a power acquired by long labor and study.

Study consists in learning to see nature [he said] and may be called the art of using other men's minds. . . . We should to the last moment of our lives continue a settled intercourse with all true examples of grandeur. Their inventions are not only the food of our infancy, but the substance which supplies the fullest maturity of our vigor.

116

On which Blake commented later:

Reynolds endeavours to prove that there is No such thing as Inspiration and that any Man of plain Understanding may by Thieving from Others become a Mich. Angelo. . . . Reynolds Thinks that Man Learns all he Knows. I say on the Contrary that Man Brings All That he has or can have Into the World with him. Man is Born Like a Garden ready Planted and Sown. The World is too poor to produce one Seed.

Reynolds was not a great artist, but he was a successful one. He had enough tricks of the grand manner to impress his contemporaries, and envelop his fashionable portraits with a flattering dignity. Through connection with the Academy and his *Discourses,* his careful cultivation of friends, and his countless commissions, he exerted an enormous influence on the London art world, and hundreds of mezzotints were made after his paintings by such skillful engravers as McArdell, Houston, Fisher, J. Watson, T. Watson, Green, Dickinson, Jones, Walker, and others. A typical example is the portrait of Mrs. Carnac engraved by J. R. Smith (illustration 295). The portrait of Dr. Johnson engraved by Doughty (illustration 297) displays more sincerity and sense of character. It was of another and earlier portrait of himself that Dr. Johnson said to Boswell: "He may paint himself as deaf as he please but *I will not* go down to Posterity as Blinking Sam." Reynolds set the style of fashionable portrait which was continued with minor variations by Hoppner (illustration 294), Romney (illustration 296), Gainsborough, Raeburn, Wright, Lawrence, and their engravers. There is a certain sameness about all these mezzotint portraits, due partly perhaps to a limitation of the medium which emphasizes softness and smoothness at the expense of honest or subtle delineation of form, but also due to the fundamentally artificial approach of the painter to his problem. It is a highly aristocratic and superficial art, grandiloquent, flattering, and sentimentalizing, and without that exquisite taste and sense of style which gives distinction to the equally aristocratic art of France.

It is with some sense of relief—a touch of reality or a breath of fresh air—that one turns to the work of Gainsborough and Hogarth. With regard to Gainsborough, it is not so much the portraits (though most of these are executed with more originality and feeling than is visible in the other portraits of his time) as it is the landscapes which he executed for his own pleasure. "I'm sick of Portraits," he wrote to a friend, "and wish very much to take my viol-da-gamba and walk off to some sweet village where I can paint landskips and enjoy the fag-end of life in quietness and ease." He made a small number of soft ground etchings which were published in 1797 by Boydell after his death. They have caught the charm and freshness of the English countryside (illustration 299b), and thus stand as precursors of the development of the English landscape school which took place in the nineteenth century. Incidentally these rare soft ground etchings are among the earliest examples of the process.

The artist who placed himself most directly in opposition to Sir Joshua Reynolds and what he stood for was William Hogarth. He espoused a popular tradition as against the aristocratic and academic tradition of Reynolds. His genius found its completest expression in the creation of universal types under the stress of dramatic situations rather than in fashionable portraits or in historical compositions in the grand manner. Hogarth was born in 1697, and like Reynolds was the son of a schoolmaster. He was apprenticed to a silversmith and later studied at the academy of Sir James Thornhill. In 1729 he ran away with Thornhill's daughter. In 1733 he moved to a house in Leicester Fields in which he lived until his death in 1764. Meanwhile he had painted in 1731, and a year later engraved, the series of six pictures entitled *Harlot's Progress*. They had such a widespread success that he became reconciled to his father-in-law Thornhill, who said "the man who can furnish representations like these can also maintain a wife without a portion." It is recorded that there were over one thousand two hundred subscriptions entered for the engravings at a guinea per set. In describing the inception of this work Hogarth wrote that portrait painting to a conscientious and self-respecting artist was "not sufficiently profitable to pay the expenses my family required."

I therefore turned my thoughts to a still more novel mode, namely painting and engraving modern moral subjects, a field not broken up in any country or any age. . . . I have therefore endeavoured to treat my subject as a dramatic writer; my picture is my stage, and men and women my players, who by means of certain actions and gestures, are to exhibit *a dumb show*. . . . This I found was most likely to answer my purpose, provided I could strike the passions, and by small sums from many, by the sale of prints which I could engrave from my own pictures, thus secure my property to myself.

The pictures were much copied and pirated; so much so that Hogarth with other artists, Vertue, Vandergucht, petitioned Parliament to pass a law vesting in the artist the exclusive right to his own designs and restraining reproduction without consent. This Copyright Act was passed in 1735, and Hogarth's next series of engravings, *Rake's Progress*, appeared under that protection, the first prints to bear the inscription *Published according to Act of Parliament*. There had been previous attempts by artists, such as Rubens and others, to prevent plagiarism of their works, and some of them were successful in obtaining exclusive privileges from the king or ruler, but in every case they were "privileges" obtained by influence or favor, as the correspondence of Rubens clearly shows. For the first time the general principle of copyright was established: any artist could avail himself of its protection. The third famous picture sequence was *Marriage à la Mode* satirizing high society in the same manner that he had dramatized episodes in the life of a harlot and a rake. The six prints were published in 1745 but were not engraved by Hogarth himself. Plate II, the *Breakfast Scene*, or the *Morning After*, engraved by Baron is reproduced herewith (illustration 258). The setting is supposed to have been copied from the drawing-room at No. 5 Arlington St., once occupied by Horace Walpole. The theme of the series is the tragic unfolding of a marriage of convenience between an earl and his rich but plebeian wife.

Hogarth was in the habit of specially engraving some little subject and presenting it to the subscribers of his various large prints or series of prints, as a subscription receipt. One of these, the receipt for *Rake's Progress*, entitled *Laughing Audience*, is reproduced (illustration 262). It is a most delightful print, perfect in composition, and expressive of character by the simplest and directest means. Hogarth engraved many famous single plates such as *The March to Finchley, Southwark Fair*,

Strolling Actresses Dressing in a Barn, Midnight Modern Conversation, Beer Street and Gin Lane, and *Garrick as Richard III. The Enraged Musician* (illustration 259) is characteristic of his rich and humorous observation of life in the London of his time. The picture, as Fielding said, is "enough to make a man deaf to look at it." Hogarth also made political caricatures, being one of the first to cultivate that form of printmaking, specially favored in England and later developed by Rowlandson, Gillray, Dighton, and others. Allied to these, though not a caricature, was his *Portrait of Lord Lovat* (illustration 266), just before his execution for high treason. It was quickly etched to satisfy a popular demand so great that he sold prints, priced at one shilling, at the rate of two hundred and forty per day for many weeks. For vigor of characterization it ranks among the greatest portrait prints of the world.

Hogarth was not a realistic artist; he worked rather in the style of the dramatist or comic writer like Fielding. He combined realistic elements for a theme that was either humorous or moral or descriptive. He was not the first artist to depict low life or the contemporary scene, nor the first to conceive of a picture sequence as connected episodes with a central theme, as we know from the many series of the Passion which preceded him. But he combined the two ideas with such vigor and dramatic power that he may be said to have perfected a new form. His painting has been called literary or didactic. This is true only of his less successful work; at his best it expresses its theme in purely pictorial terms rich in observation of life and character. His book *The Analysis of Beauty* shows him to have been a theoretician and technician of considerable ability and common sense. To say that his work has mankind for its central theme is merely to point out that it has social content. This is thoroughly within the legitimate province of art, although many critics disagree, just as in literature the purists are more likely to relish "Kubla Khan" than *Tom Jones.* For a print or picture to have a meaning should be an advantage not a disqualification. Hogarth was in many respects typically English: he had the Englishman's contempt for foreigners as his caricatures of the French testify. His training was more or less indigenous; he never traveled abroad. He allied himself with the democratic tradition of Bruegel and the seventeenth century Dutch. He aimed for expressive character, never for ideal beauty or elegant style, though, as Dobson says, when beauty came his way he drew it. It was a curious quirk of his character that although he despised the historical painters, he tried to beat them at their own game—with lamentable results. His genius was of a different order. One of the first great partisans of the bourgeois or middle class, he found his patrons among the many instead of the few.

Life in eighteenth century Venice—if we believe the memoirs of Casanova, Carlo Gozzi, and Goldoni—was one long *fête galante* or carnival interrupted by short periods of Lent equally picturesque and beautiful. At any rate it was somewhat in this spirit that Giambattista Tiepolo (1696–1770) worked at his decorations for villas and palaces and occasionally for churches. He was a facile painter and draughtsman, and inventions came bubbling from his fertile brain. In the midst of a busy career he found time to etch about thirty-eight plates. They are truly what he called the two leading series of his etchings: *Capricci* and *Scherzi*, or whimsical inventions (illustration 282). The subject matter is most varied and fanciful, scenes of magicians, occultism, satyrs, Roman soldiers, Pulchinello, and the like, all executed with a light and airy grace, with much spirit and little meaning. The Tiepolos must have been a happy jolly family: Giambattista married Cecilia Guardi, the sister of the painter Francesco Guardi. It is said that she was such a gamester that once during the absence of her husband she gambled away all his sketches and even their country house with all his frescoes in it. They had nine children, two of whom, Domenico and Lorenzo, assisted their father with his decorations, and etched a number of plates after his paintings. Domenico was an able artist in his own right, and composed a series of twenty-five etchings entitled *Idee Pittoresche sopra La Fugga in Egitto*, 1753 (illustration 283), an elegant and fluent lenten meditation suffused with soft Italian atmosphere and charm.

If the Tiepolos may be said to have pictured the actors in the Venetian carnival, then Canaletto may be said to have provided the setting or backdrop. His thirty-odd etchings, also made in the intervals of a busy painting career, depict scenes in and around Venice, and are filled with brilliant sunshine and quivering atmosphere. Such plates as the *Torre di Malghera* and the *Porch with the Lantern* are justly famous, but some of the smaller plates, the *Terrace* (illustration 281), the *Prison* (illustration 280), the *Market on the Giudecca*, are equally attractive. Canaletto had numerous contacts with English connoisseurs and collectors, and the collected edition of his *Vedute* or etchings was published with a dedication to Joseph Smith, the British Consul at Venice.

The third great name in eighteenth century Italian etching was Giovanni Battista Piranesi. He too was a Venetian, born in 1720, the son of a stone mason. He was educated to be an architect but the great passion of his life was Roman antiquities. And passion was a mighty force in a man of his fiery temperament if one can judge from the anecdotes told of him. How for instance when sketching in the old Roman Forum he saw a young girl who he was convinced was descended from the noble Romans and how after a cyclonic courtship lasting five days was married to the daughter of the gardener of Prince Corsini. How he threatened to kill the doctor called in to minister to a member of his family if the patient did not recover within a few days. How when he was absorbed in the making of an etching, his wife and five children suffered agonies of hunger, not daring to disturb him or eat without him. It was in Rome, the city of his dreams, that he spent most of his life, pursuing his archaeological researches and bringing to completion his stupendous *œuvre* of over one thousand three hundred huge etchings. He became an authority on Roman archaeology throughout Europe, and exercised an influence on the development of the classic style in the France of Louis XVI and in England through his friendship with Robert Adam. His mastery of draughtsmanship and perspective, his knowledge of Roman antiquities, the sense of drama suggested by the picturesque figures with which he peopled his romantic ruins, and above all his epic imagination all combine to make his etchings the most effective dramatization of Rome's past grandeur ever known (illustration 277). Piranesi also made many etchings of the Rome of his day; a typical and skillful example, showing the home of the French Academy in Rome from 1725 to 1800 on the Via del Corso, is reproduced (illustration 278). Early in his career he etched a series of fourteen (later sixteen) large etchings called *Carceri d'Invenzione* or *Prison Scenes* (illustration 279). They seem to have been caprices in which he allowed his imagination to run riot in a fantastic interplay of light and shade among architectural forms. De Quincey in his *Confessions of an Opium Eater* mentions these prints in a celebrated passage, which probably reads into it meanings which were not in Piranesi's mind. In spite of its distortions it does manage to convey something of the spirit of these etched phantasmagoria:

Many years ago, when I was looking over Piranesi's *Antiquities of Rome*, Mr. Coleridge, who was standing by, described to me a set of plates by that artist, called his *Dreams*, and which record the scenery of his visions during the delirium of a fever. Some of them . . . represented vast Gothic halls, on the floor of which stood all sorts of engines and machinery, wheels, cables, pulleys, levers, catapults, etcetera, expressive of enormous power put forth and resistance overcome. Creeping along the sides of the walls, you perceived a staircase; and upon it, grasping his way upwards, was Piranesi himself; follow the stairs a little further, and you perceive it comes to a sudden, abrupt termination, without any balustrade, and allowing no step onwards to him who had reached the extremity except into the depths below. . . . But raise your eyes, and behold a second flight of stairs still higher, on which again Piranesi is perceived, by this time standing on the very brink of the abyss. . . . With the same power of endless growth and self-production did my architecture proceed in my dreams.

6. Nineteenth Century

THE nineteenth century was a drama of personalities, and Goya, working in two centuries, wrote its prologue. The outstanding qualities of the nineteenth century were its diversity and its emphasis on personality. There were, to be sure, movements and schools of artists, plenty of them in bewildering succession, but they were usually grouped around a few outstanding personalities. Hitherto an art style or epoch lasted for a century or longer, now it lasted for a generation. Once the epoch molded the artist, now the artist created the style. Classicism, Romanticism, Realism, Barbizon, Impressionism, post-Impressionism all had their say within a hundred years. The nineteenth was the century of rugged individualism.

Francisco de Goya y Lucientes was a picturesque and outstanding personality who in expressing himself also expressed truths about mankind. He was a combination of court-painter and satirist, of philosopher and *aficionado* of the bull-ring, that could occur only in Spain. Spain has always been a strange and mysterious land where all things are possible. As Joseph, who tried to rule the country for six years, ruefully said to his brother Napoleon: *"L'Espagne n'est pas un pays comme les autres."* A backward and reactionary country, priest-ridden and king-ridden, its peoples displayed in many respects an astonishing wisdom of life, a real feeling for life as a fine art. Its beggars had the manners of grandees. Nowhere in Europe were bourgeois ideas and ideals so completely discounted and ignored as in Spain.

Goya was born in Fuendetodos in Aragon in 1746. There are many legends of his early life, a record as violent and vivid as Cellini's, filled with love affairs, murderous quarrels, exploits in the bull-ring, travels in Italy. In 1776 he was settled in Madrid, married to Josepha Bayeu who was to bear him twenty children, leading an active, hard-working life, designing cartoons for tapestries saturated with the gay spirit of Madrid life, painting murals and portraits of the nobility and the royal family. In 1780 he was elected to the Academy of San Fernando; in 1789 he was made *Pintor de Camara;* in 1799 he was *Primer Pintor de Camara,* chief painter to the king. He enjoyed the friendship and patronage of the Duke and Duchess of Ossuna; he had an intense love affair with the alluring but fickle Duchess of Alba. In all these years he drew and painted incessantly, tried his hand at etching, copies of Velazquez. But his direct and passionate temperament also had opportunity to reflect on the pageant of human folly as he saw it: greed, fickleness, pride, lust, cruelty, stupidity. In 1791 Le Prince's secret of aquatint etching had been published to the world in the *Encyclopédie Méthodique.* Goya must have come across it, and in the aquatint process he found a medium eminently fitted to reproduce his pen and wash drawings. In the last years of the century there began to crystallize in his mind the idea of a series of satiric compositions executed in etching and aquatint. The miracle of it was that he should want to publish to the world, in Spain of all places, such a series of prints. Perhaps he had to do it to keep his self-respect amid the corrupt and artificial surroundings of the court, perhaps he was a bit *afrancesado,* tinged with French revolutionary ideas. In any case the series was announced to the public in 1797 in a prospectus containing the following explanation written, if not by Goya, by Cean Bermudez under the inspiration of his ideas:

Believing that the criticism of human errors and vices, although first and foremost the business of rhetoric and poetry, may also come within the province of painting, the author has chosen as subjects for his work some of those extravagances and stupidities, common to all classes of society, some of those prejudices and falsehoods, hallowed by custom, by ignorance or by interest, such themes indeed as seemed to him to offer matter for ridicule and scope for the free play of the artist's imagination. As the subjects are idealized it may not be too daring to assume that their faults will be leniently judged by people of intelligence. . . . I crave the public's indulgence in consideration of the fact that the author has made use of no strange models, nor even of studies from nature. The imitation of nature is as difficult as it is admirable if one can really attain it and carry it through. But he also may deserve praise, who has completely withdrawn himself from nature and has succeeded in placing before our eyes, forms and movements which have hitherto existed only in our imagination. . . . Painting, like Poetry, selects from the universe what she can best use for her own ends. She unites, she concentrates in one fantastic figure circumstances and characters which nature has distributed among various individuals. Thanks to this wise and ingenious combination the artist merits the title of an inventor and ceases to be a mere subordinate copyist.

Two years later the set of eighty plates of the *Caprichos* was put on sale at 320 reals (about $25.00)—one of the world's masterpieces of graphic art, a savage yet detached commentary on human kind. For once the façade was ripped off and the essential type laid bare. Yet not only types were attacked, but society, which allowed certain things to happen—*Because She Was Sensitive* (illustration 311), or the fickleness of fortune in *To Rise and Fall* (illustration 312). In spite of Goya's disclaimer that the satire was general and not particular there were rumors—as was natural in a society where gossip and the malicious story were raised to a fine art—that certain reigning court favorites and even the king and queen were attacked. Furthermore there were certain inquiries and investigations by the Inquisition, for some of the shots at superstition and fanaticism had hit a bull's eye. Goya deemed it prudent to dedicate the series to the king, Charles IV, who graciously accepted it and duly rewarded the artist. Nowhere but in Spanish countries could such a thing have happened, in Spain where the technique of the deadly thrust in the bull-ring is appreciated with discriminating connoisseurship, where scepticism and faith, idealism and materialism, Don Quixote and Sancho Panza go hand in hand, and where flourishes the ironic laugh, the *vacilada* of the Mexicans, that laugh that is relished by its victims if only the sally be delivered with sufficient art. The frontispiece of the set was a portrait of Goya himself (illustration 364). We see him as he appeared at the height of his powers, the piercing, all-seeing eyes, the protruding underlip, the determined chin—the master of illusion and disillusion. Deafness was already upon him, that deafness which was eventually to cut him off from all society except a few intimates. Meanwhile things were happening in Spain. In 1808 Napoleon invaded Spain

126

to establish his brother Joseph upon the throne. The Spaniards should have welcomed him, for any rule would have been preferable to the old regime of Spain, but most of them did not, and there ensued a guerrilla warfare of unparalleled savagery on both sides. For six long years it lasted, aided by Napoleon's implacable enemy, England, until finally reaction, bigotry, cruelty, and the Inquisition returned triumphantly in the person of Ferdinand VII in 1814. Goya watched it all and set it down in a series of etchings which were not published until long after his death as the *Disasters of War*. Not all the plates refer to the Napoleonic War; several are covert satires against the French and against Ferdinand; still another group refer to the great famine of 1812, indirect consequence of the war, when over twenty thousand people died in Madrid alone. A reflection of this is given in that magnificent composition *Thanks to Millet Seed* (illustration 316). "Men women, and children," says Romanos in his *Reminiscences*, "lay dying in the streets, they begged for a scrap of green stuff, for a potato, for a drop of soup, however thin and bad. It was a scene of despair and pain." But most of the etchings relate to the invasion (illustrations 317 and 319), a terrific and awe-inspiring indictment, not of the enemy, but of war itself, its senselessness and incredible brutality. Only a Voltaire in *Candide* could do justice to the scope of Goya's savagely ironic portrayal:

He crept over a heap of dead and dying and at last reached a neighboring village which he found in ashes. It was a village of the Avares and the Bulgarians had burnt it down according to the rules of the international game. Here aged men, sinking beneath the blows that were showered upon them, saw their wives throttled to death, pressing their children to their bleeding breasts to the last. There girls lay dying, their bellies ripped open when they had served to satisfy the lust of conquering heroes; others, half burned, begged for death. On the ground one saw splashes of scattered brains and limbs lopped from bodies.

Goya worked on, more and more withdrawn into himself in the Quinta del Sordo, the deaf man's villa. On one of his *Caprichos* there was an inscription, "The Sleep of Reason produces Monsters." Dreams

127

and nightmares seemed to haunt him, visions far more fantastic and monstrous than those he pictured in the *Caprichos*. Out of pleasure or necessity he recorded them on the walls of the Quinta and in the series of twenty-two etchings and aquatints known as the *Disparates*, or *Extravagances*. Like Titian and Rembrandt, Goya suffered no diminution of imaginative power in his old age. The *Disasters* were realistic, the *Caprichos* were a mixture of realism and fantasy, but the *Disparates* were pure fantasy, a direct outpouring of his unconscious. What powerful and haunting visions they are, a group of people huddling on a rotten branch, a stallion biting a woman, flying men (illustration 313), a man haunted by demons! One of them, entitled *Disparate de Bestia* (illustration 315), shows priests and lawgivers anxiously holding a law code before an elephant who may or may not symbolize the People unconscious of their strength. It is a superbly vital composition.

In 1825 he was in Bordeaux for his health—old, in a strange land, deaf, with eyesight failing, "but very pleased with life and anxious to meet people." "He obstinately continued to work," wrote his friend Moratin, "painting everything that comes into his head and unwilling ever to correct what he paints." In his seventy-ninth year he made a number of lithographs, then a comparatively new medium, including the four great bull fights (illustration 314). He had already etched forty good-sized plates (thirty-two of which were published in 1815) as a sort of illustrated history of the *corrida de toros* and its heroes. But his invention continued undiminished. These four great stones are a veritable orgy of bull fighting, the compositions built up with broad strokes and large masses, brimming with energy. They are amazingly spirited achievements from a man almost eighty and count among the great masterpieces of lithography. Goya had extraordinary energy and an indomitable will; in a letter he excused his bad penmanship, "I have neither sight, nor pulse, nor pen nor inkpot, I lack everything, only my will survives." But even the will to live was quenched by a stroke in 1828 brought on, it is said, by joy over the arrival of his son Xavier.

On one of the preliminary drawings for the *Caprichos*, the one which originally was to serve as the frontispiece, Goya wrote "*Idioma Universal.*" Universal language, the ultimate aim of the print, that was what was in the back of his mind, and he came as close to it as any print-maker ever did. His only peers are Rembrandt and Daumier who approached humanity from the side of love and understanding. Goya perhaps probed deeper into the unconscious, into those devious but powerful forces which motivate our every action. He has brought into the light of day and made concrete in the shape of recognizable types certain essential drives that lie buried in most of us, impulses of vanity, pride, greed, gluttony, lust, cruelty, and the like. There is nothing like war or the vision of sudden death for uncovering the essence of man. This is strong medicine and bitter: many people will be repelled by Goya's work. But for those who can accept one aspect of reality with-out sugar-coating, it can become a most illuminating catharsis.

Another personality who was active in two centuries was Thomas Rowlandson. He was born in London in 1756, the son of a fairly pros-perous merchant. He studied at the Academy School for a short time. In his sixteenth year, about 1771, he was sent to Paris to live with his aunt, née Mlle Chattelier, whose favorite he became. He learned to speak French like a native, plunged with eagerness into the life of the gay capital, and entered the École de l'Académie Royale to continue his art studies. He became acquainted with Debucourt, and with Janinet, a fellow pupil at the École. In 1775 when he was nineteen, he returned to London and continued his studies at the Royal Academy. Angelo in his *Reminiscences* recounts:

Bannister and Rowlandson were prankish youths. The latter once gave great offense by carrying a pea-shooter into the life academy, and, whilst old Moser was adjusting the female model and had just directed her contour, Rowlandson let fly a pea, which, making her start, threw her entirely out of position, and interrupted the gravity of the study for the whole evening.

In spite of such pranks Rowlandson was well liked; and a great future was predicted for him by the academicians, two Presidents, Reynolds and West, having expressed the greatest admiration of his talents. In 1775 he exhibited for the first time at the Royal Academy, and continued to do so for about a dozen years. He gradually, however, lost interest in the so-called serious or historical art in favor of a more free and easy

129

and rollicking social commentary, partly through the influence of such friends as Bunbury, Wigstead, and Gillray, and partly through the bent of his own temperament. He launched into a career of extravagance and dissipation aggravated by the receipt of a legacy of over seven thousand pounds from his French aunt. Yet his wild life did not interfere with his production: it rather spurred him on to tap the apparently inexhaustible springs of his fancy. His work combined French elegance with English animal spirits. He had a ready gift for characterization combined with a rich knowledge of life gained from actual experience. His opulent and exuberant forms exactly mirrored his uncommon zest for life. His *Vauxhall Gardens* (illustration 290) has been mentioned as having influenced Debucourt. Vauxhall was a famous London amusement resort of the eighteenth century, and Rowlandson is supposed to have introduced caricatures of many well known people in his picture. The two fashionably dressed women under the singer on the balcony are supposed to be the Duchess of Devonshire and her sister Lady Duncannon. Farther to the right the man whispering into the ear of a lady linked to a deformed husband is the Prince of Wales, afterwards George IV. In a supper box Dr. Johnson is oblivious to everything but the pleasures of the table, with the ever-watchful Boswell diagonally on his left. On the right of Johnson, the blue-stocking Mrs. Thrale may be seen talking to Oliver Goldsmith. Rowlandson made many illustrations, chiefly for Ackermann's publications, the *Dance of Death*, the *Dance of Life*, the various *Tours of Dr. Syntax*, and the *Microcosm of London* (illustration 302) in collaboration with Pugin who supplied the architectural features. This last is a survey of the activities of a great city in 104 plates, furnishing a wealth of information regarding the manners of the time. He made a number of genre scenes, the *Cries of London*, such as the charming *Ballad Singers* (illustration 304). For such publishers as Ackermann, Fores, and Tegg, he produced several political caricatures (illustration 303) and countless social caricatures, etched on copper and crudely colored by hand. *More Miseries or the Bottom of Mr. Figg's old Whiskey* [*a type of carriage*] *Broke Through* (illustration 305) is typical of these and of the robust humor of the

130

time. The caricatures of Gillray, Bunbury, Dighton, and Cruikshank are in the same vein.

Rowlandson also did a few sporting prints, a genre that was popular in the early nineteenth century in England. The hard-drinking, hard-riding English country squires and the young bucks of the city were collecting art, and the demand was ably supplied. The appreciation of these connoisseurs, however, was strictly limited: they demanded that a picture be factual, accurate, and pleasant, and, in subject matter, entirely within the range of their experience, either genre pictures of the English countryside (Morland and Ward), or sporting pictures, hunting, shooting, racing, or coaching prints. A large group of able, decorative but esthetically limited prints were produced by Alken, Pollard, Wolstenholme, Howitt, and others. Two prints, *Hare Hunting* by Hodges (illustration 307) and *False Alarm on the Road to Gretna Green* by Newhouse (illustration 306), may serve as representative of the class. There were other groups of prints appealing to a specialized public, such as flower prints, here typified by Redouté's charming color print of *Roses* (illustration 308) or natural history prints, represented by a plate from the monumental *Birds of America* (illustration 309), the life work of J. J. Audubon. Mention should also be made of the lithograph genre subjects, popular in America, and published by Currier and Ives, and others. Many of these have little artistic merit but the best of them have both decorative charm and historical interest. The clipper ships especially bring back the thrill and glory of a vanished era (illustration 310). Thousands and hundreds of thousands of specialized prints have been made, relating to science, natural history, travel, genre, illustration, which in their humble way have contributed to the amusement and instruction of mankind.

A new and cheap printmaking medium was perfected at the beginning of the century which was greatly to extend the range of popular prints—lithography. The inventor was Aloys Senefelder. He was not an artist, but was ambitious to write for the stage. Being poor, he saw no way of getting the world to look at his work unless he became his own publisher. In the course of his attempts to find a cheap method of printing plays with engraved plates, he happened upon the germ of lithography. In his own words:

I had just ground a stone plate smooth in order to treat it with etching fluid and to pursue on it my practice in reverse writing when my mother asked me to write a laundry list for her. The laundress was waiting but we could find no paper. My own supply had been used up by pulling proofs. Even the writing ink was dried up. Without bothering to look for writing materials, I wrote the list hastily on the clean stone with my prepared ink of wax, soap and lampblack, intending to copy it as soon as paper was supplied.

Curiosity as to the possibilities of this chance application of ink and stone led him to further experiments till he had evolved the complete process. Later unscrupulous promoters were to defraud the unworldly inventor of some of his just benefits and dues, but in the end he received a pension from the King of Bavaria, and painstaking biographers and autobiographers have set the whole record straight for the benefit of grateful posterity. In Germany and Austria the new medium did not stimulate any far-reaching response. At the beginning of the century these countries were in a state of depression artistically, economically, and politically. Schinkel made a few prints and the Quaglios some romantic scenes including an interesting portrait of Senefelder printed with two stones like a chiaroscuro (illustration 320). The portrait, dated 1818, was undoubtedly done from life and thus punctures the legend that Hanfstängl's lithograph of 1834 was the only life portrait. The legend is that Senefelder had a deadly fear of having his picture taken; Hanfstängl persuaded him to sit for a portrait, and three days later he sickened and died. Strixner, Piloty, and Hanfstängl used lithography to reproduce paintings. Portrait lithographs were made by Reuter, Krüger, Schadow, and the Viennese Kriehuber, who drew the charmingly romantic *Une Matinée chez Liszt* (illustration 324) with portraits of Liszt, Berlioz, the pianist Carl Czerny (remembered for his Études), the violinist Ernst, and Kriehuber himself. It is one of the most famous of musical portraits.

It was in France, however, that lithography first came into its own.

132

Not only was art in demand there, but there were also distinguished artists who were willing to try their hand with the new medium, Prud'hon, Guerin, Géricault (illustration 325), Baron Gros, Boilly (illustration 321). Distinguished amateurs took it up (as they had the physionotrace). They included the Duc de Montpensier, brother of the future king Louis Philippe, and Vivant-Denon, one of Napoleon's savants who gathered together in the Louvre famous paintings from all over Europe as spoils of war, and of whom it was said that his chief occupations were *"la gravure et les femmes."* But lithography flourished in Paris chiefly because it satisfied a popular need. Amid all the ups and downs of the Revolution, the Directorate, the Empire, and the Restoration, the middle class had been slowly and steadily gaining in power and influence. A quick and inexpensive reproducing medium was needed in order to reach the bourgeoisie for purposes of propaganda. Woodcut and etching, as Edouard Fuchs has pointed out, were too complicated and costly; lithography was as if made for the purpose. Political caricature flourished as never before at the beginning of the reign of *le Roi Bourgeois*. Furthermore, the middle classes had still other uses for lithography beside political propaganda; they wanted pictures, decorations for their walls and illustrations for their books. Thackeray in his *Paris Sketch Book* has drawn a pretty picture of this aspect of French bourgeois culture:

The same love of ornament which is shown in their public places of resort, appears in their houses likewise; and everyone of our readers who has lived in Paris, in any lodging, magnificent or humble with any family, however poor, may bear witness how profusely the walls of his smart *salon* in the English quarter, or of his little room *au sixième* in the Pays Latin, have been decorated with prints of all kinds. In the first, probably, with bad engravings on copper from the bad and tawdry pictures of the artists of the time of the Empire; in the latter, with gay caricatures of Grandville or Monnier: military pieces, such as are dashed off by Raffet, Charlet, Vernet; or clever pictures from the crayon of the Deverias, the admirable Roqueplan, or Decamps. . . . We get in these engravings the *loisirs* of men of genius, not the finikin performances of labored mediocrity, as with us: all these artists are good painters, as well as good designers; a design from them is worth a whole gross of *Books of Beauty*. . . . Can there be a more pleasing walk in the whole world than a stroll through the Gallery of the Louvre on a fête-day; not to look so much at the pictures as at the lookers-on? Thousands of the poorer classes are there: mechanics in their Sunday clothes, smiling grisettes, smart dapper soldiers of the line, with bronzed wondering faces, marching together in little companies of six or seven, and stopping every now and then at Napoleon or Leonidas as they appear in proper vulgar heroics in the pictures of David or Gros. The taste of these people will hardly be approved by the connoisseur, but they have *a* taste for art. Can the same be said of our lower classes, who, if they are inclined to be sociable and amused in their holidays, have no place of resort but the tap-room or tea-garden, and no food for conversation except such as can be built upon the politics or the police reports of the last Sunday paper? So much has Church and State puritanism done for us—so well has it succeeded in materializing and binding down to earth the imagination of men, for which God has made another world (which certain statesmen take but too little into account)—that fair and beautiful world of art, in which there *can* be nothing selfish or sordid, of which Dulness has forgotten the existence, and which Bigotry has endeavored to shut out from sight.

Thackeray, in speaking of onlookers, might also have been describing the group in front of *Delpech's Lithograph Shop* (illustration 327), so apt is his account. It is interesting to note the boy carrying a lithograph stone on his head. Carle Vernet who drew the lithograph was of a long line of artists reaching back to the *Ancien Régime*. He also was one of the artists, along with Raffet, Charlet, Marlet, and Bellangé, active in building up what was called the Napoleonic Legend. Almost a generation had passed since the great wars, and the old soldiers now indulged in fond and pleasant recollection. Nor was the comfortable bourgeois averse to tasting a little vicarious glory. And so the idea went over big, as they say. Hundreds of lithographs were brought out, anecdotes of the war, details of uniforms, of battles, anecdotes of the Emperor, presenting him in a grand or kindly light, all executed with zest and a big dash of sentimentality. One of the most imaginative is Raffet's *Revue Nocturne* (illustration 318) where a phantom Emperor nightly reviews his phantom troops. The reality of the Napoleonic Legend we get in Goya's *Disasters*.

134

Another large-scale enterprise carried through with the aid of lithography was the *Voyages Pittoresques et Romantiques dans l'Ancienne France*, in twenty-four huge folio volumes brought out by Baron Taylor, Inspector General of the Fine Arts and of the Museums of France. Taylor was quite alive to the possibilities of lithography: "Bourgeois showed me his first lithographs. I saw in this new art a means of realizing an idea which was to occupy the greater part of my life: I believed I could foresee that lithography was to be for the arts of drawing almost what typography had been for literature." The 2700-odd lithographs included in this stupendous work cover every part and province of France, recording picturesque scenes and romantic ruins, and were made by the best artists of France and England, Ciceri, Isabey, Charlet, Vernet, C. Nanteuil, Ingres, Bonington, Prout, Boys, Harding, Haghe, and others. Two examples of this work, which did so much for landscape lithography, are reproduced (illustrations 328 and 329), Bonington's *Tour du Gros-Horloge* at Evreux, and Eugène Isabey's *Église de St. Nectaire in Auvergne*, of which Pennell wrote: "The gems of the collection are the drawings of Eugène Isabey. The way he could seize upon the most pictorial point of view and use chalk, stump and scraper, or anything to work up his design until one hardly knows how his effect has been obtained, how he managed to fill it with color and light and air and beauty, is truly marvelous."

The technique of color lithography had been developing along with lithography in black and white, and reached perhaps its highest technical proficiency in the Paris portfolio of Thomas Shotter Boys (illustration 330). Color lithography later was to fall into the hands of commercial printers and artists without any taste, and to acquire the opprobrious label of chromo. Color printing as a sensitive art was again revived at the end of the century by such artists as Toulouse-Lautrec, Bonnard (illustration 331), Vuillard, and Signac. Lithography found another great field in the genre pictures, the social commentary, the gay caricatures which Thackeray speaks about, by Monnier, Lami, Decamps, Deveria, Beaumont, Travies, and Gavarni.

Sulpice-Guillaume Chevalier, called Gavarni, was born in Paris in 1804 and died there in 1866. In him the wit and elegance and feminine grace of Parisian life found a worthy interpreter. One of his most famous prints is his portrait of the two De Goncourt brothers (illustration 376). His name is often coupled with that of Daumier. In a sense they complement each other: although Gavarni has none of the virility or depth or grandeur of Daumier, he has a delicacy and a flair for a pretty woman and a modish dress that is lacking in the work of the great caricaturist (illustration 348a).

It is said that when Balzac saw some of Daumier's work he exclaimed: "This fellow has a lot of Michelangelo inside of him." It is quite true that there is much of Michelangelo's heroic and plastic monumentality in his work, as there is of Rembrandt's deep feeling for humanity. Daumier presented the complete drama of humanity in the dress of the middle class. Never has the life of the solid bourgeois and his equally solid wife been presented in greater detail or with greater understanding and humor. All its hopes and fears, its virtues and prejudices, its little crises of happiness or unhappiness found expression in Daumier's crayon. As Baudelaire pointed out, Daumier was the pictorial complement to Balzac's *Comédie Humaine*. There were limitations to his range: neither the extremes of proletarian poverty, starvation, and degradation nor the elegance of the demi-monde (so delightfully portrayed by Gavarni) and luxuries of the ruling class were pictured by Daumier. Daumier was the middle class writ large, the bourgeois in his noblest aspect, the tireless fighter for political freedom against censorship and monarchical reaction, against war and extreme exploitation, ecclesiastical obscurantism, against police brutality and the venality of the law. In so far as the middle class represented the ideals of humanity —and it has come as close to it as any single class ever has—Daumier was a universal artist. "*Je suis de mon temps*," he said—I am of my own time. No heroics, no ideal figures, no search for the beautiful or the sublime, merely scenes and incidents of daily life, topical, factual, often of ephemeral interest. But through his genius he has made these scenes live for all time. We turn to them again and again, long after the stimulus that gave them birth has been forgotten, as inspiring and illuminating pages in the history of mankind—fresh and pertinent today as they were the day they were published.

Honoré Daumier was born in Marseilles in 1808, the son of an impecunious glazier with poetic aspirations. In 1814 the family moved to Paris and young Daumier grew up in the great city whose life he so heroically depicted. He wanted to draw; the family finally consented, but not until he had served his term as a bookseller's clerk and as a process-server in a lawyer's office (where perhaps he got his first insight into the legal mind). He entered the studio of Lenoir and drew ears and noses from casts. But this was not to his liking either, and he went out into the streets of Paris to watch and observe and store his memory with impressions of life. He had a visual memory astonishing even for an artist. An anecdote is told of him later, that illustrates this forcibly. He was out one Sunday with the Daubignys at Valmondois. He asked if there were any ducks to be seen, since he had to draw some in one of his lithographs. They led him to the canal where there was a whole flock of the birds, and after he had observed them for a few minutes, they asked him if he did not want a pencil and paper to make some sketches. Smilingly he said, "No thanks, you know I cannot draw from nature." A few days later the lithograph appeared with the ducks drawn to the life. What he meant when he modestly said that he could not draw from nature, was that he did not have to.

One does not know what turn the career of young Daumier might have taken if the times had not been crying out for an outstanding political caricaturist. France was getting heartily sick of the stupid and reactionary king Charles X. Political pamphleteering and caricature were in a ferment. In 1831 Daumier met Charles Philipon, founder and editor of *La Caricature* and *Le Charivari*, militant fighter for liberal democracy, ardent republican (which in 1835 excited the same opprobrium that the epithet communist does today); and so began the collaboration of these two kindred spirits which lasted a lifetime. Daumier found his metier. He was perhaps the greatest political caricaturist the world has ever seen; he had the faculty of dramatizing an abstract or political idea and clothing it in such convincing and universal terms that it still has meaning for us. Has there ever been a more vivid and complete embodiment of a prostitute press than in the picture of *Mlle Constitutionnel*, the "official" newspaper (illustration 339)? Look at those two great masterpieces, *Le Ventre Législatif* (illustration 332) and *Rue Transnonain* (illustration 333). They were separate prints issued by *La Caricature* at one franc apiece in order to defray the expense of fines that had been imposed upon the periodical. The *Ventre Législatif*—as superb in design as a grand fresco—was the caricatured portrait of a corrupt Chamber of Deputies. Daumier had made many careful studies of the members by visiting the Chamber day by day and returning to his studio to model busts of nearly everyone in clay (these busts exist today), and finally he composed the lithograph from these modeled sketches. It was by this means perhaps that he attained that plastic feeling, that tactile sense which is so marked a characteristic of his work. *Rue Transnonain* represented an incident of police brutality in which a whole family, man, woman, and cihld, were murdered by the civic guard. Burning with indignation Daumier drew the scene, so charged with emotion yet so grandly simple and monumental in feeling that it is one of the most moving pictures of all time. It is said that people lined up daily in long queues to see the picture when it was exhibited in Aubert's window in the Galerie Vero-Dodat. From this time on, Daumier's fame was secure. He had already served a six months' term in the prison of Ste. Pélagie in 1832 for a caricature against Louis Philippe. This king with liberal pretenses had been swept into power by popular discontent in 1830, but he soon proved to be as reactionary as Charles X, and in 1835 he clamped down a censorship of the press so severe that any political caricature was quite out of question. Daumier therefore turned to social caricature and began the huge opus of over three thousand lithographs which appeared in *Charivari* from 1833, off and on, to 1872. He received at first forty and later fifty francs per stone, and his work for *Charivari* constituted his chief source of income during his life. He often brought out series of from ten to fifty lithographs on the same subject, as for example *Blue Stockings, Les Artistes, Le Bon Bourgeois, Les Beaux Jours de la Vie, Histoire Ancienne, Croquis Parisiens, Landlords and Tenants, Hunting, Country Life, Railroads* (just being built), *Les Papas, Théâtre, Mœurs Conjugales, Bathers* (copied by Delacroix as studies of the nude), *Professeurs et Moutards, Croquis Musicaux* and many others. There was one class which he was merciless in satirizing,

138

Les Gens de Justice (illustration 338). Another famous series was that of Robert Macaire, a type whose adventures gave a complete picture of the rascality of the time. He also designed a large number of woodcut illustrations for books, notably the *Nemesis Médicale, Les Français Peints par Eux-mêmes* (illustration 79), *La Grande Ville*, and the various *Physiologies*, and for magazines such as *Le Monde Illustré* in the years 1862-8 (illustrations 75a, 335). But in spite of his manifest achievements Daumier never felt quite at home in this medium. He told Théodore de Banville that "he was sick and tired of designs on wood and did not wish to do any more; the lithographic crayon alone followed his thought, whereas the lead pencil was refractory and would not obey him; in short he had a violent dislike to this kind of design where nine times out of ten one is betrayed and dishonored by the engraver."

Daumier lived quietly and modestly on the Ile St. Louis. He liked to go to the theater and to chat with a few intimate friends far into the night; or on a Sunday excursion, he would be with such confrères as Delacroix, Corot, Millet, Rousseau, Dupré, Daubigny, and Geoffroy-Dechaume. He painted also in his leisure moments and in those years (1860–1863) when there was no demand for his caricatures. In his painting and drawing, *Don Quixote, Les Blanchisseuses, Christ Presented to the People,* he voiced those deep and moving intuitions which somehow never found expression in his lithographs. In his later years the style of his lithographs changed. Color, rich blacks, and minuteness of form, no longer were important; the figures became bathed in atmosphere and light; only the barest essentials were given. His line became fluid, form-enclosing, and supremely vital. He always had the gift of creating types. His distortions, his deviations from the norm, always were convincing: every figure he ever drew had in it the breath of life. But now his expression became truly monumental. Take for example the *European Equilibrium* (illustration 336) or the *Witnesses* (illustration 337), an unpublished lithograph said to be the last one he made: grandeur of conception and inspired breadth of execution lift them out of the limbo of ephemeral caricatures into the small class of the elect of all time. The *Witnesses* with its group of skeletons of men, women, and children picketing, as it were, the Council of War, is one of the grandest war pictures ever made. Great and satisfying as were these paintings and lithographs of Daumier, they brought him little material recompense. Old and blind, he eked out a modest existence with a tiny pension from the government in a cottage at Valmondois generously given to him by his old friend Corot. He died in 1879. Van Gogh in a letter has perhaps summed him up as well as anyone:

But I remember being so very much impressed at the time by something so strong and manly in Daumier's conception that I thought: it must be a good thing to think and to feel in that way, and to overlook or to pass by many things, in order to concentrate oneself on things that furnish food for thought, and that touch us as human beings much more than meadows or clouds.

A number of the great painters of the time also tried their hand at printmaking. Ingres made a notable portrait etching of Pressigny and several lithographs including an *Odalisque* (illustration 374) similar to one of his paintings. It is a miracle of tight drawing and carefully built up effects. Ingres, the brilliant pupil of David, broke from the classical tradition of his master, and was considered a "Gothic" by him and others. However, as the Romantic School gained in favor and influence, Ingres became the chief bulwark of classicism against the Romantic vagary. His work was based on line and drawing highly finished, and, within its narrow limits, attained a rare perfection, but in Delacroix's words, it was "the complete expression of an incomplete intelligence." His great rival was Delacroix, the champion of the Romantic School. Eugène Delacroix was born in 1798, the natural son—according to one rather credible story—of Talleyrand. Delacroix was one of the most richly endowed personalities in the history of art. He was passionately devoted to music; he had a gift for writing, published many articles and from his twenty-fourth year kept a diary which is a most revealing document on the temperament and character of an artist. "He was a man of general education," wrote Baudelaire in a sensitive appreciation of his genius, "unlike the other modern painters who are for the most part either illustrious or obscure daubers, sad specialists old or young, or pure artisans, some making academic figures, others fruits, and still others animals. Delacroix loved everything, and surrendered his mind to every kind of impression." His writings on art praising order, reason, and clarity, Baudelaire continues, reveal that duality in most great artists, "which compels them, as critics, to praise and analyze with all voluptuousness the qualities of which as creators they are most in need, and which are the antithesis of what they possess in abundance."

If Delacroix had praised and extolled what we specially admire in him, the violence, the precipitateness of his gestures, the turbulence of his composition, the magic of his color, we would indeed be astonished. Why search for something one already has abundantly? . . . In the last years of his life all that might be called pleasure had disappeared from his life, a single, avid, exacting, terrible passion having taken its place—work—which was no longer merely a passion, but would have been better described as a fury.

In his one hundred and twenty-six etchings and lithographs Delacroix spoke the language of the Romantic artist. The Romantic School of artists, in reaction against the growing crystallization of bourgeois culture, sought either to combat it or shock it (as did Berlioz or Victor Hugo) or to run away from it to exotic lands or to a Gothic Middle Ages of their own imagination. Delacroix, although not indulging in the excesses and exaggerations of some of the Romantic fraternity, nevertheless was one of their acknowledged leaders. We find therefore in his work many of the leit-motifs of Romanticism, the portrayal of the elemental qualities of wild animals, the exotic note of African sketches, and illustrations for *Les Chroniques de France*, for *Hamlet,* and for *Faust.* The lithograph, *La Sœur de Dugesclin,* from *Les Chroniques de France* (illustration 323) is a most inspired reconstruction of medieval romance. It has color, movement, drama, it is beautifully drawn; in a word a *chef d'œuvre.* Eckermann in his *Conversations with Goethe* in 1826 records the poet's reactions when the first proofs of the *Faust* lithographs (illustration 322) were sent to him from Paris:

The longer this excellent design was looked at, the greater seemed the intelligence of the artist; who made no figure like another, but in each expressed some different part of the action. "M. Delacroix," said Goethe, "is a man of great talent who has found in Faust his proper nourishment.

The French censure his wildness, but it suits him well here. He will, I hope, go through all Faust, and I anticipate a special pleasure from the witches' kitchen and the scenes on the Brocken. We can see that he has a good knowledge of life, for which a city like Paris has given him the best opportunity." I observed that these designs greatly conduce to the comprehension of the poem. "Undoubtedly," said Goethe, "for the more perfect imagination of such an artist constrains us to think the situations as beautiful as he has conceived them himself. And if I must confess that M. Delacroix has in some scenes surpassed my own notions, how much more will the reader find all in full life and surpassing his imagination."

Delacroix's aquatint of *The Blacksmith* (illustration 348) shows that he could treat an everyday scene with dignity and grandeur.

In the career of that short-lived genius Théodore Chassériau (1819–1856) the conflicting principles of Ingres and Delacroix were resolved and blended. He combined the purity of Ingres with the richness of Delacroix. His print *œuvre* consists of a series of etchings for *Othello* and a few other etchings and lithographs, of which the *Venus Anadyomène* is an outstanding example (illustration 371). It is interesting to discover that in the nineteenth century artists made more and more use of the nude as a compositional element. They might call their composition by some fancy name such as *Odalisque, Olympia, Venus, Bather, The Horoscope*, but the chief interest after all was in the nude human figure. A half-dozen prints (illustrations 368, 369, 370, 371, 374, and 375) give an idea of the great variety of approach to a single theme. The point of view expressed by these artists begins to approximate the conception of art for art's sake: subject matter is less important than the personality of the artist and a new and original manner of expressing it. Whistler was to establish the doctrine in its most complete form. The theory works successfully in those cases where the artist's personality is richly endowed, where the artist's mentality and feelings become the lens which concentrates some leading idea of humanity or nature as a whole, a definite *Weltanschauung*. In the hands of a petty or incomplete personality, the result becomes banality.

The great painter Gustave Courbet (1819–1877) made only one lithograph, *The Apostle Jean Journet Setting out for the Conquest of*

Universal Harmony (illustration 377). Courbet, an expansive, robust, somewhat demagogic personality, championed the doctrine of realism (which viewed in the perspective of time turns out to be far from photographic realism). Not abstract or ideal or exotic subjects, he maintained, but real life was important. However, when he thought that he was copying nature, he really was being only an honest, vigorous, and skillful painter. He was filled with the radical and humanitarian notions current in his time, was persecuted for his active participation in the short-lived Paris Commune of 1871, and died in exile in Switzerland.

One offshoot of the realistic movement was the program of the Return to Nature which animated a group of artists who went to live around the Forest of Fontainebleau. The leading members of this School of Barbizon, as they were sometimes called, were Jacque, Millet, Daubigny, Théodore Rousseau, and Dupré. The names of Corot, Diaz, Barye, and Daumier, are often associated with them. They produced landscapes and rustic scenes in much the same spirit as the Dutch landscape etchers and painters of the seventeenth century. Charles Jacque, an industrious landscape and genre painter, made almost a thousand etchings which, though not deep or profound, nevertheless exhibit a great variety of technical approach in etching, drypoint, and roulette work. His etching, *Pastoral* (illustration 362), portrays the peasants' noonday rest with great economy of means. Jean François Millet (1814–1875) in his dozen important etchings shows a greater depth and nobility of feeling. Norman, peasant-born, Millet, after years of struggle in Paris, returned to the country to consecrate himself to the epic of the soil.

Peasant subjects [he wrote] suit my nature best, for I must confess, at the risk of your taking me for a socialist, that the human side is what touches me most in art, and that could I only do what I liked, or at least attempt to do it, I would paint nothing that was not the result of an impression directly received from Nature, whether in landscape or in figures. . . . I have been reproached for not observing detail; I see it, but I prefer to construct the *synthesis* which as an artistic effort is higher and more robust. You reproach me with insensibility to charm; why, I open your eyes to that which you do not perceive, but which is none the less real: the dramatic.

143

Many of his famous prints were variations of subjects used in his paintings: the etchings of *The Gleaners, The Diggers* (illustration 360),
*The Churner, The Man with the Wheelbarrow, The Shepherdess Knit-
ting, Woman Feeding a Child, The Woolcarder*, and the lithograph of
The Sower. Millet's work in a sense was a reflection of certain social
theories of the time, as promulgated for example by P. J. Proudhon:

To paint men in the sincerity of their nature and their habits, at their
work, accomplishing their civic and domestic duties, with their actual counte-
nances, above all without posturing; to surprise them in the undress of their
consciousness, as an aim of general education: such seems to me to be the
real starting point of modern art.

The purely landscape aspect of the Barbizon School was expressed
in the few etchings of Rousseau and the thirty-four etchings and lithographs of Jean Baptiste Camille Corot (1796–1875). Once during a
discussion of Delacroix, Corot said, "He is an eagle and I am only a
skylark." In a sense this gives the keynote of his character and achievement, at least as far as his prints are concerned. In his prints he is never
the great figure painter, but rather the lyric poet celebrating the delicate
and subtle moods of nature (illustration 361). In his etchings he built
up his effects with a free, almost careless interweaving of lines which
suggested rather than defined the forms. He always painted from imagination rather than *en plein air*. When Corot was asked by a colleague
for the secret of his painting he replied, "All you have to do is to look
at the large masses with half closed eyes." Yes and when you want to
see the details? "Then I close my eyes completely." He always had
trouble with the biting of his plates, and this service was usually performed for him by his friends Bracquemond, Michelin, or Delaunay.
Similar in spirit to the Barbizon landscapes, though not by an artist
associated with them, are the thirty-odd etchings of the Dutchman
Johann Barthold Jongkind (1819–1891). Like Corot's, his effects are
built up by wild and wayward lines, though with greater economy
than Corot and with a more vital and nervous stroke. The *Porte d'Honfleur* (illustration 355) is a marvel of direct and forceful approach to
a landscape scene.

The discussion of landscape painting and etching inevitably leads us to England, for English poets and artists, especially in the last two hundred years, have shown a notable and sensitive appreciation of landscape. At the beginning of the century the activity in oil and watercolor painting was paralleled by the production of many prints, etchings by Crome, Daniell, and Read, soft ground etchings by Cotman, Girtin, and J. R. Cozens, aquatints by Alexander Cozens, Prout, and David Cox (the *Treatise on Landscape Painting* of 1814). But the two most important artists in landscape were Turner and Constable. Turner's *Liber Studiorum* was projected in direct emulation of Claude's sketches in his *Liber Veritatis* which had been translated into etching and mezzotint by Earlom in 1777. The set was planned to consist of one hundred combined etchings and mezzotints but the project was abandoned by Turner owing to lack of popular support after seventy-one had been formally published between the years 1807 to 1819. In most cases the preliminary etched outline was made by Turner himself and proofs exist of the plates in this state. In ten subjects, including the one here reproduced (illustration 300), Turner then added the tone and washes by means of mezzotint. For the balance of the plates he employed such mezzotinters as Charles Turner (no relation), Say, Dunkarton, Clint, Lupton, and others. The *Liber Studiorum* expressed not Turner the great colorist and pathfinder admired by the modern artists of today, but Turner the traditionalist who summed up the landscape schools of the past (especially of Claude) and, in his delineations of wild scenery, the Romantic School current in his day. In his "Prospectus" to the series in 1807 he announced that he "intended in this publication to attempt a classification of the various styles of landscape, viz. the historic, mountainous, pastoral, marine, and architectural." It is as examples of composed or heroic landscapes rather than for their direct observation of nature that Turner's plates are valued today. For direct transcripts from nature, for the moving and subtle delineation of atmospheric effects, for wind and clouds and rain, for sunset and dawn, for the freshness of dew and the brightness of sun, we turn to the collaboration of the painter John Constable and the mezzotinter David Lucas. The first set, *Various Subjects of Landscape,* from which *Summer Evening* is

145

taken (illustration 301), was published in its completed form in 1833. In a tribute to Lucas, Constable wrote, "His great urbanity and integrity are equaled only by his skill as an engraver; and the scenes transmitted by his hand are such as I have ever preferred. For the most part, they are those with which I have the strongest associations—those of my earliest years, when in the cheerful morn of life, I looked to nature with unceasing joy." Constable as a painter was to have considerable influence on Delacroix and others of the French School, for the freshness of his color and the fidelity of his obsérvation of nature. It is to be regretted that Constable did not make more than two or three original etchings, for his *Milford Bridge near Salisbury* (illustration 299a) is a vigorous work filled with atmosphere and light.

The revival of interest in the woodcut began in France and England in the 1830's. The way had been prepared by Thomas Bewick of Newcastle (1753–1828). This provincial engraver began in the tradition of the crude and popular woodcut, but in the course of his long life perfected a new style of xylography, the white line engraving. He was not the first to have made such engravings but he was the first to have worked up the technique into a practical method. By working on end grain wood with engraving tools instead of a knife, he was able to build up compositions in which white lines of hitherto unachieved fineness became the dominant motive. This procedure was more in the true spirit of the medium since it is easier to work from black to white on wood and engrave high-lights and break up black masses with fine white lines than it is to scoop out wood on both sides of a black line. His two most famous works were the *History of British Birds*, 1797–1804, and the *History of British Quadrupeds*, 1790, written and illustrated by himself. His plates of natural history are interesting for their able rendering of textures, plumage, and the like. But we turn especially to the tailpieces and vignettes which he inserted at various places in his books. They are filled with charming, racy, and humorous observation of English country life (illustrations 77 and 78). It is England seen by a man of the people, which Bewick always was. In the hands of his followers in England and France white line wood engraving became an efficient reproductive medium especially in connection with book illus-

146

tration. Xylography had always had this great advantage over lithography and the intaglio process—the cuts could be printed simultaneously with the letter press. The regular woodcut, however, had the disadvantage of being crude and lacking in subtlety. With the new method this disability was obviated, since wood engraving could reproduce tonal effects with great flexibility. The impulse of a new technique combined both with the demand of the rising middle-class culture for cheap illustrated books and the existence of a flourishing school of artists produced the so-called renaissance of French book illustration. In 1835 appeared *Gil Blas* with Gigoux's romantic illustrations; in 1838 Curmer's edition of *Paul and Virginia;* in 1842 Grandville's sprightly *Les Scènes Privées des Animaux* (illustration 74). There is not space enough to consider all the charming and interesting works that came out in the first half of the century with illustrations by Vernet, Raffet, Meissonier, Grandville, Daumier, Gavarni, the Johannots, and others. The name of Doré is associated with imposing illustrations of the Bible, Dante, Coleridge, Rabelais, and Balzac's *Contes Drolatiques*. Doré (1833–1883) was an exuberant, fantastic, and at times melodramatic and superficial illustrator. His fertility of invention was remarkable. Less known are his extraordinary illustrations to Blanchard Jerrold's *London* (illustration 83), a spirited, comprehensive, and somewhat lurid commentary on the heights and depths of a great city. One of the most striking of his designs of their series, the *Prisoners Taking Their Exercise in a Courtyard*, was the inspiration for one of van Gogh's famous paintings.

In Germany woodcut illustration also was popular. Inspired by Vernet's *Napoleon*, Kugler and Menzel brought out in 1840 their monumental *History of Frederick the Great* (illustration 70). Adolph Menzel (1815–1905) was in many ways an amazing artist, amazing in his mastery of minute and factual detail, which he marshaled, by patient research, into some of the most extraordinary historical reconstructions the world has ever seen. He had what might be called a factual imagination: facts inspired him to his highest flights. His reconstruction of the life and times of Frederick the Great in the aforementioned history as well as in the illustrations to Frederick the Great's literary works, and the costumes of his army, was truly unique. Other outstanding works

147

out of an unusually productive *œuvre* are his illustrations to Kleist's *Der Zerbrochene Krug* and the series of lithographs entitled *Versuche auf Stein mit Pinsel und Schabeisen*. The popular uprisings throughout Europe in 1848 found a satiric reflection in Alfred Rethel's *Auch ein Totentanz, Another Dance of Death* (illustration 102). These six woodcuts, though conceived in a hostile spirit, have in the course of time lost something of their partisan animus and remain as a moving and dramatic portrayal of stirring and turbulent times. Ludwig Richter (illustration 82) stands revealed in his work as a charming, benevolent, and sentimental personality, a child who never grew up. It is interesting to note that in his drawings there are no grown-ups: his men and women are never of adult stature, they are merely bigger children. He is at his best when illustrating folk song or fairy tale. A sweet and sentimental charm shines through all his work, a nostalgia for the good old times when life was *gemütlich* and pleasures simple. The complement to Richter's pious and sentimental picture of German life is provided by the woodcuts and text of Wilhelm Busch (1832-1908). Here we find gentle satire and good-humored insight into the foibles of Herr Biedermeyer and his family (illustrations 73, 80). The pictorial adventures of his characters, Max and Moritz, were prototypes of our comic strips. Although the new technique of wood engraving was perfected in England, it did not at first stimulate the artists in the production of illustrated books; it was used rather in the interests of factual journalism such as the *London Illustrated News*. In the sixties many designs were made on wood by Rossetti, Sandys, Whistler, Keene and other *Punch* artists. Later William Morris, Walter Crane, Shannon, and Ricketts revived the use of the woodcut for book illustration. *When Adam Delved*, designed by Burne-Jones, with the decorative border by William Morris, was the frontispiece to the Kelmscott edition of Morris's stirring socialist romance, *A Dream of John Ball* (illustration 84).

The name of William Blake carries with it the magic of an ineffable secret: he was a man apart, a mystic whose values were created not of this world but of an inner and transcendent light. He would have been the same had he been born at any time and place. It was one of the ironic touches of history that he was born in 1757 and lived for seventy

148

years in the city where Reynolds and Stothard were great and popular. He was an engraver by profession and spent a large part of his life doing hack-work for publishers to earn his daily bread. At the age of fourteen he was apprenticed to a second rate engraver named Basire, whose rather mechanical system of engraving he absorbed. It is unfortunate that he had no better model, for it was not until the end of his life that he was able to shake off some of these mechanical mannerisms and evolve a more beautiful and flexible medium for the expression of his ideas. After his apprenticeship he studied for a time at the Royal Academy School. He already had very definite ideas about art and recounts an anecdote about Moser the academician (of whom we have already heard in connection with Rowlandson):

I was once looking over the prints from Rafael and Michel Angelo in the library of the Royal Academy; Moser came to me and said, "You should not study these old, hard, stiff and dry unfinished works of art. Stay a little and I will show you what you should study." He then went and took me down Le Brun's and Rubens' galleries. How did I secretly rage. I also spoke my mind. . . . I said to Moser, "These things that you call finished are not even begun. How can they then be finished? The man who does not know the beginning never can know the end of art. . . . I am happy to say that Rafael never was from my earliest childhood hidden from me. I saw, and I knew immediately the difference between Rafael and Rubens."

These two artists symbolized for Blake the difference between good and bad art. Drawing, the firm and precise outline, was to him more important than color, tone, and chiaroscuro; in this he was truly Gothic. Art was never the imitation of natural objects, always the expression of an abstract idea. For this reason the sensuousness of Rubens repelled him.

Blake had two great vehicles of expression, poetry and art, and they went hand in hand. He had a momentary flash of acclaim with his *Poetical Sketches* in a circle of fashionable ladies and bluestockings. But the productions of his genius were not understood and he was driven to find a cheap way of setting down in permanent form the thoughts and images that teemed in his consciousness. To this end he perfected the method of "relief etching." John Thomas Smith describes it as Blake told it to him:

Blake, after deeply perplexing himself as to the mode of accomplishing the publication of his illustrated songs, without their being subject to the expense of letter-press, his brother Robert stood before him in one of his visionary imaginations, and so decidedly directed him in the way in which he ought to proceed that he immediately followed his advice, by writing his poetry, and drawing his marginal subjects of embellishments in outline upon the copper plate with an impervious liquid, and then eating the plain parts or lights away with aqua-fortis considerably below them, so that the outlines were left as a stereotype. The plates in this state were then printed in any tint that he wished, to enable him or Mrs. Blake to color the marginal figures in imitation of drawings.

In this manner he produced whole books with text, illustrations, and marginal decorations. The first work to be published was the *Songs of Innocence* in 1789. In 1794 he finished the complement to this, the *Songs of Experience*, in which appears that superb poem on the nature of evil, "Tyger Tyger" (illustration 345). He made numerous other books, *The Book of Thel*, 1789, *The Marriage of Heaven and Hell*, 1793, and the various *Prophetic Books* ending up with the *Milton* of 1808 and the *Jerusalem*, finished in 1821. As illustrated books they are perfection, for the artist-author has completely realized his intention. If much of his writing and visual symbols are seemingly obscure, it is because we have not taken the trouble to learn his language or are not sensitive to mystical experience. Blake had a definite world-conception that was as complete as any single man has ever worked out. It was, however, so far beyond the ken of his contemporaries that he was for the most part misunderstood and neglected. Even when Blake exhibited and later engraved his large picture of the *Canterbury Pilgrims* (1810) —surely understandable enough in its delineation of types—he met with failure. He was given a commission to illustrate the first Eclogue of Virgil for an edition of translations published by Dr. Thornton in 1821. He made seventeen small wood engravings which narrowly escaped recutting since they were not in the style of the mechanical wood engravings of the time. Underneath the first cut the following apology was printed:

The Illustrations of this English Pastoral are by the famous Blake, the illustrator of Young's Night Thoughts and Blair's Grave; who designed and engraved them himself. This is mentioned, as they display less of art than genius, and are much admired by some eminent painters.

Today the book is remembered only because of these wood engravings, for they are among the most lovely designs ever made (illustrations 345a and 345b).

Blake's last years would have been passed in abject poverty, had it not been for the friendship and generous aid of John Linnell. It was he who commissioned Blake to engrave the *Illustrations of the Book of Job*, published in twenty-one plates in 1826. This is unquestionably Blake's masterpiece and one of the choicest treasures in the world of art. It is an epic of the imagination, outstanding in pictorial design and felicity of execution, and endowed with a profundity of hidden meaning which only years of study will reveal. Blake has made the problem of Good and Evil the central theme of his drama, for such it may properly be called; and he has resolved this everlasting problem by departing somewhat from the original Bible story and conceiving the conflict in terms of man himself, by making it, in the words of Joseph Wicksteed, "a primarily subjective experience; the account of a man's inward struggle and triumph; the conflict between his indwelling Good and Evil powers." It is Blake's great achievement, alas not recognized during his lifetime, that he not only conceived this stupendous cosmic drama of the human soul, but he also carried it out in a moving and beautiful and precise formulation. One of the loveliest engravings of the series is number fourteen, *When the Morning Stars Sang Together*, and it is reproduced herewith (illustration 344). Two years later Blake died while he was working on a series of engravings for Dante's *Inferno*. Samuel Palmer thus gives his recollection of the man:

He was energy itself, and shed around him a kindling influence, an atmosphere of life, full of the ideal. . . . He was a man without a mask, his aim single, his path straightforward, his wants few, so he was free, noble,

151

and happy. His voice and manner were quiet, yet all awake with intellect. Above the tricks of littleness or the least taint of affectation, with a natural dignity which few would have dared to affront, he was gentle and affectionate, loving to be with little children and to talk about them. . . . Those may laugh at this who did not know such a one as Blake, but of him it is the simple truth.

A small band of young artists gathered with John Linnell in admiration of the venerable Blake. Chief among them were Edward Calvert, George Richmond, and Samuel Palmer. Blake the mystic they did not understand, but they loved and revered the pastoral Blake of the *Songs of Innocence*, and Virgil's Eclogue. Under the direct inspiration of Blake (for he never made a print after 1830) Calvert made a dozen engravings on copper and wood and two lithographs. *The Bride, The Cyder Feast, The Brook*, and *The Return Home* (illustration 75) are filled with sweet arcadian charm. The *Chamber Idyll* (illustration 345c) in particular for its delicacy and ecstatic mood and masterly execution is one of the most perfect little prints ever made. Calvert lived until 1883, very much introverted, destroying almost more than he produced. Samuel Palmer (1805-1881) continued the pastoral tradition in his elaborate, minutely worked out etchings (illustrations 350a, 351). "Those who have seen him," wrote his son, "sitting, sable in hand, hour after hour behind tissue paper, pencilling, in varnish, silver cloudets round a moon; or have seen him revelling in the ferocity of seething mordant with which he sometimes loved to excavate an emphatic passage, will not wonder that he achieved only thirteen etchings." He was a typical Victorian artist; and the *Memoir of Palmer* written by his son gave Victorians an insight into what they thought was artistic temperament.

In every century, as we have seen, there are one or two artists who stand apart from the main current of their time by the intensity of their inner life or their difficulties in adjusting themselves to their surroundings. In the fifteenth century there was the Master of the Amsterdam Cabinet; in the sixteenth Duvet and Baldung Grien; in the seventeenth Elsheimer, Seghers, and Rembrandt; in the eighteenth Gabriel de St. Aubin and possibly Goya; in the nineteenth Blake and possibly Calvert.

To this company of what might be called the Brotherhood of the Inner Life four more names must be added, Meryon, Bresdin, Redon, and Ensor. Charles Meryon (1821–1868) had a tragic life: there was in him a strain of morbid melancholia, he suffered poverty, and he died insane. But no one has ever drawn a portrait of a city with such vivid intensity, or endowed every brick and stone with such personality. And this in spite of the fact that he had no great technical facility in etching. Such etchings as the *Petit Pont*, the *Galerie de Notre Dame*, the *Rue des Mauvais Garçons*, the *St. Etienne du Mont*, the *Abside de Notre Dame*, all etched in the years 1850 to 1854, are immortal. Especially moving is the *Morgue* of 1854 (illustration 340) as successful in its evocation of a mood as it is in its superb rendering of buildings. Jules Andrieu reports Meryon's comment on his etching, *Le Stryge* (illustration 341), which gives a clue as to why his prints have such a moving effect: it is because he was a visionary who lived not in the present but in the past or in a world of his own. Picking up an impression of *Le Stryge*, Meryon said:

You can't tell why my comrades, who know their work better than I do, fail with the Tower of St. Jacques. It is because the modern square is the principal thing for them, and the Middle Age tower an accident. Even if they saw, as I see, an enemy behind each battlement and arms through each loophole; if they expected, as I do, to have the boiling oil and the molten lead poured down on them, they would do far finer things than I can do. For often I have to patch my plate so much that I ought indeed to be a tinker. My comrades are sensible fellows. They are never haunted by this fellow [Le Stryge]. The monster is mine, and that of the men who built this Tower of St. Jacques. He means stupidity, cruelty, lust, hypocrisy; they have all met in that beast.

A legend has been built up by certain critics around the name of Rodolphe Bresdin (1825–1885). They nicknamed him Chien-Caillou and endowed him with an ultra-bohemian character and a garret to live in after the manner of Murger. Redon, whose teacher he was, gives a more sensitive and reasonable estimate of his character. Like Redon himself, he was a gentle visionary, and Redon recounts how "his words directed the painter's eye toward the two worlds of life, toward two realities which it was impossible to separate without a diminution of

153

our art." *La Comédie de la Mort* (illustration 346) is characteristic of his miniature-like workmanship and his fantastic and subtle humor. Redon's own expression is more austere and noble. He sought to give form—always in plastic terms—to the contents of dream and to flights of imagination, inspired by Poe, Goya, the Bible, and Flaubert's *Temptation of St. Anthony.* Among his hundred lithographs are many of startling originality, notably the *Pegase Captif, Yeux Clos, L'Aile* (illustration 347), *Buddha, L'Arbre, Le Jour,* and *La Mort.* Technically they exhibit a range from delicate greys to rich vibrant blacks. Walter Pach has pointed out the extent to which Redon was a precursor of certain modern movements. Blake, of course, had said many of the same things as Redon, but Blake was not known in France. James Ensor, the last of the great visionaries, was born in 1860 and is still alive today. His highly personal and somewhat macabre art is represented in a characteristic etching, the *Cathedral* (illustration 343).

In 1862 Baudelaire wrote an article with the title *"L'Eau-forte est à la Mode"*—Etching is in Fashion—in which he speaks of the work of Meryon, Legros, Manet, Ribot, Whistler, and Jongkind and of the activities of the print-publisher Cadart. Quite a number of professional etchers were attracting notice: the amiable and accomplished Bracquemond (1833–1914), who etched some interesting birds and two striking portraits of Edmond de Goncourt and Meryon (illustration 367), and who gave technical instruction to Corot, Millet, Rousseau, Manet, and Degas. There was Lalanne, who produced a new textbook on etching and many uninspired plates, and Felix Buhot (1847-1898), who etched a number of picturesque and whimsical scenes in Paris and London in the seventies and eighties (illustration 350). This print of the *Débarquement en Angleterre* is technically of interest because it is a counter-proof. Such a proof is made by placing a clean sheet of paper on top of a freshly printed proof and running the two through the press. Most of the design will come off in offset, and since the image is always reversed in printing, the design appears as it does on the original copper. Alphonse Legros (1837-1899) started by making crude but powerfully felt etchings of monastic life; later he went to England and turned out soft, innocuous landscapes. The etching, *The Pit and the Pendulum* (illustration 350b), inspired by Poe's tale, is an early work. The leading British etcher of the time was an amateur, the well-known surgeon Sir Francis Seymour Haden (1818-1910). He was an able and somewhat dictatorial Victorian gentleman who had very definite ideas and knew how to express them both with his pen and his etching needle. He liked etchings and collected them. He did not like engravings and reproductive work in general, and he wrote against them, exalting etching at their expense, and making a fetish of spontaneous originality. Perhaps a reaction against mediocre reproductive engraving was needed, but he went too far and condemned it all from Marcantonio to Moreau-le-Jeune. He himself also etched and used to carry around with him in his carriage a copper plate, ready to draw upon. He made over two hundred etchings and there was nothing amateurish about them except that they were done in his leisure time. Like many English country gentlemen he had a real feeling for landscape, and since he was never at a loss to express his feelings positively, the best of his etchings are vigorous and even tender transcripts from nature. Rembrandt was his master, and he made good use of his instruction. Such plates as *Egham, Water Meadow, Egham Lock* (illustration 354), the five Welsh plates, *Sunset in Ireland, Kensington Gardens, Windmill Hill No. 1, Nine Barrow Down,* and *Challow Farm,* are a contribution to landscape etching.

Haden's brother-in-law was the American James A. McNeill Whistler, and as they both had rather peppery personalities they did not get along very well together. Whistler was born at Lowell, Massachusetts, in 1834. He attended West Point for a while, but not finding military discipline to his liking, went to Paris to study art. He made friends with Legros, Bracquemond, Degas, and Fantin-Latour. In 1858 he published a set of etchings, *The French Set,* containing such notable plates as *The Kitchen, La Vieille aux Loques, The Mustard Woman,* and *Street in Saverne.* In some of them the influence of Jacque's and Meryon's etchings is visible. In the same year he went to London which became more or less his headquarters until his death in 1903. He was as able with his tongue and pen as he was with his brush and etching needle, and remained a thorn in the flesh of British philistinism all his life. In his famous lawsuit with Ruskin, resulting in an award of one

155

farthing damages, he scored a moral triumph over the very British dictator of prevailing taste. Shortly after his arrival in London he made a series of sixteen carefully worked out etchings known as the *Thames Set* (published in 1871), of which the outstanding examples are the *Black Lion Wharf, Rotherhithe*, the *Limeburner* (illustration 349), the *Hungerford Bridge*, the *Thames Police*, and *Limehouse*. In these early etchings, inspired by the bustle of London's shipping and industry, he made a complete statement of what he saw. In his painting he was influenced to a certain extent by Velasquez and Rossetti, by the Impressionists, and by Japanese prints. He painted a number of well-known portraits including *Carlyle*, his *Mother, Duret*, and the *Leylands*. A reflection of this phase of his activity is seen in the dry point of his niece Annie Haden (illustration 359). He was very fond of this plate, and wrote on the proof in the Avery collection, "One of my very best." Mansfield quotes him as saying that if he were required to rest his reputation on any one print, as a matter of technical achievement, he would be willing to rest it on that. Other notable portrait prints are *Bibi Lalouette, Becquet, Riault the Engraver, Drouet*, and *Fanny Leyland*. In the course of the years his artistic expression changed. His signature developed from the name Whistler into a stylized Butterfly. He became interested not in portraying a scene in its detailed form but in suggesting a mood, in rendering and setting down a definite "impression" from which all but the contributing details were tastefully excluded. In this he was allied to the French Impressionists, but where their leading motive was a greater sense of reality or scientific management of light, his keynote was largely decorative, a poetic impression of exquisiteness and irresponsible beauty. He truly became the Butterfly that composed lyrics in a lighter vein. His etchings have all the spontaneous charm of an improvisation, but many of his lesser plates suffer from this very quality, for the sketch can easily become trivial. "Taste," wrote Arthur Symons, "in Whistler was carried to the point of genius and became creative." The full expression of this attitude appeared in the twelve etchings known as the *First Venice Set* published in 1880, and which contained the *Palaces*, the *Nocturne* (illustration 353), the *Traghetto*, the *Doorway*, and the *Riva*. He repeated this success with another *Venice Set*, the *Twenty-six Etchings of 1886, San Biagio, Turkeys, Nocturne: Palaces, Upright Venice, The Garden, The Balcony, Nocturne: Furnace,* and *Lagoon: Noon.* In these etchings the effect is greatly enhanced by Whistler's masterly printing. Indeed so dependent was he on printing that an etching like *Nocturne* is practically a monotype. In addition to his four hundred and sixty etchings he made about one hundred and sixty lithographs which have much the same qualities, fugitive visions, delicate and poetic effects of atmosphere, such as the *Thames, St. Giles in the Fields, Little Evelyn, Steps: Luxembourg Gardens, The Horoscope, Dancing Girl,* and *Old Battersea Bridge.* The effect produced by a lithotint such as *Nocturne: The Thames at Battersea* (illustration 352), he has also produced in words:

And when the evening mist clothes the riverside with poetry, as with a veil, and the poor buildings lose themselves in the dim sky, and the tall chimneys become campanili, and the warehouses are palaces in the night, and the whole city hangs in the heavens, and fairy land is before us—then the wayfarer hastens home; the working man and the cultured one, the wise man and the one of pleasure, cease to understand, as they have ceased to see, and Nature, who, for once, has sung in tune, sings her exquisite song to the artist alone.

Whistler, in his writing and in his work carried to its extreme the doctrine of art for art's sake, where the artist's personality and taste become the sole source of value. In his reaction against the stodginess of the Victorian story-telling picture he went to another extreme. In spite of his ruthless wit and striving for effect, he had his integrity as an artist, and he was a patient and tireless and fastidious craftsman.

A picture is finished [said he] when all trace of the means used to bring about the end has disappeared. To say of a picture, as is often said in its praise, that it shows great and earnest labor, is to say that it is incomplete and unfit for view. Industry in Art is a necessity—not a virtue—and any evidence of the same, in the production, is a blemish, not a quality; a proof, not of achievement, but of absolutely insufficient work, for work alone will efface the footsteps of work. The work of the master reeks not of the sweat of the brow—suggests no effort—and is finished from the beginning.

Whistler has his place in history as an aristocratic and exquisite poet, a high priest of Personal Art, that "goddess of dainty thought—reticent of habit, abjuring all obtrusiveness, purposing in no way to better others —seeking and finding the beautiful in all conditions and in all times."

In France a group of Whistler's contemporaries were making art history. They were all great painters, and because they were distinguished artists their prints have an importance and significance greater than that of the often larger production of the professional printmakers. First there was Manet (1832–1883). In his famous *Manifesto to the Public* in 1867 he wrote: "M. Manet has always recognized genius wherever he found it and he has never aimed to overthrow an ancient tradition of art or to establish a new one. He has merely sought to be himself and no other." This sums up his achievement in a few words. In neither his life nor his works was Manet deliberately subversive of tradition; viewed in the perspective of time, much of his art, that was so excoriated by contemporary criticism, is seen to be merely a purification of the academic tendencies of his day. The one thing he insisted on was that art be true to life and to the personality of the creator, and he sought for a technique which would most adequately give expression to this for himself. Manet had independent means and was essentially a gentleman of the world. He went to his studio and painted pictures, "as regularly," said Zola, "as other people go to their offices and counting-houses." He made seventy-five etchings and twenty-one lithographs. His etchings are typically painter's etchings: he was more interested in color and tactile values than in line work as an end in itself. He had what Baudelaire called *"un gout decidé pour la realité."* With Manet this enhanced vision of form was instinctive and immediate: he did not have to perform a laborious synthesis in order to give it expression, and it is this that gives his prints their vigor, spontaneity and verve (illustration 357). His etching, *Olympia* (illustration 375), a free translation of his famous painting, was etched as a frontispiece to a pamphlet which Zola wrote in defense of Manet's art.

Degas, like Manet, had independent means, but he was more aloof and sardonic in temperament. He had an absorbing passion to draw and paint, a passion to capture the elusive, to set down for all time the fleeting moment, to immortalize the significant gesture or movement. "You know how I hate to sell my work," he grumbled. "I always hope eventually to do better." Degas had a trenchant wit and many stories are told about him. Vollard relates:

Suddenly we heard someone call Monsieur Degas! It was Vibert, the well-known painter of the Cardinals. You must come to see our exhibition of watercolors, he said. Then he gave a sidelong glance at the old mackintosh Degas was wearing, and added: "You may find our frames and rugs a little too fancy for you, but art is always a luxury, isn't it?" "Yours, perhaps," retorted Degas, "but mine is an absolute necessity."

He painted and made pastels; he modeled in wax; he made drawings, countless studies which he hoarded in his studio; he experimented with etching and aquatint and lithograph. He made about sixty prints altogether, some of them frankly experimental but others among the most perfect and completely realized prints ever made. Take for example the lithograph, *Mlle Bécat aux Ambassadeurs* (illustration 378); how complete and moving is the evocation of the scene in the *café chantant*, the sight, the smell, the sound of it; or the *Sortie de Bain* (illustration 368); what wealth of meaning there is in that intimate picture of a fat woman. The etching and aquatint, *Au Louvre* (illustration 358), contains a portrait of his friend and fellow-artist Mary Cassatt. "Cassatt has infinite talent," Degas remarked musingly. "I remember the time we started a little magazine called *Le Jour et la Nuit* together. I was very much interested in print processes then, and had made countless experiments. . . . You can get extraordinary results with copper." Mary Cassatt, though American born, lived most of her life in France and painted chiefly mothers and children. She made a number of charming etchings and drypoints and some aquatints in color inspired by Japanese prints (illustration 356).

Pissarro had the largest print *œuvre* of any of the Impressionists, having made 127 etchings and 67 lithographs. His best work, as exemplified by the charming *Goose Girl* (illustration 363), has the smell of earth and moist fresh dew upon it. Renoir, the healthiest and most sensuous and natural of the group, put the stamp of his expansive personality

159

upon everything he touched, be it oil painting, pastel, sculpture, or his few etchings and lithographs (illustration 370). He created instinctively and elementally. He loved color and sunlight and children and motherhood and the ruddy skin and rounded forms of buxom women; and this love of his radiated from his every work. No greater contrast can be imagined than between Renoir and van Gogh, both sun-worshipers. But where Renoir just basked in the sun, van Gogh reached for it passionately to illumine the dark night of his soul. Van Gogh made only one etching, the striking portrait of Dr. Gachet (illustration 366). Van Gogh wrote to his brother:

I have seen Dr. Gachet, who gives me the impression of being rather eccentric, but his experience as a doctor must keep him balanced enough to combat the nervous trouble from which he certainly seems to me to suffer at least as seriously as I do. . . . When he spoke of Belgium and the days of the old painters, his grief-hardened face grew smiling again, and I really think that I shall keep on being friends with him and that I shall do his portrait.

Dr. Gachet was the same doctor who knew Meryon at the asylum of Charenton.

The name of Gauguin has been surrounded with a halo of romantic legend. His life, to be sure, was picturesque enough, wild adventures between Europe and South America, a successful business career, the renunciation of business and family for the pursuit of art, and finally the renunciation of a whole civilization in favor of a savage Eden which Strindberg dramatically rejected: "You have created a new heaven and a new earth, but I do not enjoy myself in the midst of your creation. It is too sun-drenched for me, who enjoy the play of light and shade." In his life there was much travail of flesh and spirit.

I have known [he wrote] extreme misery, that is to say I have been hungry and I have been cold and all that follows therefrom. That is nothing or almost nothing; one gets used to it. But what is terrible in one's misery is the frustration of one's work, and of the development of one's intellectual faculties. It is true that suffering sharpens the faculties. But it must not be too much, otherwise it kills you.

160

There is no trace of poverty, suffering, and sickness in his works from the South Seas: the forms are big and serene, the mood exalted. Out of odd flat bits of wood he made wood engravings such as never had been made before, blocks that were cut and scratched and sandpapered in unconventional ways, forms that were distorted in the interest of design or emotive effect, subjects that were taken from Tahitian life and legend.

It is because these prints go back to the most primitive time of engraving [he wrote to de Monfried] that they are interesting. Wood engraving for illustration has become like photogravure, detestable. A drawing by Degas beside a copy of the drawing done by hatchers! I am sure that in time my wood engravings being done now will have a certain value.

(At the time there were no buyers at eight francs apiece.) The best of these, such as *The Night, Maruru, Fair Land, Te Faruru,* and *Te Atua,* have a strange and moving beauty. *Mahna no Varua Ino* (illustration 373) is filled with the magic and mystery of the jungle at night. Stripped of legend and fable the story of Gauguin is simply the story of a man with a terrific urge to create, the triumph of a demonic will.

Spend yourself, spend yourself again! . . . I believe that life has no meaning unless one lives it with a will, at least to the limit of one's will. Virtue, good, evil are nothing but words, unless one takes them apart in order to build something with them; they do not win their true meaning until one knows how to apply them.

Cézanne was the painter's painter, that is to say his great contribution was technical and only indirectly in terms of the human spirit. He was absorbed during his whole life in what Read calls "the knitting together of form and color into a co-ordinated harmony," or as Cézanne himself put it "to make a Poussin out of nature," to combine the architectonic concept of the classical painters with the color perception of the Impressionists.

Everything we see [said Cézanne] is dispersed and disappears. Nature is always the same, but nothing remains of it, nothing of what we see. Our art should give to nature the thrill of continuance with the appearance of all its changes. It should enable us to feel nature as eternal.

All this is related to the problem of Cézanne as a painter, but some reflection is given in his prints—he made but six—such as the color lithograph, *The Bathers* (illustration 372). Here the artist has created a microcosm, as Wilenski calls it, of planes and forms and color in which each part is pleasurably and vitally connected with every other part. To do this successfully, to make the parts all fit together harmoniously, a certain amount of distortion is necessary. The distortion which most people notice is the deviation from their preconceived notion of the appearance of the human figure, although there are equally wide deviations from the appearance of other natural objects. If these people would stop fixing their eyes on the figures in their effort to correct the supposed defects of anatomy, and, instead, look directly into the picture beyond the figures and enjoy the pleasurable perspective of space, then the figures would take their proper place and seem strangely solid and real. This is the beginning of an adventure in perception and appreciation which will bring great delight and continued satisfaction to the seeing eye. The people who are bothered by distortion are like the people who refuse to enjoy Chaucer because the words are so queer.

And now we come to the Gay Nineties. There were the posters, a new and fascinating art by Lautrec, Steinlen (illustration 381), Cheret, Willette, and Léandre. There were the woodcuts and wood engravings which the etcher and engraver Auguste Lepère (illustration 394) and his associates were trying to revive as a popular art in the publication, *L'Image*. Bonnard and Vuillard were setting down their breezy impressions of Paris in color lithographs (illustration 331) so different from the precise statements of Boys or Girtin. Fantin-Latour was still making his soft lithographs inspired by the music of Berlioz and Wagner (illustration 383) and the young Swede Zorn was already etching his brilliantly superficial plates (illustration 382). Forain was drawing and etching (illustration 392) and Vallotton cutting bold woodcuts (illustration 104). Across the channel Beardsley and Max Beerbohm were making drawings, and Conder and Rothenstein and Shannon making their lithographs (illustration 419). But the artist who perhaps best summed up the period, its odd mixture of glamor and tinsel, its decadence and *fin de siècle* pose was Henri de Toulouse-Lautrec. He was born in 1864, a descendant of the famous Counts of Toulouse. He died of drink and dissipation at the age of thirty-seven. He was crippled and conspicuously ugly: fate cast him for the role of observer. He watched life, but was never of it, the sporting life at the race course (illustration 380), the gay life of the theater, music hall, and cabaret (illustrations 365 and 379). He lived for a while in a *maison close* and became the friend and confidant of the inmates. It was out of this intimate knowledge that he drew the set of ten lithographs, *Elles,* and the vividly realized *Étude de Femme* (illustration 369). He started making lithographs in 1892 and in the next nine years drew more than three hundred and fifty. He had a trenchant and vital line and a sardonic sense of character. *"Vraiment, vous êtes le génie de la déformation,"* exclaimed Yvette Guilbert when she saw one of his caricatures of her, but she grew to like it just the same. Yvette Guilbert, the greatest of music hall singers, summed up the period, too, in her way. "Yvette begins to sing," wrote Arthur Symons, "and immediately the gay world that you see across the smoke of your cigarette, seems to unmask itself, becomes too suddenly serious, tragic, a piece of real existence."

So we come to the end of the nineteenth century, extraordinary in its variety and complexity, and brimming over with startling contrasts. No century has had richer material. There was a great impetus to printmaking not only through the enlargement of the buying public but also through the invention of new techniques, lithography and aquatint and the new wood engraving. But the technique which was to have the widest influence on nineteenth-century art was photography. It is less than a hundred years since the perfection of its technique by Wedgwood, Davy, Niépce, Daguerre, Talbot, and others, but it has already completely revolutionized printmaking. Through the development of photo-engraving, the line cut and the halftone, it stripped regular printmaking completely of its reproductive function. It could make a facsimile of an artist's drawing more quickly and more cheaply than the other processes, and it had the further advantage that it could be printed simultaneously with letter press. It was the Gillotype or early version of the line cut, that supplanted lithography as the medium for political caricature in the fifties. Photography, as an art for itself,

163

has passed through stages of experimentation, of commercialization, and of creative mastery. It is foolish to maintain that photography can never become an art because of the mechanical elements inherent in the process. If one does so, one must logically banish all the print processes for lithography, engraving, and the rest of them, also make use of mechanical aids, and are capable of indefinite reproduction. Many of the old woodcuts and engravings which we so admire as works of art, were commercial productions in their day. A photograph is as much of a "print" as an etching or a lithograph. The essential element in every case is the conscious use of common materials by the human mind and imagination. There are photographs by recognized masters that have a singing quality of perfection as obviously and definitely as any etching or woodcut. Out of the wealth of material at hand three examples have been chosen to typify the achievement of photography in three classes, the portrait, the documentary, and the work of conscious art. No attempt has been made to trace the enormous development of the art in the twentieth century through all its phases—that would require a separate book. The first is the *Portrait of Mrs. Anna Jameson* (illustration 384) by David Octavius Hill (1802-1870). Hill was a Scotch painter who turned to photography in collaboration with the chemist Adamson, to help him in his painting. Now he is remembered for his photographs and not for his paintings. Eugène Atget (1856-1927) devoted most of his life to making a straightforward portrait of every aspect of Paris life with stand camera and dry plate. In his photograph of a shop window on the Avenue des Gobelins (illustration 385), the skillful use of the accidentals of window reflections contributes greatly to the vividness of the scene. Another genius of photography in technical skill, psychological insight, and creative vision is Alfred Stieglitz (1864-1946). His control of every detail of selection, angle of vision, exposure, and printing builds up in *The Hand of Man* (illustration 386) definite esthetic and psychological values that haunt the imagination. A born experimenter and keenly alive to the significant currents of his time, he was among the first to photograph night and rainy scenes, airplanes, skyscrapers, and industrial scenes. His portraits and those interpretations of nature's moods called *Equivalents* are among the great achievements of the camera.

164

Photography functions at its best as a more or less faithful transcript of external reality. Only in the hands of a few masters have its limitations been transcended. Photography is of the moment, a snap-shot, an instantaneous cross-section of the outward aspect of things. It records behavior not motives. By its success in objective documentation it has driven the artist to find an outlet on a subjective plane, as it were, to analyze and synthesize his own feelings, to explore the resources of symbolic expression and psychological nuance—the very things which the camera can not do. The effect of photography on print-making has been tangible and definite. Photo-engraving has made print-making less of a business and more of an art. The artist who now makes prints, as we shall see in the next chapter, speaks not as a copyist but as a creative artist working directly in a graphic medium. This has necessitated a new orientation, a new justification for prints. They must stand or fall as an independent art. Photography has had still another effect on art and culture. Photo-mechanical processes have made the arts of all the world, even the most obscure and exotic, and also of the totality of the past, readily accessible through reproduction. This has made for an easy eclecticism and a melange of many styles.

7. Twentieth Century

Modern   Art—Abstraction—Distortion—Hayter—Surrealism—English—French—Matisse—Rouault
—Picasso—Expressionism—Chagall—Mexican—U. S. A.—Modern Lithography—Wood-Engraving
—Serigraph—Graphic Illustration

IF the keynote of the nineteenth century was personality, the keynote of the twentieth century is flux. The tempo of civilization has
been steadily accelerating: lightning changes, violence, tumultuous
upheavals, epoch-making discoveries are the order of the day. An
old order is crumbling. The individual is being submerged in the coales-
cing of vast collective forces. Two of the greatest and most devastating
wars the world has ever known were fought in this century; perhaps
they are but successive chapters of a world catastrophe, the climax of
which is yet to come. Countries, nations, and peoples are shuffled about
on the world map as never before. Treaties are made to be broken, wars
are waged without being declared. Human beings are exterminated on a
scale that staggers the imagination. International morality is declared
bankrupt; diplomacy becomes a sordid and shoddy piece of chicanery.
Individual heroism, self-sacrifice, and idealism flourish side by side with
cruelty, profiteering, and exploitation. Speed and more speed, power and
more power! Man talks to man in the antipodes. We travel across a continent in a few hours, and around the world in a few days. Supersonic
speed and transcendent power have been gained under the stimulus of
war, that is to say, of mass murder. The fission of the atom has become
a reality. The Frankensteins of destruction are creeping up on mankind,
while it plays with power politics. Man has become master of stupendous
forces which he knows not how to use. Nature is in harness for nation-
ality and monopoly, and not for humanity at large.

Values are shifting from day to day: concepts of morality, of courts
and justice, of property rights and human rights, movements of labor, of

the individual and totalitarianism—nothing is stable and secure. Everybody is bewildered—or indifferent—the leaders as well as the led. *We don't know where we are going but we are on our way*. Orozco made a powerful lithograph, *Leaders*—a restless sea of sombreros above which, through the exigencies of time and chance, there have been tossed up two or three other sombreros, no bigger or better than the rest: these are the leaders (illustration 463). Values are changing in literature, music, and art. The artists are searching, perhaps in vain, for a unifying or stable principle. Styles are born and flourish in bewildering succession. In addition to the older styles still current, there have appeared in the course of the century such movements as Pointillism, Fauvism, Cubism, Expressionism, Futurism, Orphism, Suprematism, Constructivism, Dada-ism, Purism, Neo-classicism, Neo-romanticism, Neo-plasticism, *Die Neue Sachlichkeit*, Social Consciousness, Surrealism, and Non-objective Abstraction. Once, as we have seen, an epoch or a century dominated the artist's expression; later he molded his own manner of speech. Now the artist—Picasso for example—runs through a half dozen styles during his lifetime. Not only in their work but also in their lives are the artists drawn into participation. They are forced to reckon with a community relatively indifferent to their contribution and welfare; to re-interpret through bitter experience the old patterns of collector, patron, and dealer; and to come to terms with society economically as well as esthetically. Gone are both the *bottega* and the ivory tower of yesterday.

Such is the background which the twentieth century artists have to reckon with. The problem of the artist and his time can be summed up in a sort of parable of river currents. Artists either swing with the current of their times, deriving power from it, or else they swim against it, if they are energetic and individualized enough. Those who add their own motive or creative power to that of the current, travel far and have much to see. Those who fight against the current either make a big splash or sink beneath the stream to find a fairy grotto; or else it is said of them after their death that they saw much and traveled in strange directions and discovered new streams. There are some who do not swim against the current nor do they ever exert much motive power of their own. These are the traditionalists. They just drift down stream, they see things, too, but not much more than others have already seen, and sometimes they land in stagnant waters.

It was during the twentieth century that the strange manifestation known as modern art burst upon the world. For those who have traced the mutations of style, century by century, the development of this so-called new phenomenon at the end of the nineteenth century and beginning of the twentieth can come as no great surprise. Its history can be interpreted in terms of action and reaction, and the impact of certain discoveries upon the creative youth of the time. There was, for example, a revolt by the Impressionists against the official Salon tradition. When the Impressionists became successful and were imitated by a host of lesser fry, a younger generation reacted against their preoccupation with surface and light, in favor of a more profound study of form and design. They turned for inspiration to a more plastic and possibly more universal art tradition than the bankruptcies of the Salon or the color researches of the Impressionists. Thus arose Post-Impressionism, which includes much of modern art. They harked back to primitive woodcuts, to folk-art in general, to the hitherto neglected sculpture and applied arts of Africa, Persia, Mexico, or the South Pacific. Thus, modern art is not really a bolt out of the blue but a logical development in keeping with the trend of the times.

For those who are confronted, as it were, with modern art for the first time, it might be well to give a few clues as to what the artist is driving at. He does not want to imitate anything: he wants to create something. His aim is not the representation of nature but its transformation: nature or life seen through temperament. The artist insists that a work of art is an entity separate from nature, an entity that has a life and function of its own, and obeys its own laws and conventions. It was Whistler, surely no wild modern, who said in his *Ten O'clock:* "Nature contains the elements, in color and form, of all pictures, as the keyboard contains the notes of all music. But the artist is born to pick and choose, and group with science, these elements, that the result may be beautiful. . . . To say to the painter that Nature is to be taken as she is, is to say to the player, that he may sit on the piano." And likewise a story is told of Matisse's reply to a question by an irate amateur at an exhibition.

168

"Monsieur Matisse," said he pointing to one of the artist's more daring distortions of the human figure, "did you ever see a woman like that in real life?" "No," replied Matisse, "I never did. But this is not real life: this is a picture."

As an introduction to the problem of modern art let us consider for a moment the state of America or Great Britain around the beginning of the century. The world was, on the whole, a comfortable and pleasant place to live in. The idea of unlimited progress developed by the Victorian Age was still dominant: no one anticipated the debacle of the second decade. Etchings were in vogue: architectural etchings and pleasant etchings of landscape or picturesque types. These prints of architecture were addressed to a lay public more or less as souvenirs of old-world monuments and places once visited and enjoyed. The pattern of subject-matter was set by the "picturesque scene" first delineated by Isabey, Bonington and the travel books of the Romantic period (illustrations 328, 329). The technique and treatment were derived from two nineteenth century etchers: Meryon by his meticulous use of detail and masterly evocation of architectural mood, and Whistler by the charm of his etched line, tasteful selection of detail, and the compositional device of the vignette. A vast amount of this kind of etching has been produced in our time. Some of it, in the hands of the great exponents, is excellent indeed, but much of it is mediocre and commercial. It is always the second and third rate imitators who dilute the achievements of the masters and bring discredit on the school. They have nothing new to say and have not even discovered a new way of saying it. When an artist works in a pattern or formula that is well established, he must speak with unusual creative intensity in order to overcome in the beholder the indifference of familiarity. As with architectural prints, so with landscapes, which had tended to become innocuous and repetitive, or with figure etching—a Head of a Girl, or a Nude, or a Figure of a Patriarch, for example—which degenerated into sweetness and sentimentality. Such were the prints which continued to be produced long after they had any *raison d'être*, and which in time were labeled as conservative. Yet, if one had grown up with such prints, and had come to find pleasure, solace, and even escape in them, it would seem quite natural to be shocked on seeing examples of modern art, and to feel that the whole edifice of familiar beauty and art was crumbling. Possibly it was; but so were many other values. The world, as I have said, was not standing still.

The moderns, then, have tried to interpret this turbulent new world in the idiom and tempo of today. To interpret, rather than portray, although portrayal or reporting also has its place. The camera has to a large extent taken over the reporting function, and left the artist free to explore new fields and to record experiences, moods, feelings impossible to express with the canons of purely realistic art. The artist's task has become not to portray an object but to dramatize his thoughts and feelings in relation to it, whether it be for stylistic self-expression or for purposes of documentation. As John Marin once wrote: "If these buildings move me . . . it is this moving of me which I try to express, so that I may recall the spell I have been under, and behold the expression of the different emotions that have been called into being." So in his etching *Downtown New York* (illustration 437) the buildings are sketched in as an undefined towering mass, while he focuses his attention on the jumble and confusion of traffic and the roar of an elevated train. Or, to give another architectural example, in Feininger's *Village Church* (illustration 94) the interest is not in the church or the emotions associated with old architecture, as there might be in an etching by John Taylor Arms, but in the abstract pattern, the dynamic balance of light and dark, the equilibrium of thrusting lines and shapes. The artist has used a building with a tower as a spring-board to create a fascinating and exciting design. In Landacre's wood-engraving *Counterpoint* (illustration 498) the chief concern is not in the figure but in its pivoting movement, the simultaneous representation of a nude in two positions.

In order to help him in this dramatization and in the reinforcement of his meaning, the artist makes use of certain qualities inherent in the conventions of art. It is known that a picture, by its design or arrangement of lines and forms, can, within certain limits, suggest distress, restlessness, serenity, ecstasy, melody, and the like, quite apart from the meaning. The medium, the form, has an evocative power of its own. A simple example is Hokusai's *Wave* (illustration 546) where a variety of curves are used with telling effect. The chief tools, however, employed

170

to impart emphasis are abstraction, distortion, and rhythm. To abstract means to draw out, to concentrate on essentials, to eliminate everything which does not contribute to the desired effect. There are various degrees of abstraction; in the most advanced state a natural form is transformed into pure geometric ornament: a mountain becomes a triangle. To distort means to deviate from an accepted norm either to emphasize the meaning or to re-inforce compositional lines. The function of abstraction and distortion is not new, though it may seem so to those who are familiar with only one kind of art—the art they grew up with. There is distortion in an Ingres lithograph (illustration 374) as well as in a Gothic woodcut (illustration 22), and, one might add, in a Salon painting based on photography. Let us look at an obvious modern example, Benton's *Going West* (illustration 424) to see how distortion can enhance the meaning. The artist presumably wished to communicate the sensation of a train rushing past at great speed. He heightened the effect by various compositional devices, such as the shape of the smoke, the curves of the bridge in front, and by making part of the locomotive project beyond itself as if straining in a mighty effort; but chiefly by bending back the telegraph poles. In deviating from the accepted norm in the relationship between horizontal tracks and perpendicular poles, he greatly increased the sense of speed and urgency. Similarly, the vibrant stylization of forms and dramatic arrangement of light and dark in John J. A. Murphy's wood-engraving (illustration 87) evoke a mood of radiance and magic and wonder, imparting a fresh approach to the oft-portrayed theme of *The Adoration of the Shepherds*. The modern artist thus has many more powerful tools at his disposal than the associative appeal which a mirror-like copy might possess. He can and does reinforce his message through form and stylization. After this rather elementary introduction to the modern point of view let us find out what the printmaker has been saying about the world we live in.

Landscape—the face of nature—is interpreted, not by a set formula, but under the impulse of a personally felt vision, to communicate a definite mood as in Hopper's *American Landscape* (illustration 425), or to project on paper a fully realized and richly organized composition combining both solidity and atmosphere, as in Dehn's *Garden of the*

171

Gods (illustration 426). Further instances of a fresh approach are afforded by Joseph Hecht's witty stylization of a familiar scene (illustration 432) or by the American Indian Twohy's sprightly design, based on his native artistic heritage (illustration 434). The profile of a big city has likewise received original treatment by such men as John Marin, Howard Cook, Stuart Davis, or Niles Spencer (illustrations 411, 412, 429, 439). The artists have found in industrial structures ample material for exciting compositions. These forms, functionally designed as they are, are in themselves new and admirably adapted for new treatment. Joseph Pennell, disciple and biographer of Whistler, was one of the first to glorify the skyscraper and the Wonder of Work, or industrial scenes in England, Belgium, and the United States. He adopted Whistler's impressionistic technique and made of it a facile descriptive formula (illustration 409). Bone's *Shipbuilding* (illustration 410) and Kravchenko's *Dnieprostroi Dam* (illustration 100) are further examples of straightforward and somewhat more solid reporting. Other artists, going beyond reporting, have offered their reactions in other terms: Victoria Huntley as lyric design (illustration 443), Louis Lozowick as synthesis (illustration 445), Jolan Bettelheim and Harry Sternberg with more critical overtones (illustrations 441, 444). The automobile as an entity in modern life is touched upon in Gertrude Hermes' *Through the Windscreen* and Benton Spruance's *Road from the Shore* (illustrations 436, 438). Similarly many facets of contemporary life and living are annotated and translated into prints: realism with Bellows or Sloan (illustrations 414, 417), dignity and monumentality with Wickey, Siporin, or Charlot (illustrations 408, 413, 482), grace and sensibility with Matisse or Kuniyoshi (illustrations 483, 485), new-fashioned rhythms with Becker or Covarrubias (illustrations 427, 428).

One salient phase of twentieth century art, as well as of literature, has been the growth of social consciousness. To be sure, the expression of social ideals had been anticipated in the work of such nineteenth century artists as Millet, Daumier, Goya, Courbet, Pissarro, and William Morris; but it received a powerful impetus through the devastating World War, the economic depression of the Thirties, and the success of the Russian Revolution. In its broadest aspect it envisages the essential solidarity of all human beings, a conviction that the world might be made a better place to live in by the abolition of injustice and discrimination and exploitation. As an ultimate goal, this quest for an Earthly Paradise would no doubt be endorsed by all men of good will. The disagreement is in the means: whether it be Marxian socialism, revolutionary communism, anarchism, social credit, economic democracy, or the primitive communism of early Christianity. The idea thus seems to be a seminal one, a fertile source of inspiration to the artist. And there is no reason why The Brotherhood of Man could not become as powerful and sustaining an emotional drive as, say, Nirvana or The Redemption. There are various levels of absorption in the theme. With most artists, as with most people, the impulse goes no farther than a generalized sympathy for the downtrodden and oppressed (illustrations 447, 449, 465, 487), and a painful realization of the horrors of war (illustrations 452, 454, 456, 457). With a limited few the attitude stems from a more specific conviction as to the cause of injustice and its eradication. The theme at this level—in so far as it is expressed in terms of art and not of mere propaganda (which is the result of convictions either ill-digested or imposed from without)—has a dual aspect. The first is critical and satirical, a denunciation of the flaws in the present social order (illustrations 101, 440, 442, 444, 446, 448, 475). The second is in a more positive vein, a glorification of the heroes of the class struggle, and a faint adumbration of a better world to come. This last must necessarily be expressed in general terms (illustrations 100a, 481) since with so complicated a structure as modern society, the artists, no more than the political economists themselves, have no clear idea of the working out of any new order. Along these lines, then, a new mythology is being built up around the left movement, with heroes and martyrs (illustrations 98, 99a, 448), and villains (illustrations 450, 451, 455), and various inspiring and edifying parables.

While some artists were trying to take the measure of a changing world, others were making research in self-expression. Numerous painters, concerned chiefly with esthetic self-expression, a new form of art for art's sake, have established a great reputation with their oils and carried over into their prints the same qualities which brought them

173

renown in their easel pictures. Conspicuous among these is Henri Matisse, who has succinctly stated the case for style over contents: "What I dream of is an art of balance, of purity and serenity, devoid of troubling or depressing subject matter, an art which might be for every mental worker, be he businessman or writer, like an appeasing influence, like a mental soother, something like a good armchair in which to rest from physical fatigue." Matisse and other artists of the *École de Paris* have achieved a personal style which is their hall-mark; collectors acquire their work not for the subject matter, but as specimens of the artists' treatment of any subject whatsoever.

Other artists have carried the flight from the subject still further, and developed an art that was almost completely abstract. Taking a cue from certain paintings of Cézanne and from Negro sculpture, they began a drastic simplification of natural forms into rough cubes and cylinders, which they organized into an esthetically satisfying whole. There were two aspects of what might be called the classical phase of Cubism. The first in the suggestion of three-dimensional design, a play of planes and their intersections, in many paintings of the epoch and in prints by Picasso, Gris, and Braque (illustration 499). The other, in flat color patterns with variations of surface texture, exemplified among prints by the *pochoirs* of Braque, Gleizes, or Picasso (illustration 488). Other directions in abstraction have also been explored: the idea of designs based on the structural essence of natural forms or movements: a pattern of ice floes in Peter Sager's linoleum cut (illustration 94b), or the graceful curves of swimming fish in Josef Albers' *Aquarium* (illustration 94a).

Mechanical forms, too, can be an inspiration, as they are to Fernand Léger: "I invent images of machines as others, with their imagination, have invented landscapes. The mechanical element in my work is not a prejudice or an attitude, but a means of giving the sensation of force and power." (illustration 94c).

A new school of engraving with abstract leanings has grown up around Stanley William Hayter. Equally at home in London, Paris and New York, he had a studio in Paris at 17 Rue Campagne Premier from 1927 to 1940, to which many artists including Picasso, Miro, Kandinsky, Masson, Ernst, Calder, and Tanguy came to get technical advice and tools and to work on plates. Through his infectious enthusiasm and instructive zeal, Studio 17 took on the aspect of a collective movement, which continued when he came to America in 1940 and initiated many Americans into the craft, including Fred Becker, Werner Drewes, Sue Fuller, Ian Hugo, Ezio Martinelli, Alice Trumbull Mason, Roderick Mead (already in Paris), Dimitri Petrov, André Racz, Abraham Rattner, Anne Ryan, and Mauricio Lasansky (illustration 476) who in turn has taught many students in Iowa. Joseph Hecht and Roger Vieillard carried on in Paris.

Hayter has undertaken, with all the fervor of an apostle, to revive and explore a creative approach to the handling of the burin. He maintains that after the great achievements of Mantegna and Pollaiuolo, the direction of line engraving was diverted by Dürer and Raimondi toward purely reproductive values, thereby ignoring the plastic and spatial resources of the medium. His comments on the engraving of the past and present are penetrating and challenging. His manipulation of the graver displays a vitality of control, a variation of linear expression, and a bravura of curve that has seldom been surpassed. He and his associates have also made researches in the textures produced on a copper plate by burnishing and by graining with carborundums, and especially by the impress on soft-ground of many materials, including textile weaves of all kinds, wood grains and other natural forms, pieces of string, crumpled paper and the like (see the impress of textile and leaf in Masson's etching, illustration 490). The artist has an all-absorbing interest in questions of technique, though he admits that technique alone will not produce a work of art. He has enumerated the operations performed in the making of *Pavane* (illustration 501) as follows: "Started with line engraving on a copper plate, whole plate then coated with soft ground and a woodgrain pressed into it, certain parts stopped out, rest bitten in Smillie's bath until almost black, work continued in line engraving, background worked back with burnisher, stone, and charcoal, certain parts darkened by planing with coarse carborundum stone (prints like drypoint), and the whites finally hollowed out of plate." *Pavane* was selected for reproduction rather than such large works as *Combat, Tarantelle, Laocoon, Flight* or *Amazon* because it would suffer less by reduction. It is characteristic, however, of the stylistic direction of his work—what he has called "the integration of space and object." Another characteristic is his use of ambiguous forms (giving the impression of now you see it and now you don't) and of the eidetic image, both of which are related to surrealist theory and will be treated below.

The question of abstract or non-representational art has been one of the most controversial issues in the modern movement. In addition to its being one of the more incomprehensible phases of art for the general public, it has been the subject of much debate by artists and critics. On the one hand Fernand Léger has promulgated a theory that an abstract esthetic is the most complete expression of our mechanized civilization; on the other hand Meyer Shapiro and the artists of the left claim that the movement appeals only to a very limited and luxurious class, carefully shielded from the realities of life, that in effect it is an escapist mechanism, a means of fleeing from unpleasant facts, indulged in both by the artist who makes it and by the collector who buys it. Both seem to be extreme statements. Although it is true that in some instances an extreme absorption in abstraction indicates a calculated avoidance of challenging issues, it does not follow that all non-objective art is evasion or repudiation. As Henry Moore once put it: "I dislike the idea that contemporary art is an escape from life. Because a work does not aim at reproducing the natural appearance, it is not therefore an escape from life—it may be penetrating into reality . . . an expression of the significance of life, a stimulation to greater effort in living." Artists have a way of formulating the intuitions of mankind. They are sensitive receiving sets which pick up, unconsciously perhaps, prevailing ideas and attitudes that are in the air, so to speak. In this sense the flux and chaos of modern art is but a reflection of its counterpart in life. And with special aptness in the case of non-objective expression—is not the artist's analytical drive, his research in the break-up of forms, his organization of abstract lines of force, simply another aspect of the scientist's delving into the forms of matter, the hidden patterns of inner structure? Thus we see an isolated visionary of the Middle West, Mabelle Stamper, steeped in a world of Baudelaire and Jeffers, also making around 1941 a lithograph such as *Abstraction Energy* (illustration 500). We see Boris Margo and other artists creating imaginative and highly abstract compositions based on forms derived from electro-magnetic research, vacuum tubes, pliotron, radar, and the like; or Diego Rivera using cell and germ patterns in his murals. The artist, sometimes in ways of which he is not aware, elucidates the drift of a period.

Earlier I touched upon the subjective approach of the modern artist, how he focuses attention on his own reaction rather than on the external object. This assertion of individuality is at the opposite pole from the medieval artist's almost complete self-effacement. Yet curiously enough the concept of art's function is similar in both eras; the expression of an idea rather than the imitation of nature. St. Thomas Aquinas's dictum, "Art imitates nature (not in its form but) in its processes," is matched by Stuart Davis's, "Our pictures will be expressions which are parallel to nature, and parallel lines never meet." We have seen how a subjectively creative attitude provides a fresh approach in the portrayal of the external world. It is equally effective in the evocation of the intangibles of thought and feeling for their own sake. Take for instance Franz Marc's *Annunciation* (illustration 88) and contrast its treatment with that of Baroccio (illustration 165). In the modern print all the emphasis is directed upon the inner feelings of Mary, feelings so exalted and profound that for the moment they have become cosmic and are shared by all creation. Everything in the picture—the design, the darting rays, the staccato accents—contribute to the feeling of tingling rapture. The artist has dramatized ecstasy. Edvard Munch in *The Cry* (illustration 467) conveys "the feel" of dread and anxiety; Max Kahn in *Judith on her Way to the Tent of Holophernes* (illustration 468) somehow manages to suggest by dramatic sky and gesture the emotions of the heroine who is about to kill the oppressor of her people. The analysis of emotions was carried to extreme lengths in Germany, where the movement was called Expressionism. The Expressionist was largely occupied with his inner psyche: he externalized his private conflicts, the tragedies and turbulences of his inner life, by projecting them outwards, by endowing nature with a pathetic fallacy. Kokoschka, for example, used the Christian legend (illustration 470) as he used the inspiration of a Bach Cantata, the framework around which to give form to his personal sensibilities.

Although Expressionism, strictly speaking, was confined to Germany, the term in its broadest sense is descriptive of much modern work. Many artists, not so exclusively concerned with their own affects, are nevertheless moved to express their reaction to the external verities in symbolic form, or to make some commentary, whether ironic, compassionate, or philosophic, on life in general. Rouault, for instance, seems to concentrate the whole misery of the world in one gigantic figure of *The Beggar* (illustration 465), or suggest the essential loneliness of man—attended only by his intimate family—in *By the Sea* (illustration 460), Benton Spruance reflects on the tragic inevitability of war in *Fathers and Sons* (illustration 461); Posada's attack on the dictator Huerta (illustration 480), transcending the ephemeral, becomes a horrifying personification of evil and the forces of destruction. Two of many moving variations on the theme of death are given by Kollwitz and Orozco (illustrations 458, 478). And exploring the antithesis of death, Munch dramatizes the lovers' sense of oneness in *The Kiss* (illustration 471), and Castellón recaptures that aeon of wonder in Eden when Adam first saw Eve (illustration 459). The attempt to record psychological truths and the whole drama of inner consciousness may be said to be one of the keynotes of modern art.

It was the Surrealists who carried the preoccupation with the inner psyche still further in the exploration of the unconscious and its deliberate use as a creative impulse. It is doubtful whether Surrealism would ever have been possible, had it not been for the discoveries of Freud and the psychoanalysts. The disclosure of man's subconscious, of his powerful irrational impulses, of the devious motivation of sex instincts, of anti-social tendencies which flare up sometimes in spite of all social conditioning, has had a tremendous effect upon the culture of our time. A vast new continent has been opened up which may have reverberations as far reaching as the discoveries of the Renaissance. It is on some such basis, combined with the ironic irrationalism of Dada born of disillusion after the first world war, that the Surrealists built their program. It is difficult often to explain clearly and logically what they are driving at, since they make a virtue of irrationality. There is no doubt that a complete philosophy of Surrealism would be exceedingly difficult to put into practice in

178

life or in art, combining and stressing as it does such elements as the Freudian subconscious, the anti-social, the pathological and insane, psychic automatism, the emotional shock for the sake of shock, the grotesque outpourings of unfettered imagination, and the attack on reason in general. Man, as we know, is an irrational as well as a rational being. He spends about one-third of his life in the state of sleep and dream where much of the Surrealist point of view is approximated. There are certain intuitions about life that can be expressed in no other manner but the Surrealist. There are elements, drawn from the unconscious or expressed more or less in Surrealist terms, in the works of Shakespeare, Swift, Coleridge, Blake, and Lewis Carroll, just as there are in the pictures of Dürer, Bosch, Bruegel, Callot, Goya, Grandville, Bresdin, and Redon.

André Breton has thus stated the fundamental aim of Surrealism: "I believe in the future transmutation of those seemingly contradictory states, dream and reality, into a sort of absolute reality, of Surreality, so to speak." The difficulty is to give free voice to the subconscious, to find some way of getting past the censor, which is conscious reason. Various methods are employed to accomplish this purpose. One is through psychic automatism, as for example the "doodles" on a telephone pad, the theory being that such forms are a true index to psychic states (illustrations 490, 493, 501). Related to this is the elaboration of the eidetic or persistent image. The Surrealists claim to distinguish between valid and invalid images by their persistence and compulsive momentum. These valid images, they say, are part of a collective human subconscious, and should therefore strike a responsive note in every beholder (illustrations 496, 501). It is an interesting theory if one grants the premise that there is a collective subconscious; psychoanalysts are not all in agreement over this point. It was more or less on this question, however, that the main body of Surrealists rejected Dali around 1936 for his exploitation of purely personal neuroses, or what he called "paranoiac-critical activity." A compositional device sometimes used by Surrealists is the juxtaposition of objects seemingly unrelated but really conjoined by unconscious motivation (illustration 491). An interesting anticipation of this principle—the unity of inner meaning—is to be found in a stone rubbing of the Han Dynasty *Five Omens of the Frog Pool* (illustration 502). Images of double meaning are often used to evade the censor; such ambiguous forms are really metaphors based on visual association, just as puns in the Freudian sense are valid through sound (illustrations 489, 491, 501). It might be added that certain ambiguous forms, especially when highly abstract, may also be produced through the effort at simultaneous representation of different facets of the same object or figure according to cubist-futurist esthetic. Finally there is the use of the hypnagogic image or remembrance of dream upon waking (illustration 494), and the development in general of material located near the threshold of consciousness (illustrations 490, 493).

Of the two main methods for producing Surrealist pictures, Breton, the orthodox theorist of the movement, maintains that psychic automatism is the surer; the other, namely the use of dream material, is more liable to error and corruption in its transmutation. There has been considerable bickering among the Surrealists—which seems natural considering the material with which they deal. One of the great schisms occurred in 1931 when Louis Arragon and his followers broke away to espouse communist theories. It was perhaps inevitable that such an antagonism should develop, for Freudianism represents about the only serious ideological challenge that communism has received. If the psychoanalysts' contention regarding the irrational factor in man's essential make-up is accepted, then the communists' extravert faith in the complete social and economic conditioning of man is untenable. So much for the artists and the problems of Surrealist expression. What of the effect on the uninitiated beholder? These pictures astonish and outrage the spectator at first; yet they exert an undeniable fascination. Picasso's *Minotauromachia* (illustration 496) merits intensive study as the pictorial embodiment of a fantasy of the unconscious. Dali's etching (illustration 491) is an example of emotional shock for the sake of shock: he has transformed a watch, with which, in everybody's mind, are associated properties of hardness and inflexibility, into an object with the soft and yielding attributes of a pillow. Dali's later work, as we have seen, has been repudiated by the orthodox group. The Surrealists are pioneers in the discovery of a new mode of expression. Some of them are pathological and extreme—exhibitionists literally and figuratively; nevertheless, they are laying the groundwork of a new symbolic language of benefit to the world at large.

II

After this exposition of the general trends of the modern movement, it might be well to give a brief historical survey by various countries. Print production has been influenced by many factors, including changes of taste, the mutations of national schools of art, the enterprise of publishers, and the demands of collectors. Thus the development in different countries has sometimes been full and sometimes meagre, yet in the main expressive of national characteristics. And may I here speak a personal word, and beg indulgence of the reader. In treating of contemporary work, the critic must of necessity make judgments that are not final. There are bound to be many errors of omission and commission, as well as the distortion of wrong emphasis. In estimating the work of living artists whose major oeuvre may still be in the future, one can not always decide whether it will wear well or be just a flash in the pan. Therefore, with an apology for the tentative nature of my diagnosis I shall plunge into my journey round the world of prints.

Haden and Whistler were still alive in Great Britain at the turn of the century. They both did much to lay down the path which British etching was to take in subsequent years, not only by their work but also by their writing and influence. Haden helped to establish the vogue of the collector's print, which has been generally regarded as characteristic of British printmaking. The subject-matter of the collector's print was usually architecture or landscape along traditional lines, executed with a high degree of technical proficiency. The printmakers were in most cases not primarily painters but specialists, that is to say they devoted themselves almost exclusively to etching and drypoint. The editions were strictly limited and meticulously printed. The prints themselves, and the speculative prices they often commanded, had a particular appeal to those collectors who liked to buy pictures for investment. Therefore these prints have been more subject to the ups and downs of speculation than most others. (It must be admitted that the paintings, and to a lesser extent the prints, of the School of Paris have also become the object of commercial enterprise.) The dean of British etchers was D. Y. Cameron, whose achievements range from the cleanly etched early London and Paris sets to more colorful combinations of etching and drypoint in architectural pieces *Doge's Palace* (illustration 400), *Five Sisters*, *Tewkesbury Abbey*, and in poetic landscapes *Ben Ledi* and *Ben Lomond*. Muirhead Bone is an equally consummate technician particularly with drypoint, and possibly a more versatile draughtsman and all-around artist, as evidenced by his drawings of the *Western Front*, his portraits of *Mrs. Drummond*, *Conrad*, and *Tagore*, his shipbuilding lithographs (illustration 410), and masterly renderings of complex structure, *The Great Gantry*, *Demolition of St. James Hall*, or such famous drypoints as *Ayr Prison, Ballantrae Road* (illustration 397), *Spanish Good Friday* (illustration 403). Two etchers stand at opposite poles in their approach: Gerald Brockhurst with his cleanly wiped and detailed elaboration of values in various idealized heads and *Adolescence* (illustration 405); and James McBey with his sketchy and impressionistic line and versatile printing, *Night in Ely Cathedral, Dawn* (illustration 398), *Gale at Port Errol, Barcarolle* and others of the Venice series. Among the etchers of landscape, portrait, or architecture may be mentioned Frank Short, Ernest Lumsden, Martin Hardie, William Strang, Francis Dodd, Stanley Anderson, Frank Brangwyn, Henry Rushbury, Edmund Blampied, Percy Smith, Arthur Briscoe, as well as Robert Austin and Stephen Gooden with burin engravings in the style of the old masters. Also, standing apart from the general trend in that they were able painters who occasionally made prints, were Augustus John, Walter Sickert, and C. R. W. Nevinson, the first with his figure etchings in the spirit of Rembrandt, the second with vibrant genre and city scenes in the spirit of Degas and the Impressionists (illustration 401) and Nevinson with his strongly designed prints (illustration 453) and occasional ventures into cubism. Mention should also be made of the Hindu etcher Mukul Chandra Dey, who received his training in England, but who lives and works in Bengal.

Following the example of Whistler and Pennell, such artists as Charles Conder, William Rothenstein, and Charles Shannon (illustration

419) took up lithography. Printing on stone, however, in spite of the efforts of the Senefelder Club, never attained the wide acclaim it had in France and later in the United States, even though F. Ernest Jackson, John Copley, and Ethel Gabain of a younger generation have produced excellent work. Next to etching, perhaps the most characteristic expression of the British School has been wood-engraving, both as single prints and in connection with book illustration. Earlier representatives were Charles Ricketts, Sturge Moore, William Nicholson with his flat-patterned portraits of celebrities, and Gordon Craig with his engravings for *The Mask* and woodcuts displaying contours sofened with sandpaper. But the fullest development came with a younger generation nurtured on the more dynamic design of the moderns. This they combined with great technical skill to produce some of the best wood-engraving being done today, such as that by Eric Gill, renowned for lettering as well as for engraving and sculpture (illustration 85), Robert Gibbings of the Golden Cockerell Press, Leon Underwood, strongly plastic Mexican subjects, Paul and John Nash, both distinguished painters, Blair Hughes-Stanton, Agnes Miller Parker, David Jones, Douglas Percy Bliss, author of the delightful History of Wood-Engraving, Gwendolen Raverat, Clare Leighton, now in America, Eric Daglish, John Farleigh, Ethelbert White, Julia Mavrogordato, J. Buckland Wright, and Gertrude Hermes, two of whose engravings are reproduced (illustrations 436, 497) *Through the Windscreen* and the imaginative and superbly designed *Adam and Eve.*

The outstanding characteristic of French graphic art, as well as of French painting, during the past fifty years has been untrammelled research into new modes of expression. Most of the new movements, as we have seen, were originated by artists living in Paris. Being all-around artists with a definite feeling for style, they had a different attitude toward the graphic arts than did, for instance, the makers of the collectors' print. They did not produce prints with a specific market in mind; they made them as they painted in oil, executed sculpture or drawings, or designed for the ballet: in order that they might try out all media and put the impress of their style on them all. Courageous and far-sighted dealers also played a positive role in French graphic art. Edmund Sagot, his successor Maurice le Garrec, Henry Kahnweiler, and Ambroise Vollard deserve special praise for their part in commissioning and publishing prints, singly, in sets, and in books. Many French painters might not have made any prints but for the intervention of Kahnweiler and Vollard.

Post-impressionist ferment began early in the century. The *Fauves* or Wild Men, so named at the *Salon d'Automne* of 1895, among whom were Matisse, Derain, Vlaminck, and Dufy, cut strongly distorted woodcuts under the inspiration of primitive woodcuts (illustration 96a). A few years later the emergence of a cubist style was reflected in prints by Picasso, Jacques Villon, Marcoussis, Braque (illustrations 488, 499). Concurrently Signac was translating the *pointillist* style into color lithography (illustration 433), Bonnard and Vuillard were continuing to make impressionist lithographs in color, Forain and Steinlen were pursuing social studies (illustration 392), Lepère, Frélaut, and Segonzac were etching landscapes based on Rembrandt and the Impressionists (illustrations 394, 395), and Laboureur was making elegantly stylized engravings on copper. Perhaps the most distinguished burinist and virtuoso of intaglio technique was Jacques Villon. It is impossible to enumerate all the artists or even the many styles. Several artists, however, deserve further mention. Dufy turned from stylized woodcuts to calligraphic lithographs (illustration 435); the eclectic Derain made prints in various styles (illustrations 484). Matisse turned from trenchant outline etchings of heads and figures to lithographs of odalisques and interiors beautifully organized and vividly suggesting color (illustrations 483, 486). He has made well over three hundred prints displaying the female figure in every conceivable pose and carried out in various ways from the incisive sketch to the fully realized composition—a magnificent set of variations on a single theme. The sculptor Maillol made some lithographic figure studies and many woodcuts for books (illustration 97). Rouault stands apart from most of the modern experimenters in that he seems to live in a medieval world of his own. Yet by his lithographs and intaglio prints of circus and religious themes he shows himself one of the greatest graphic artists of our time. His prints are intensely felt and executed by methods all his own. They combine a tragic sense of life with a feeling of monumental grandeur. Perhaps his greatest work is the set of *Miserere et Guerre*, in fifty-seven large copper plates from which our illustrations are taken (460, 465, 466). Of the French Surrealists only Yves Tanguy, Jean Arp, and André Masson (illustration 490) have made a few prints. The creative ferment of the early part of the century simmered down after the world war. The great figures have become old masters, as it were, and there seems to be no younger generation to carry on. Nevertheless the last fifty years in France have had a fructifying influence on art in the United States, in Germany, to a lesser extent in Great Britain and elsewhere.

Paris has been a Mecca for many foreign artists. Severini and Chirico (illustration 492) were as much at home in France as in Italy. Nearly all the great Spanish artists have lived in Paris. Witness Juan Gris with lithographs, Joan Miró with stencils, etchings, and lithographs (illustration 489), Manolo with woodcuts, and Salvador Dali with etchings. Indeed the etcher Quintanilla is almost the only one who shows no trace of the School of Paris. Picasso, however, is the most famous artist of Spanish birth. His graphic production has mounted to over 300 prints in all mediums. As one surveys his work, one is struck by his relentless drive to fathom every metamorphosis of visual representation: outer form, inner form, abstract form, broken-up form, movement, simultaneity. *Repas Frugal, Salomé La Source, Minotauromachia, Sueño y Mentira de Franco*, the sequence of states of *Le Taureau*, and the books *St. Matorel, Chef d'Oeuvre Inconnu, Les Metamorphoses*, and Buffon's *Histoire Naturelle*, give a fair sample of his manifold achievements (illustrations 487, 488, 496).

In Germany there also was a creative ferment around the turn of the century. Impressionism had been welcomed there chiefly through the championship of Liebermann; and there likewise had been a reaction to the surface aspects of Impressionism similar to Post-Impressionism in France. It took a different turn in Germany. The French had emphasized chiefly the formal architectonic elements, adopting what might be called the classical attitude, whereas the Germans emphasized the psychological approach, an almost Gothic pre-occupation with inner meaning. Out of such distortion and abstraction—for emotive effect rather than for sheer joy of organizing formal elements—grew what is loosely called the Expressionistic School. It happened in several stages. Around 1903 the group known as *Die Brücke*, Nolde, Kirchner, Schmitt-Rotluff, Pechstein, and Heckel, first reacted against the Impressionist group or *Secession*, Liebermann, Slevogt, Corinth, and Meid. The rebels found inspiration among other things in Munch's strongly emotionalized paintings and prints. Around 1911, Marc (illustration 88), Kandinsky, Klee, Macke, and Jawlensky coalesced into the *Blaue Reiter* group, mingling mysticism with inspiration drawn from primitive art and cubism. In Vienna Kokoschka evolved from the decorative stylizations of the *Wiener Werkstätte* to such highly-charged subjective expression as the lithographs to the *Bach Cantata* (illustration 470). All these movements reached their fullest development during the febrile post-war years. There was terrific emotional tension all over Germany, which found one outlet in feverish activity by artists good, bad and indifferent. Inflation and the consequent urge to convert money into tangible objects caused a great demand for works of art. Such dealers as Paul Cassirer, Hans Goltz, J. B. Neumann, and A. Flechtheim, also helped to encourage modern printmakers by exhibitions and the publication of editions. The older artists who had survived the war continued to produce prolifically. Klee (one of the most original and sensitive of modern artists), Marcks, Kandinsky, Feininger, Albers, and others of the *Bauhaus* group pursued their researches in modern idioms, first at Weimar and later at Dessau (illustrations 95, 94, 94a, 493). The painter Karl Hofer made some lithographs similar in classic feeling to his oils. Käthe Kollwitz, apart from all movements, made her simple but deeply felt prints of sorrowing humanity (illustrations 99a, 447, 449, 456, 458). The New Objectivists saw life in a more bitter mood: Grosz in his satiric lithographs executed with a deceptively child-like schematic line (illustrations 446, 455), Dix in his gruesome set of war etchings (illustrations 387, 452), Beckmann in his harshly ironic etchings and lithographs (illustration 469), Karl Rössing in satiric wood engravings. In Germany as in France there were relatively few professional printmakers (as for instance Hermann Struck, Emil Orlik, H. A. Mueller, or Max Slevogt). It was as painters that they made their prints. The sculptors—and there was a strong school of sculpture there—Lehmbruck and Barlach notably (illustration 430), and also Sintenis, Kolbe, Mataré, and Marcks, have made a distinct contribution to graphic art. All this creative activity came to an end with the advent of the Nazi regime. The artists were silenced, exiled, or died; and there seems little spark left alive today.

In Russia at the beginning of the century there was little professional print activity. Several artists connected with the Russian Ballet in Paris, Goncharova, Larionov, and Grigoriev made a few prints. Marc Chagall first came to Paris about 1910, and has been there, off and on, ever since. With the exception of the early series of *Mein Leben* (illustration 494) and a few miscellaneous things, all of Chagall's four hundred etchings were commissioned by Vollard as sets of illustrations to Gogol, La Fontaine and the Bible (illustration 495). Chagall's work has a unique, almost magical quality, a seemingly naive yet esthetically sophisticated charm based on folk art, a fantastic dreamlike humor, a wealth of imagery drawn from Jewish life and mysticism. His illustrations to the Old Testament are perhaps the most truly Hebraic interpretations of the Bible ever made.

After the Revolution, there was for a while a bewildering succession of extremist schools, such as Suprematism and Constructivism, which found no expression in prints. Lissitsky and Achipenko made some abstract color lithographs in Germany. Later, a more realistic art, which could be understood by the people, was encouraged. The great demand for illustrated books stimulated graphic production, first along the lines of folk art in lithograph with Vladimir Lebedev, Konstantin Kusnetsov, and E. I. Charushin; but chiefly in wood-engraving which fitted easily with type. Foreign as well as Russian classics, often in cheap but excellent editions, were published: Shakespeare, Homer, Chaucer, Fielding, Dickens, Heine, Zweig, de Maupassant, Mark Twain, as well as Pushkin, Gogol, Gorky, Tolstoy, and Chekov. In the hands of such artists as Vladimir Favorsky, Alexei Kravchenko (illustration 100), Mikhail Pikov, Pyotr Staronossov, David Sterenberg, Nikolay Piskarev, E. Budogosky, Olena Sakhnovskaya (illustration 98), Sergey Pozharsky, Fedor Konstantinov (illustration 100a), and many others, the Soviet wood-engraving school has grown into one of the strongest movements of today, combining vigor and taste and technical skill. During the German invasion of the Soviet Union, book and print production was necessarily suspended; it has since been resumed. One of the interesting manifestations of the war years were the posters or *Tass Windows*, as they were called, which did much to bolster morale, and which were incidentally among the best posters made anywhere. They were executed in the cut stencil technique, and were designed by Gorayev, Sokolov-skalya, and notably by Kukryniksy, that pseudonym covering an amazing collaboration of three able artists, Kuprianov, Krymov, and Nikolai Sokolov.

After the first world war and the reconstitution of the Polish nation, a flourishing wood-engraving school was launched by W. Skoczylas (illustration 92), S. Mrózewski, S. Ostoja-Chrostowski, T. Ciéslewski, T. Kusiliewicz, W. Podoski and others. The prints were sometimes decoratively heraldic, sometimes in the vein of religious images, and sometimes executed with all the resources of modern technique. This promising movement was nipped in the bud by the Germans. Mention should be made of the Polish artist, Joseph Hecht, resident in Paris, one of the leaders in the revival of burin engraving (illustration 432), and of Jacques Lipchitz and Jankel Adler who have made prints.

In many of the other European countries printmaking has not attained the scope of a national school. There may be a few outstanding but isolated artists working in prints, but no great body of printmakers. In Hungary, for instance, there were Pal Molnar, George Buday, Bella Uitz, and Nandor Varga; in Czechoslovakia Max Svabinsky, Jan Rambousek, and Vladimir Silovsky; in Jugoslavia the sculptor Mestrovic. In Switzerland Hodler made several lithographs with his usual emphasis on repetitive rhythm; Steinlen and Vallotton (illustration 104) drifted to Paris, and Klee to Germany. The Greek, Demetrios Galanis (illustration 90), and the Turk, R. Ben Sussan, likewise made Paris their headquarters. Belgium had strong ties with Paris. Frans Masereel, who developed a new kind of illustrated woodcut novel without words (illustration 99), Nicolaas Eekman with his strongly designed wood-engravings, and Edgard Tytgat with his charmingly naive woodcuts, were perhaps as well known in France as at home. James Ensor was perhaps better known in Germany than in France since his painting and etching had psychological

188

overtones anticipating Expressionism. Dutch etchers range from Joseph Israels and Jan Toorop of an older generation to J. Mankes and Lodewyk Schelfhout. Marius Bauer (illustration 396), a prolific draughtsman and etcher of oriental subjects, had a genuine if Rembrandtesque charm, but he never went beyond his early promise. Among the wood-engravers may be mentioned Jan Franken, B. Essers, and J. Ten Klooster, who often used Javan motifs.

Outstanding in Swedish graphic art were the genial etcher Carl Laarson, and Anders Zorn (illustration 382), whose brilliant but superficial technique, adapted from the Impressionists, has made him internationally known. The Norwegian Edvard Munch was undoubtedly a more creative artist; and his influence on other artists has been more widespread. His lithographs (illustration 467) and especially his woodcuts (illustration 471) executed in bold and seemingly crude flat patterns—always directed toward the expression of inner psychological reactions—were one of the foundations of the Expressionist School. His work is original and of a Strindbergian emotional intensity. In the 1940's a Latvian living in Sweden, Adja Yunkers, has started making color woodcuts of unusual imaginative power. Partly abstract or expressionistic in approach, they are sensitive in color and fertile in their play upon fantasy.

In Mexico during the past forty years there has been a resurgence of creative activity that has made the Mexican School one of the most vital in our day. It has been primarily a social art, of which the human figure —humanity—has been the keynote. Landscape, still life, and all the technical virtuosities of the School of Paris, have found comparatively little favor. The latent pictorial genius of the Mexicans flared up during the storm and stress of the Revolution, and was fortunately encouraged by mural commissions and by other indirect means. Its influence in the United States was considerable, and the States in turn did much to keep the movement alive by the purchase of pictures. The existence of a graphic tradition is demonstrated by the wood and metal cuts of the folk artist José Guadalupe Posada from 1887 to 1913 (illustrations 103, 480). Rivera and Orozco have testified to the influence which Posada had upon the direction of their own art. Nearly all the great painters of the Mexican Renaissance have made prints as well: José Clemente Orozco with his intensely felt and powerfully stylized lithographs (illustrations 462, 463, 478), Diego Rivera with his adeptly organized scenes of Mexican life and history (illustration 481), David Alfaro Siqueiros with his colossal heads and compositions (illustration 477). Jean Charlot is perhaps the most prolific printmaker of the group, working in wood but chiefly in lithograph, including color prints made by lithographic offset (illustration 482). Emilio Amero has made color lithographs and instructed many other artists in the technique of lithography. Among the painters who have made few, but still important, prints may be mentioned Carlos Merida, Rufino Tamayo, Miguel Covarrubias (illustration 428), and Julio Castellanos. Francisco Diaz de León, as director of the *Escuela de las Artes del Libro*, has initiated many into the graphic arts. Perhaps the strongest group among the younger generation is the *Taller de Gráfica Popular* (Workshop of Popular Graphic Art). Among its members may be cited Leopoldo Mendez (illustration 479), José Chavez y Morado, Francisco Dosamantes, Jesús Escobedo, Gonzalo de la Paz Perez, Antonio Pujol, Alfredo Zalce, Luis Arenal, Ignacio Aguirre, Raúl Anguiano, Angel Bracho, Fernando Gamboa, and the American-born Pablo O'Higgins. They are all more or less socially conscious; they make posters, booklets, and prints, chiefly lithographs, in great numbers.

In the countries of Central and South America, the graphic arts are just beginning to come into their own. A growing cultural nationalism is gradually overcoming the provincialism which has dominated them for a century. So far we can speak of names rather than movements, for example, Candido Portinari of Brazil, Luis Acuña of Colombia, José Sabogal of Peru, Joaquín Torres-Garcia of Uruguay, Hector Poleo of Venezuela. In the Argentine there are perhaps a few more: Alfredo Guido, Pompeyo Audivert, Demetrio Urruchua, and Mauricio Lasansky (now in the U.S.A.). The same holds true for Canada. Outside of the old master, Clarence Gagnon, and a few wood-engravers, notably Edwin Holgate (illustration 97a), Walter Phillips, Thoreau MacDonald, Carl Schaeffer, and Peter Sager (illustration 94b) there are relatively few printmakers. Certainly there is no great body of prints that are racy and uniquely expressive of the character of the country as there are in Mexico and the United States.

Finally there is the United States. Somewhat more emphasis in word and picture is given to American printmaking in this book—designed primarily for an American audience—because the American school, although important in its achievement, has received relatively little documentation at home and none abroad. Early in the century the collector's print had considerable vogue. Not only were etchings by the British school eagerly sought for and speculated in, but also the work of Whistler, Zorn, and the native architectural etchers, Herman Webster, D. S. MacLaughlan, Ernest Roth, Louis Rosenberg, Samuel Chamberlain, and John Taylor Arms (illustration 399). Though the subject matter of the latter group was largely European, they were not much collected in Europe, because American art has not as yet attained an international market. Other American etchers of traditional tastes have also achieved success with non-European subjects: Frank Benson (illustration 402) and Richard Bishop with etchings of ducks and sporting scenes, G. E. Burr with prints of the Arizona desert, Ernest Haskell with etchings of California and Maine, or Kerr Eby with New England landscapes. Around 1910 a movement in reaction against academicism was started by the New York Realists who found their material in the homely, sometimes sordid, but always vital realities of city life. Several of the painters also made prints: John Sloan (illustration 414), Edward Hopper (illustration 425) and Jerome Myers made etchings; George Bellows (illustration 417) and, later, Glenn Coleman made lithographs. The 225 etchings which John Sloan has made, place him in the forefront of American printmakers, not only because of their content— transcripts of life vividly drawn—but also by reason of the formal relations exhibited in the later works—the sense of color and plastic solidity. The tradition of genre and urban life was carried on in varied ways, with compassion, with humor, with monumentality, or with rowdy gusto, by other printmakers: Raphael Soyer (illustrations 416, 420), Mabel Dwight (illustration 422), Hayes Miller, Isabel Bishop, Paul Cadmus, Reginald Marsh, Peggy Bacon (illustration 391), Harry Wickey (illustration 413), and others. The American Impressionist painters, J. Alden Weir, John Henry Twachtman, and Childe Hassam also have transferred their particular idiom to the copper plate.

The prestige of etching, however, was challenged by the rising star of lithography. George Bellows, along with Joseph Pennell and Albert Sterner, was pioneer in the revival of lithography in America after its lapse into commercialism and disfavor. Bellows was not our greatest artist, but he was in many ways characteristic of the emergence of an American art. His boyish enthusiasm, his discovery of new subject-matter, and the vigor of his execution drew the attention of artists and public to the possibilities of lithography. Almost all of the younger generation of artists took to the medium with enthusiasm, approaching it not as craftsmen but as artists, that is to say with a sense of creative adventure. Another factor which contributed was the existence of able lithographic printers such as George Miller and Bolton Brown (both of whom printed for Bellows), Theodore Cuno (who printed for Pennell) in Philadelphia, Lynton Kistler in California, and Lawrence Barrett in Colorado. The artist-lithographers, Emil Ganso, Russell Limbach, Francis Chapin, Max Kahn, and Will Barnet also helped by their own work and by their teaching. As a result, in addition to countless artists who have made prints sporadically, there has emerged a group of varied aim, such as Adolf Dehn, dean of lithographers (illustrations 426, 450), Wanda Gág (illustrations 91, 423), Francis Chapin, George Biddle, William Gropper (illustrations 440, 448), Rockwell Kent (illustration 415), Yasuo Kuniyoshi (illustration 485), Max Kahn (illustration 468), Stow Wengenroth, Albert Barker, Robert Riggs, and Benton Spruance (illustrations 438, 461), all of whom have done very special things with the lithograph stone. During the 'Thirties two separate trends were in evidence. One was a revolt against the domination of the big cities, New York and Chicago, by the regional artists of the Middle West and elsewhere, and their determination to use hitherto neglected material for pictorial use close to home. This regional recording of American life was carried out in all graphic techniques but chiefly in lithography by such artists as Harry Wickey, Thomas Benton (illustration 424), John Steuart Curry, Grant Wood, Alexander Hogue, Jerry Bywaters, Merritt Mauzey, Clement Haupers, Caroline Durieux, Henry G. Keller, William Givler, Hubert Davis, Malette Dean, and many others. The other manifestation, occurring chiefly in the big cities where the incidence of economic depression was greatest, was the spread of socially conscious art. In spite of its great vogue, the interest of many artists in it was either temporary or half-baked, since when conditions changed the movement dwindled to a relatively few class conscious artists.

The first great stimulus to the expansion of graphic art came through the spread of the dynamic idea that printmakers could find their subjects close at hand, that their own way of life, their own background and distinctive customs could furnish esthetic material of a most exciting kind. They discovered that a skyscraper or a steel mill might have a beauty of its own, different from that of a cathedral; that a Kansas harvest or the Rocky Mountains or the stylized contours of the Southwest could speak to them more vividly than the Alps or Flanders Field. It was the re-discovery of a continent, the unfolding of a great pageant: landscape, people, city and country life, industry, transportation, social forces—portrayed in a myriad different ways, factually, heroically, sketchily, lovingly, humorously, satirically. Here were graphic illustrations of the Face of America so eloquently described by Walt Whitman. Just about one hundred years previously there had been a similar outburst of national documentation, but not on so grand a scale. It was the period of the topographic and historical views, the genre prints after Bingham, Mount, and others, the beginnings of Currier and Ives lithographs (illustration 310). Perhaps the Civil War checked a movement which might have expressed, in Whitman's words, "the underlying and typic aspiration of the land in a spirit kindred to itself." Certain it is that after the Civil War the energies of America were directed more toward the exploitation of material resources, whereas the arts, with a few notable exceptions (illustration 76), sank into unreality and futility. The modern artist at last rebelled against this.

Coinciding with the discovery of new subject matter, was the discovery of new modes of expression, a fructifying impulse which had much the same effect that the discovery of antique art had upon the Italians of the fourteenth century. It opened new horizons and drew upon a grand tradition as opposed to an outworn minor one. As early as 1910 American artists who had studied abroad came back with reports of the ferment in Paris. Such artists as John Marin (illustrations 411,

193

437), Arthur B. Davies (illustration 418), Walter Pach, Walt Kuhn, Ralph Pearson, Max Weber (illustration 86), and Stuart Davis (illustration 429) began to make experiments of their own in a modern idiom. The creative approach of the new movement, its preoccupation with style and design and new techniques, its courageous acceptance of the rhythms of today, gradually brushed aside the stereotypes of the Academy and, in prints, the equally sentimental conception of the "picturesque scene." It provided a whole orchestra of expression in place of one single cloying instrument. By the end of the 'Twenties, the battle for freedom of expression had been won. Henceforth the conservatives were on the defensive. The expansion of the new movement has proceeded so rapidly that detailed exposition is impossible. Among the artists, not mentioned elsewhere, whose work seems to have qualities which stand apart may be mentioned: Armin Landeck, George Constant, Maxil Ballinger, Prentiss Taylor, Nahum Tschacbasov, James Steg, Kornig Nalbandian, Thomas Handforth (illustration 390), Andrée Ruellan, Lamar Baker (illustration 389), Richard Correll, Philip Evergood, Frances Mitchell, Harold Keeler, and Emil Ganso (illustration 406). The stimulus of Studio 17 on abstract and surrealist printmaking has already been noted. This influence expanded enormously when Maurice Lasansky and others became established in the Middle West and began teaching a younger generation at the state universities.

Under the leadership of Rudolph Ruzicka, Allen Lewis, J. J. Lankes, Rockwell Kent (illustration 89), Thomas W. Nason (illustration 93), Fiske Boyd, Fritz Eichenberg, Lynd Ward (illustration 101) and Paul Landacre (illustration 498), a strong school of wood-engraving, though not as extensive as lithography, also arose to challenge etching in its hold on public interest. Linoleum blocks in color were used by Alfred Frueh to produce some excellent caricatures of theatre folk. Will Barnet and H. Warsager have made some notable expressionistic color woodcuts. Two other xylographers deserved further mention. John J. A. Murphy has combined the use of religious and modern subject-matter with important research in technique and optics, in the breaking up of forms for emotive effect, and in the application of optical focus for the suggesting of planes in recession (illustrations 87, 96). Louis Schanker's abstract color woodcuts have an appealing quality—a gesture or a rhythm filtered through the imagination, the telescoping of numerous visual impressions—expressed in form-shaping line and patterns of subtle or exciting color (illustration 431).

Perhaps the most important technical development in recent years has been the perfecting of the serigraph or silk-screen-stencil technique. This medium, an extension of an old stencil method used commercially, was adapted for artists' use chiefly by Anthony Velonis on the New York Art Project around 1938. Velonis is an engaging personality, a tireless experimenter for whom the search is perhaps the prime incentive. Like S. F. B. Morse, he has gifts both as an artist and as an inventor. Though he has made some notable prints, he modestly claims that whatever qualities of art they may possess are incidental to his exploration of the resources of the medium. There can be no doubt as to his far-seeing vision or his practical ability to organize and adapt means to an end. Among the early pioneers in the process were Guy Maccoy, Elizabeth Olds, Harry Gottlieb, Ruth Chaney, Eugene Morley, Hyman Warsager, Harry Sternberg, Mervin Jules, Chet La More, Ruth Gikow, Mildred Rackley, Leonard Pytlak, and Edward Landon. In its perfected stage the method offers a freedom of line and a variety of textures and effects, undreamed of in commercial practice. Transparent and opaque colors can be used, in either oil or water mediums. The illustrations selected (472, 473, 474, 475) give no idea of the richness of color but they do suggest the autographic quality and range of effects that are possible. The essence of the stencil is a flat uniform application of color, and it has been effectively employed in Robert Gwathmey's print. Tonal gradations of a single color are difficult except by the superimposition of many stencils or the successive stopping out of portions of one stencil. On the other hand, stylized abstractions with emotional interplay of color are possible and effective, as in Morley's *Execution*. Broad impressionistic renderings of landscape can be very successfully made as in Pytlak's *Rockport*. Velonis' still life is rich in texture and color, including some subtle blended effects. The greatest virtue of the serigraph is color, and its greatest triumphs will come through the creative use of color, color in the rendering of form, color for emotive effects.

195

The name serigraph (silk-drawing) by analogy with lithograph (stone-drawing), was invented to avoid the awkward term silk-screen-stencil print and to distinguish between commercial productions and original color prints made by artists. Knowledge of the technique and its manipulation has been spread over the United States by the Art Project, by personal instruction and demonstrations by artists, by several technical handbooks, and especially by the activities of the Silk Screen Group which was founded in 1940 and which in 1944 changed its name to the National Serigraph Society. (This change might well serve as the terminal date for the incunabula of the art.) The Society, an enterprising artists' cooperative, has done a great deal to further the cause of serigraphy. Among its activities may be mentioned the establishment of an exhibition gallery, the distribution of prints by its members, the maintenance of standards of quality and fair trade practice, and the publication of the Serigraph Quarterly. Among those prominent in the Society and not already mentioned are Doris Meltzer, Harry Shokler, Ernest Hopf, Bernard Steffen, Frank Davidson, and Ruth Starr Rose. Serigraphy has enormous and still untried potentialities as a creative color print medium, for it is simple, flexible, and capable of a multitude of effects, always under the artist's control.

In completing the round-up of contemporary prints, a word should be said about graphic art and books. As in the past, numerous books containing etchings, woodcuts, and lithographs have been issued in the twentieth century. The enterprise of publishers has always been an incentive in the production of prints. The subject is capable of extended study, but can be treated only briefly here. Of our illustrations the following prints appeared in books: Maillol's for Virgil's *Eclogues*, published by Count Kessler, Weimar (illustration 97), Léger's for Malraux' *Lunes de Papier*, published by Kahnweiler, Paris (illustration 94c), Pascin's for *Cendrillon*, published by Trémois, Paris (illustration 421), Dali's for *Les Chants de Maldoror*, published by Skira, Paris (illustration 491), Chagall's for *The Old Testament*, unpublished at Vollard's death, Paris (illustration 495). Most civilized countries have produced enormous quantities of illustrated books, whether in popular or in limited editions, containing process illustrations or original prints. One would wish that there were fewer and better. How can one define the perfect illustration? First of all it should be an integral part of the book; it should fit in harmoniously on the printed page in scale and color and weight, or, if the text is subordinate to the illustration, as might happen with a distinguished original print, then the typography should be built around the picture. But beyond all technical or typographical considerations, there is required a certain quality of pertinent inevitability: not just *an illustration* but *the illustration*, the perfect interpretation of the spirit and content of the writer. As a norm for the ideal illustrated book of the twentieth century one might suggest the following works, as interpreted in original graphic productions by great artists: Bonnard for Verlaine's *Parallèlement*, Derain for Apollinaire's *Enchanteur Pourrisant*, Dufy for Apollinaire's *Bestiaire*, Matisse for Mallarmé's *Poésies*, Segonzac for Phillipe's *Bubu de Montparnasse*, Rouault for Suares' *Passion*, Léger for Cendrars' *Fin du Monde*, Picasso for Ovid's *Métamorphoses*, Maillol for Virgil's *Eclogues*, Pascin for Heine's *Schnabelowopsky*, Barlach for Goethe's *Walpurgisnacht*, Masereel for Coster's *Tyl Ulenspiegel*, Chagall for *The Old Testament*, Eric Gill for *The Four Gospels*, Hughes-Stanton for Lawrence's *Birds, Beasts and Flowers*, Agnes Miller Parker for *The Fables of Esope*, Mendez for Cabada's *Incidentes Melodicos del Mundo Irracional*, John Sloan for Maugham's *Of Human Bondage*, Adolf Dehn for *de Maupassant's Tales*, Kravchenko for Sholokhov's *Quiet Don*.

In conclusion, I should like to quote a few reflections (adapted from Siren's and Waley's) translations of a Chinese artist of the seventeenth century, Tao-chi, for they seem to touch on the problem of the artist and his work as it relates to the works of the past and to his own creative impulse:

The works of the old masters are instruments of knowledge. To transform means to understand these instruments, but not to be as they. One may imitate the old masters' methods of brushwork; but still one has not painted "their landscape". By categories and rules one becomes a slave to the old masters, and is reduced to feeding upon scraps from their table.

One may know the old masters but not know one's self. I am always myself and must naturally be present in my work. The whiskers of the

Ancients can never sprout on my cheeks. I express my own lungs and bowels (thoughts and feelings) and show my own beard and eyebrows.

Once my motto was *My own way*. But now I realize that, after all, there is only one way; and that which I discovered for myself and called my own way, was really the way of the Ancients.

And so out of flux and ferment and transvaluation of values, the art of the twentieth century is being born. Whither it will lead we know not, nor wherein its true greatness lies. We are too close to it, too much a part of it, to view it with a detached and appraising eye. At the moment the so-called modern idioms are in the ascendent, and there is always the danger that its successes will crystallize into a New Academy. Whatever posterity may decide as to the merit of these works, one thing is clear: there has been an enormous expansion of techniques and of the modes of expression; the languages of Cubism and Abstraction, Expressionism, Surrealism, and others, give future artists a greater range of expression than they ever had before. It must be left to time to add weight and substance to what will become the major works of art of the century. But meanwhile we can be moved and enlightened by the prospect of these stirring times as they are mirrored in the prints of today. We can see in them the faithful reflection of our own hopes and fears and indignations, of our own confusion and doubt, of our dreams and sympathies, our sense of play and fun, our quest for happiness and peace and understanding.

In the view of a Soviet critic, A. Solodovnikov, there is "a clash of two general trends in art. One of these trends is founded on the principle that the chief purpose of art is to carry man away from reality, to provide amusement and relaxation; the other claims that art is called upon to educate society." In my opinion both alternatives are but partial statements. Art ministers to the whole man, to the play instinct as much as to the serious business of life. Propaganda (or education) has its time and place, but it is not the whole story of art. Pure escapism, likewise, is infantile and unworthy of any mature conception of art. The artist, less bound by the interests and prejudices of a class, and infinitely curious about all phenomena, contrives to render a fairly impartial cross-section of life as a whole. In one respect only, may the true artist be called partisan: in the assertion of his individuality and freedom, in his faith in the integrity of his expression. The world is witnessing an unparalleled aggrandizement of the forces of regimentation and collectivization. This anti-individualistic tendency may eventually be disclosed as the major trend of the century, overshadowing the conflicts of rival nations or economic theories, because it is universal and functions as much under capitalism as under communism. The individual is being submerged in the mass, his life regimented, his outlook and tastes standardized, as much through the by-products of capitalist democracy—radio, cinema, newspaper syndicates, mass production and assembly lines, book clubs and digests, national advertising and packaged products—as through the plan and program of a totalitarian state. The artist by instinct and training stands apart from this collective drift. He believes in freedom (which does not mean economic *laisser faire*); and individuality, that is to say, a personal viewpoint, is his greatest asset. The artist's is one of the few voices today that can speak for freedom and the individual.

8. China and Japan

Part I

The Six Essentials—The Invention of Woodcuts—Stone Rubbings—Wu Tao Tzŭ—Su Tung-P'o —Confucianism, Taoism, Buddhism and Their Influence—Distinctive Conventions—The Ten Bamboo Print Collection—The Mustard-Seed Garden

Part II

Ukiyo-ye—Standards of Print Quality—Hishikawa Moronobu—Torii Kiyonobu and His School —Kiyomasu—Kwaigetsudo—Masanobu—Brocade Pictures—Harunobu—Shunsho—Kiyonaga—Sha- raku—Utamaro—Toyokuni—Hokusai—Hiroshige

I

AFTER the turbulence of the twentieth century, we return, for a moment, to the past and to the detachment and remoteness of an alien civilization. We journey to a far distant continent whose philosophy and thought-forms, whose total outlook on life differ widely from our own occidental culture. The East possesses many secrets not easily revealed—that East where all things have been done, all emotions felt, all thoughts expressed from time immemorial. The East of asceticism and sensuality, of mysticism and rationalist ethics, of fecund life and the equally overwhelming sense of the futility of life, of experiments and theories of government from absolute monarchy through theocracy, aristocracy, militarism, and socialism to anarchy. The East of the great inventions, gunpowder, the compass, printing, and paper money. "To look for the first time at the art of Asia," said Coomaraswamy, "is to stand at the threshold of a new world. To make ourselves at home here requires sensibility, intelligence, and patience." The East that expresses itself in prints is China and Japan; the graphic arts for one or another reason did not flourish in India, Persia, and the Mohammedan countries. Here we are face to face with one more esthetic that definitely subordinates realistic representation to contemplative insight, metaphysical vitality, a quest for essentials or the innate spirit of things. There is an analogy, as Coomaraswamy has pointed out, between oriental art and Gothic or Scholastic art: they both contain linear, calligraphic, and symbolic elements, and are expressive of inner truth rather than external reality. And, as we have seen, modern twentieth century art in many of its aspects seems to be approaching the oriental conception. The emphasis on the creative rather than the imitative can be illustrated by a dialogue from an *Essay on Landscape Painting* by the Sung painter Ching Hao, translated by Siren.

When an old sage meets in the forest the young painter who tells the story, he asks: "Do you know the method of painting?" To which I answered: "You seem to be an old uncouth rustic; how could you know anything about brushwork?" But the old man said: "How can you know what I carry in my bosom?" Then I listened and felt ashamed and astonished; he spoke to me as follows: "Young people like to study in order to accomplish something; they should know that there are six essentials in painting. The first is called Ch'i (spirit or vitality), the second is called Yün (resonance or harmony), the third is called Ssu (thought or plan), the fourth is called Ching (effect of scenery or motif), the fifth is called Pi (brush), and the sixth is called Mo (ink)." I remarked: "Painting is to make beautiful things, and the important point is to obtain their true likeness, is it not?" He answered: "It is not. Painting is to paint: to estimate the shapes of things, to really obtain them; to estimate the beauty of things, to reach it; to estimate the reality (significance) of things and to grasp it. One should not take outward beauty for reality. He who does not understand this mystery will not obtain truth, even though his pictures may contain likeness." I asked: "What is likeness and what is truth?" The old man said: "Likeness can be obtained by shapes without spirit, but when truth is reached, both spirit and substance are fully expressed. He who tries to express spirit through ornamental beauty will make dead things." I thanked him and said: "From this I realize that the study of calligraphy and painting is an occupation for virtuous men."

The Chinese invented paper and printing and the technique of making woodcuts. The earliest dated woodcut extant appeared in the *Diamond Sutra*, a Buddhist scripture with the date 868, discovered by Sir Aurel Stein in the Cave of Ten Thousand Buddhas at Tun Huang in Chinese Turkestan and now in the British Museum. But there must have been other and cruder woodcuts before this, cuts similar to the tenth century Buddhist image (illustration 106) printed by stamping. We can therefore safely say that the Chinese have been making woodcuts for well over a thousand years. The earliest woodcuts here reproduced are the above image and another block print inspired by Buddhism, with woodcut and text combined, *Manju-sri*, the personification of transcendent Wisdom (illustration 108), a votive offering similar to European indulgences, also found at Tun Huang and probably made around the middle of the tenth century. Printmaking in China was largely interpretive or didactic, and not an instrument for original creative work. Paintings and drawings were reproduced in woodcut by specialized craftsmen. Since so few of the early paintings have survived, the print often remains the only record of an artist's pictures or style, still existing. The technical competence of these woodcut craftsmen varied greatly. Many of the blocks were very crudely cut and none too faithful in their interpretation of the original. Nor can productions be dated on the basis of cruder or more primitive style. Exquisitely cut blocks are to be found in early times as well as crude work in later eras. It depended upon the skill of the individual craftsman.

The vast majority of Chinese woodcuts were made for books. The earliest printing of books occurred in the eighth century, when the idea of taking impressions on paper from wooden blocks seems to have arisen, chiefly in connection with Buddhist tracts and images. A large number of these early books were destroyed in 845 during the reign of the Taoist T'ang Emperor Huei Ch'ang, who ordered the destruction of over 4,500 Buddhist temples. Production of printed books, however, did not become general until 932 when the Confucian Canon, and 972 when the Buddhist Canon or Tripitaka, were printed for the first time. In these early days a page of text was cut on a single block; these books were what we would call block-books. Movable type of baked clay was invented about 1043, and some centuries later was made of wood or metal; but its use was never so general as the block-book method. T'ang, Sung, and Yüan illustrated books are now very rare. During Sung times it became customary to fold over the sheets and tie together the loose ends to make pages—a style of binding that has continued in use ever since. Previously books were in the form of rolled hand scrolls or were folded in bundles accordian-fashion. There was a great expansion of illustrated book production during the Ming dynasty, particularly during the reign of Wan Li (1572-1622). The earliest illustrated books were almost all religious in character. In the Ming and succeeding dynasties the field was enlarged to include history, poetry, encyclopedias, drawing manuals, and other books on the arts and sciences.

There was another print medium used in China long before the invention of the woodcut—the stone rubbing, *T'a*. About the year 175 the six Confucian classics were engraved on stone by Imperial authority, and the slabs set up at the entrance of the Academy in order that scholars might have the benefit of an accurate and enduring text. Copies were struck off for the use of scholars when lampblack ink was perfected during the fourth and fifth centuries, and it was discovered that impressions of inscriptions and designs incised in flat slabs of rock could be obtained. A dampened sheet of thin but tough paper was laid on the stone and forced into all the incisions, whereupon black ink (occasionally red or green or blue) was applied with a flat pad to the surface of the paper (that side of the paper which we would call the back). Because the ink could not reach into the incisions, the design appeared in white against a background of black. In this way was avoided that reversal of image which always takes place when ink is applied *between* the block and the paper. Although there are references to stone rubbings in early Chinese literature, the earliest actual stone rubbing now in existence, discovered by Pelliot at Tun-Huang, dates from the reign of T'ai Tsung (627-649). In 992 there is a record of the publication of books of stone rubbings after calligraphy of the Tsin and Wei dynasties.

It is not known when stone engraving was first used for the reproduction of designs by well-known artists; possibly it was as early as T'ang. Tablets exist dating from Sung times with engravings supposedly after originals, now lost, by Wu Tao Tzǔ and other artists. From the Ming dynasty onwards stone engravings were made to perpetuate famous paintings in increasing numbers. In certain places, such as The Grove of Stone Tablets (Pei Lin) at Sian-fu or the Confucian Temple at

203

Ch'ü-fu, whole collections or museums of incised tablets exist, from which stone rubbings are still taken. Rubbings were made not only from stones prepared for this purpose but also from famous sculptured monuments, wherever flat incised or low relief stones existed. For instance as early as 1064 the famous Sung scholar Ou-yang Hsiu referred to stone rubbings in his possession from the funerary chamber of the Wu Family (illustration 111). Similarly, rubbings have been made of sculpture in the caves of Yün Kang in Shansi (illustration 506) or of Lung Mên near Lo-yang in Honan (illustration 505).

One of the most famous and seemingly authentic designs ascribed to Wu Tao Tzǔ is the *Snake and Tortoise*, symbol of the North (illustration 503) taken from a stone in the Municipal Office at Ch'êng-tu, capital of Ssechuan. Another famous work, a Kuan-yin, exists in several stone versions. Wu Tao Tzǔ is perhaps the most famous of all Chinese painters, and many fantastic legends are told of him, though no authentic work of his (much of it having been in fresco) exists today except for such translations as the stone rubbings. As early as 1085 the Chinese painter and critic Su Tung P'o could write that he knew of only one or two genuine pictures by Wu Tao Tzǔ. In a reconstruction from various sources Waley describes his style as realistic, strongly sculpturesque and three dimensional, imaginatively original and facile in technique; he quotes Su Tung P'o's estimate: "Wu Tao Tzǔ's figures might have been drawn from lantern shadows on the wall. They seem to walk out of the picture and back into it; they project, can be seen from each side. The flat planes and tilted angles fit into one another as though by a natural geometric law." The T'ang Dynasty during which he worked was one of the most creative in Chinese history. Among his famous contemporaries were the landscape painter Wang Wei, the poets Li Po and Tu Fu, and the Emperor Ming Huan, poet and musician, whose mad infatuation for the concubine Yang Kueifei, "the most beautiful woman in the world," led to his tragic downfall.

Of Wu's rival and contemporary, Wang Wei, equally known as a poet and a painter, likewise, no authentic original has survived, and we can estimate his greatness only by his reputation and influence, which has been enormous. He has been called the father of the Southern Sung

Landscape School and of poetic landscape in general. His mature paintings, chiefly in monochrome (p'o-mo or broken ink style), were of a subtlety and delicacy which made translation into another medium well nigh impossible. A section of the famous Wang Ch'uan hand scroll, an early work in miniature style, portraying his villa and gardens, from a Ming stone rubbing (dated 1617), based probably on a Sung copy of the original, is reproduced (illustration 113c). As Tung Ch'i Ch'ang, the Ming critic said, the beloved contour lines were there but the execution was so poor that the engraving could not be made the standard for Wang's style.

The stone-rubbing, the *God of Fortune* (illustration 113), is attributed to the renowned Su Tung-P'o (1036-1101), a universal genius of the Sung Dynasty, a poet, essayist, art critic, calligrapher and painter. The print, distinguished for its exquisite placement of seals, design, and script, illustrates the close relation between calligraphy and drawing in Chinese art. In his practice with written character, every Chinese scholar acquires a sensitive appreciation of the formal and artistic aspects of writing, of individuality of brush stroke, rhythm, symmetry, asymmetry, balance, and vitality of line. Where every written character is in itself a work of art, calligraphy ranks as a fine art. In China there are people who collect examples of writing as we collect works of art. In this picture the artist first drew an ideograph or written character, and then upon that drew a head, thus creating the character of the God of Fortune, both as symbol and as representation. Another example of this kind of artistic punning is a stone rubbing dated 1864 of *Chung K'uei* (illustration 110) after a painting by K'uei Hsing. The portrait is a fanciful adaptation of the ideograph for Chung K'uei, the Demon Queller, whose effigy is often hung at the portal of houses to ward off evil spirits.

Three cultural traditions run through Chinese art and history, and are, in a sense, recapitulated in the personal attitude of cultivated Chinese: Confucianism, Taoism, and Buddhism. The modern scholar T. C. Lin's dictum: "We are socially Confucian and individually Taoist", is matched by the T'ang poet Po Chü Yi, who wrote in his epitaph that he used Confucianism to order his conduct, used Buddhism to cleanse his mind, and then utilized history, paintings, mountains, rivers, wine, music and song to soothe his spirit.

Confucianism has been a force in China for about twenty-five hundred years—the Doctrine of the Golden Mean (the Mean-in-Action or morality), a system of rational ethics, a reliance on good breeding, art and ritual for the cementing of human relations. When asked if there was not one word which could be the keynote to conduct, the Master said: "Is not reciprocity such a word? What you do not wish done to yourself, do not do to others." Pragmatic in his attitude, Confucius was quoted by his grandson Tsesze as saying: "I know now why the moral life is not practised. The wise mistake moral law for something higher than what it really is; and the foolish do not know enough what moral law really is. I know now why the moral law is not understood. Noble natures want to live too high, high above their moral ordinary self; and ignoble natures do not live high enough. There is no one who does not eat and drink. But few there are who really know flavor." Such in brief was the teaching of Confucius, projecting the ideal of a cultivated man true to his own nature, aiming neither too high nor too low, and enjoying the pleasant life of a scholar and a gentleman. As early as Han times, the great historian Ssuma Ch'ien could say: "All people in China who discuss the six arts from the Emperor down regard the Master as the final authority." Significant, too, is the examination system for public office, instituted in the T'ang Dynasty and in use ever since, whereby candidates for public service are selected on the basis of their knowledge of the Confucian Classics. Everything relating to the life and works of Confucius has been the subject of diligent compilation by Chinese scholars. It is natural therefore that many books exist portraying his life in word and image. The portrait of Confucius (illustration 112) is a characteristic example of the use of a flowing linear rhythm and the emphasis on an inner likeness. The Chinese ideal of portraiture is expressed by a writer of the twelfth century, Hu Ch'üan. How different it is from Albrecht Dürer's dictum engraved on his portrait of Philip Melanchthon: "The trained hand of Dürer can depict the features of the living Philip but not his mind."

206

There is no branch of painting so difficult as portrait painting. It is not that the reproduction of the features is difficult; the difficulty lies in painting the springs of action hidden in the heart. The face of a great man may resemble that of a mean man, but their hearts will not be alike. Therefore, to paint a likeness which does not exhibit these heart-impulses, leaving it an open question whether the sitter is a great man or a mean man, is to be unskilled in the art of portraiture.

Taoism, in contrast to the urbane worldliness of Confucianism, represented a mystical strain, in the direction of simplicity and passivity in harmony with a universal principle, Nature. Convinced of the relativity of all attributes, the pure Taoist turned away from the rational and intellectual: he desired to *be* rather than to know or to do. In the *Tao Te Ching*, attributed to that mythical personality, Lao Tzŭ, and in the delightfully written and profound parables and reflections of Chuang Tzŭ (ca.300 B.C.), this contemplative and unwordly ideal is expounded in such maxims as "Those who know do not speak; those who speak do not know", or "The sage does nothing but achieves everything", or the following, in Hughes' translation:

"To know men is to be wise,
 To know one's self is to be illumined.
 To conquer men is to have strength,
 To conquer one's self is to be stronger still,
 And to know when you have had enough is to be rich."

There were, however, other aspects to Taoism beside a mystical philosophy. Taoism as a mythology and a special technique of soothsaying, dated back to before Han times. This established religion degenerated —as did Buddhism, each borrowing from the other—into the practice of meaningless ritual, magic incantations, and a superstitious belief in demons and sorcery. Taoism in this debased form bore no relation to lofty concepts of Lao Tzŭ and Chuang Tzŭ; the purer strain of their teaching was carried on in the appreciation of nature and the cult of mystical simplicity of many poets and artists, and in particular was to have considerable influence on Sung landscape painting. Among our illustrations are several which exhibit Taoist influence. One is a rubbing from the relief sculptures in the funerary chamber of the Wu Family at Chia Hsiang in Shantung, dated A.D. 147, depicting in a courtyard the Ho Huan Tree (illustration 111) with forked trunk and interlacing branches, the sacred cosmic tree of Taoist lore. Another rubbing, likewise displaying the vigor of Han Dynasty art, is the so-called Li Hsi Stone at Chien Hsiên in Kansu, which has been dated A.D. 171. *Five Omens of the Frog Pool* (illustration 502) is one of the earliest representations of landscape and of the dragon, chiefly a Taoist symbol, here representing beneficent rain. Among the other omens may be recognized a deer bespeaking length of days, two trees growing together, a stalk laden with ears, and a man in a votive gesture. A world of magic and myth, of animals and demons is revealed in the next illustration. Readers of Wu Ch'êng-ên's folk novel *Hsi Yu Chi*, Record of a Journey to the West, translated by Arthur Waley under the title of *Monkey*, will remember it as a fantastic mingling of Taoist and Buddhist lore. The framework of the novel is based on an historical fact, the pilgrimage of Hsüan Tsang (Tripitaka) to India in the seventh century in order to gather Buddhist scriptures. By the tenth century, as Waley points out, Tripitaka's pilgrimage had become the subject of a whole cycle of legends. The woodcut *Scene in a Spiral* (illustration 508) from a *Shu I Chi* or Record of Marvels, has been identified by Dr. Fêng Yu-lan as being related to the corpus of legend associated with the monkey hero. It is not an illustration to Wu Ch'êng-ên's novel, since the author lived in the sixteenth century, and this woodcut dates from very early Ming times (reign of Hung Wu, 1368-1398). It is interesting technically, too, in that the red and yellow coloring seems to have been applied through stencils.

Buddhism was officially introduced into China during the reign of Ming Ti, who in A.D. 61-67 had sent a mission into India to procure, as the legend runs, the god whose golden image had been revealed to him in a dream. Buddhism, first regarded as an alien religion, gradually grew in power and influence. The form of Buddhism current in China was the Mahayana, or Great Vehicle, with a wider scope and larger pantheon of divinities than the austere intellectual doctrine of Nibbana taught by Gautama himself, and thus more sympathetic to plastic expression

208

in the arts. Most Chinese sculpture reveals Buddhist elements. The stone rubbing of *Buddha* (illustration 506) from the caves at Yün Kang shows a strong Indian influence. This carving is in higher relief than most others from which rubbings have been taken—which accounts for the almost completely white background. It was under the Bo or Bodhi tree, the Tree of Wisdom at Bodh Gaya, that Shakyamuni after a colossal mental struggle attained Buddhahood. From another cave, Lung Mên, comes a stone rubbing of *Maitreya* dated A.D. 542 (illustration 505). It is indeed a most moving dramatization of a hermit's rapt contemplation. Completing a trio of pictures of the Buddhist inner life is a *Lohan* (illustration 504) after the Buddhist priest, poet, and painter Kuan Hsiu (832-912), from a sixteen-sided stele in Hang-chou engraved by order of Ch'ien Lung and dated 1764. In Buddhist mythology, the Lohan or Arhats were the sixteen disciples commanded by the Buddha to remain in the world without entering Nirvana until the coming of the future Buddha Maitreya, to protect his Law. One is impressed by the powerful characterization of these grotesque ascetic types, who are supposed to have appeared to the artist in a vision. Of a different order of appeal, namely in sensuous, poetic charm, though still Buddhist in impulse, is the rubbing *Procession* from the base of a stele now in the University Museum (illustration 105). Equally exquisite and charming is the woodcut *Kuan-yin* (illustration 114) from the set *P'u-sa Hsiang-tu* (Images of Bodhisattvas). It dates apparently from early Ming times (there is an attribution to the reign of Hung Wu 1368-1398), and thus is an earlier version of a similar set entitled *Tsu Yung Wu-shih-san Hsien* (Fifty-three Manifestations of Kuan-yin), dating from the second half of the seventeenth century. It is sensitively cut by an expert craftsman and, like the rest of the set, the result of special care in production, since each bears the inscription "Joyfully dedicated by the Marquis Huai Hsi, of Sei Yang, a disciple of Buddha." It likewise differs from the later set in that each Bodhisattva (including others beside Kuan-yin) is attended by a Lokapala or Guardian of the Four Corners of the World. Buddhism was a great stimulus to the graphic arts. From the earliest known woodcut onwards countless prints have been produced to illustrate the Sutras, to recount the life of Buddha, and to portray the hierarchy of Buddhist divinities.

Bodhidharma, the great apostle of Dhyana Buddhism, came to China from India in A.D. 520. A native strain of this same school of Contemplative Buddhism developed in China under the name of Ch'an (and Zen in Japan). It taught that monastic rules and ascetic practices belonged to the World of Being; salvation was only through mystic contemplation: Buddha was pure thought, Buddha was the Way. Ch'an Buddhism, mingled as it was with the individualistic and mystic elements of pure Taoism, had a great influence on Sung landscape painting and indeed on all subsequent landscape painting. It gave the artist that spiritual background and emotional *timbre* essential for *feeling-into* a landscape, and for the imaginative and sympathetic apprehension of the forces of nature—the grandeur of mountains, the softness of mist, the silence of snow, the music of a waterfall, the innate character of pine or plum or bamboo (illustrations 113a, 113b, 114a).

There are certain conventions used by Chinese landscape artists that often prove a stumbling block for Western appreciation. One of these is what is assumed to be absence of or ignorance of perspective, but which in reality is the use of a system of perspective different from the Western geometric convention. In Chinese pictures distant objects do not recede along converging parallel lines, but are merely placed a little higher up in the picture. The convention of superposed registers, as Vernon Blake points out, dates back to Egyptian and Assyrian times, and is, in the hands of its practitioners, quite as flexible and expressive an instrument as the equally artificial geometric convention which we have come to regard as infallible. To a certain extent the customary shapes of Chinese pictures were a determining factor, either very tall and narrow or the very wide and not so tall, in neither of which would Western perspective have been very effective. An approximate way of explaining Chinese perspective is to assume that one is on a vantage point and looking down at the picture; in other words that the horizon line is high. Sometimes when the distortions inherent in the system might become unpleasant, the artists will resort to the device of breaking up the whole composition by means of cloud bands and sheets of water into several smaller units each with its own perspective system. This is one of the reasons for the frequent use of bands of cloud and mist; and they, together with the perspective which, for example, makes mountains even more awe-inspiring than they are, add greatly to the mystery and dreamy unreality of Chinese landscape art.

The Chinese also made color woodcuts. Already in Ming times books were printed in black and red, the red being used for notes and comments. Toward the end of the Ming Dynasty experiments in color printing with woodblocks to reproduce designs and paintings were being made, culminating in the publication in 1643 of a landmark, the *Shih Chu Chai Hua P'u* or Collection of Prints from the Ten Bamboo Studio. It was a collection in sixteen volumes of designs by Hu Yeh Tsung and others of birds, flowers, rocks, bamboo, prunus, orchids, and fruit (illustration 507), with an accompanying text of notes and advice to artists. Some time later, from 1679 to 1701 the first three volumes of the *Chieh-tzu-yuan Hua-chuan*, or Painting Manual of the Mustard-Seed Garden, were issued. This was specifically an encyclopedia on painting for artists, with many woodcuts in color and monochrome in the style of various painters, and with instructions on how to paint bamboo, pine, landscape, etc. The color woodcut *Squirrel-shrew and Grapes* (illustration 509) is based on a composition by the Sung artist Chao Ch'ang. Both works, and others like them, were popular and exist in numerous editions. The color work and technique, particularly in the early editions, were of a high order. The colors were delicate and subtle. Many of the pictures were executed in the "boneless style," that is to say without the use of a black key block. Some very interesting textures were achieved perhaps by wiping the blocks in a special way or by cloth impresses before printing.

Single prints in color were also produced during the late seventeenth century, possibly to be used as wall decorations. There are a number in the British Museum which were purchased by the traveller Kaempfer in Japan before 1693—still lifes of vases and baskets of flowers with other accessories, elaborately printed in color, including *gauffrage*. It is strange that so few have survived. Nanking and Soochow were the great centers of printing, and no doubt many prints of theatrical subjects or popular superstition were produced for general consumption during the eighteenth and early nineteenth centuries. In fact, there is a type of woodcut known as the Soochow Print. One great factor which contributed to the deterioration of the art was the Tai Ping Rebellion (1851-1864) which completely devasted Nanking, Soochow, and Hangchow. Most of the craftsmen were killed and the traditions of the technique interrupted and in many cases lost. The popular prints of today are undistinguished in design and garish in color.

Chinese prints, by and large, seem somehow to lack print quality, that personal touch which works out a conception purely in terms of the medium. They were a means to an end, never an end in themselves. Great artists never worked directly on or for wood. Printmaking in China was a minor art, reproductive, a surrogate for something greater than itself. Nor was it ever popular art in the sense that is was cherished by the people: it was a scholars' art, remote from everyday life and closely bound up with books. Within the last twenty years a Chinese artist, Teng K'uei, has used a Western medium, the lithograph and lithotint, to make a series of original and technically accomplished prints (illustration 510). Conceived in the great tradition of Chinese painting, they have, nevertheless, the vitality and freshness of a personal approach. Likewise, during the Japanese invasion, numerous woodblocks were cut by Chinese artists, chiefly in the Western manner, for documentation and propganda. It is possible that out of the chaos of China a new and more widely popular print art may emerge.

II

Much of Japanese art and culture was derived indirectly from Chinese sources. As far as the graphic arts are concerned, the basis of woodcut technique, and probably of color printnig (there was a reprint of the Mustard-Seed Garden in Japan in 1748, and Chinese editions must have penetrated even earlier) came from the Chinese. The art took a different turn in Japan, however, and was animated by a different purpose. Japanese prints of the Ukiyo-ye School, which is the glory of Japanese graphic art, were specifically designed to be cut on wood

212

and were definitely produced for a popular audience. Simultaneously with Ukiyo-ye, some prints and albums were published, which reproduce drawings and designs by famous Japanese artists who were primarily painters and not print designers, such as Korin or Kanō Tanyu (illustrations 114c, 116a). Yet if Japanese graphic art were to be judged solely by these reproductive examples, it would rate a position not much more important than a minor adjunct to the Chinese School.

The best Japanese printmakers, then, followed a graphic rather than a reproductive tradition, and made full use of the esthetic conventions inherent in the woodcut medium. Japanese prints were the result of the skilled cooperation of three people, a designer, a woodcutter, and a printer. In the Orient there was always a division of labor: the designer never cut his own woodblocks, nor did he ever attend to the printing. In general only the name of the designer has been recorded. Around the beginnings of the full polychrome woodcut with Harunobu, the name of the cutter or printer was sometimes given, probably because the importance of their share in the perfection of the technique was recognized. Later, however, the practice was seldom observed, and the cutter and printer remained anonymous though technically accomplished craftsmen.

A word about the names of Japanese artists. In Japan the patronymic or family name comes first and the given name comes second. According to Western nomenclature Torii Kiyonobu should read Kiyonobu Torii. Through a misunderstanding of Japanese terminology we in the West have fallen into the habit of calling all Japanese artists by their first or given names, as we might say Raphael (Santi) or Rembrandt (van Ryn). Also one might add, the Japanese (and the Chinese) adopt and discard names in ways that are somewhat incomprehensible to the occidental mind.

The Japanese have definite names for the various sizes of prints. Since these are often referred to in the literature, it might be well to give the names and approximate dimensions of the commonest shapes: *Hoso-ye*, about 12 x 6, much used, for instance, by the Primitives or Shunshō; *Chūban*, about 11 x 8, as used by Harunobu and many others; *Ōban*, about 15 x 10, used on larger Kiyonagas, for example. Frank modern reproductions and deceptive forgeries, as well as late reprints of many important prints exist, and the collector must be on guard against them. The real collector of Japanese prints is very much concerned about standards of print quality. Louis V. Ledoux has summarized the matter as follows: "In selecting prints, distinction of subject, excellence of impression, excellence of condition, loveliness of color, all have been considered." In addition to the defects to be avoided, common to all prints, such as holes, mended spots, rubbed areas, trimmed margins, impressions from blocks in which lines are worn or broken, there are several considerations which refer particularly to Japanese color prints. The chief of these are accuracy of register in the successive color blocks, and condition of the coloring. Some of the pigments, particularly the violet, were fugitive, and seldom are found in their original hue. A harmony of colors, as opposed to crude or harsh contrasts, is considered eminently desirable, and appears only in the best of prints. Pristine condition—cleanness of paper and freshness of coloring—is highly prized, perhaps because it is so rarely to be found after the vicissitudes of a century or two.

The prints of the Ukiyo-ye School, or Pictures of Transient (or Floating) World of Everyday Life, are among the most beautiful and original manifestations of popular art in the history of prints. It was an impulse toward vitality in the midst of decadence, toward realism as against idealism, but a realism of subject, never of treatment, which remained symbolic and suggestive as in all oriental art. Arthur Davidson Ficke has aptly described the imaginative appeal inherent in the Japanese print:

This almost symbolic quality is the chief element of the pleasure to be derived from Japanese art. Japanese designs are metaphors; they depict not any object, but remote and greater powers to which the object is related. Often the artist produces his effect by the exaggeration of certain aspects, or by expressing particular qualities in the terms of some kindred thing. If his subject happens to be an actor in some great and tragic role, he will not hesitate to prolong the lines of the drapery unconscionably, to give the effect of solemn dignity, slow movement, and monumental isolation. Westerners may smile at the distortion of such a figure; but they must acknowledge that

214

an atmosphere of lofty and special destiny surrounds the form, precisely because the artist has dared to use these devices. The Japanese artist will draw a woman as if she were a lily, a man as if he were a tempest, a tree as if it were a writhing snake, a mountain as if it were a towering giant. This is the very essence of poetical imagination; and the result of it is to endow a picture with obscure suggestions and overtones of infinite power. Symbols of existence beyond themselves, these designs are charged with an almost mystical command upon the emotions of the spectator. Western art has employed such a method comparatively little in painting. In poetry it appears frequently. The poet, when he wishes to convey the impression of a beautiful woman, does not set out her features and her stature and all the details of her aspect. He tries to awaken some realization of her by a bold and fantastic leap of the imagination straight to the heart of the matter—he makes her a perfume, a light, a music, a memory of goddesses. The prosaic mind will never greatly care for work produced in accordance with this principle; the conventions will seem distortions, the imaginative generalizations will seem inaccuracies, and the transcending of reality to shape a more universal and significant statement will appear nothing more than ineptitude in grappling with fact. But to the poetical mind, all these things will come with a unique and irresistible fascination.

Ukiyo-ye prints were a popular and ephemeral art similar to the theatrical posters and "funnies" of today. They were sold for a few *sen*, and little value was attached to them; they were pasted on wooden pillars and on the screens that protected the kitchen fire; they were bought, as are picture post cards today, by visitors as souvenirs to take back to the provinces; they were used as costume plates or as advertisements for houses in the Yoshiwara or other licensed quarters. It is extraordinary that a popular art should exhibit such refinement and subtlety of treatment. The rise and development of the Ukiyo-ye School occurred entirely within the period of the Tokugawa Shoguns (1603-1867), when the urban or middle class was growing in wealth and power. Trade and manufactures flourished during the long peace which followed the devasting civil wars that were ended by the accession of Tokugawa Iyeyasu. The prosperous city dwellers of Yedo, Kyōto, or Ōsaka, shut off by a rigid code from aristocratic pleasures, began to devise for themselves their own pastimes and amusements. The rise of the popular theatre (*Kabuki*), as opposed to the *Nō* drama of the aristocracy, coincided with the development of the Japanese print. Well known historical legends, such as the *Chūshingura* (Forty-Seven Ronin), the vendetta of the *Soga Brothers* or the vicissitudes of *Sugawara Michizane*, as well as other even more lurid and melodramatic themes were dramatized. The acting likewise was melodramatic and colorful, with much recourse to *aragoto* (rough business), sound and fury and vehement gestures, or to *nuregoto* (moist business). Actors, in spite of being at the bottom of the social scale, were immensely popular; and pictures of them in characteristic roles were eagerly sought for. The other popular class of subject-matter was the *Bijin-ye* or Pretty Girl Picture, either as models of dress and fashion or as frank advertisements for houses of assignation. The inhabitants of the Yoshiwara and other licensed quarters, were in no sense considered merely as prostitutes; they were more like the *hetairae* of the Greeks, professional entertainers, boon companions, women of wit and culture, accomplished poets and musicians. The tea-houses, too, were centers of elegance and gaiety and cultured amusement. An eighteenth century Japanese writer thus describes the quarters of the Yoshiwara: "their splendor was by day like Paradise and by night like the Palace of the Dragon King." The most famous of the courtesans—they were called *Oiran*—lived in indescribable luxury. They set the fashion in costume and elegant manners for the demi-monde; their appearances on the streets were triumphal processions. The situation was not without its sordid aspects, but the whole was invested with a glamor and elegance that has never been surpassed in its particular sphere.

Thus the theme of Ukiyo-ye was the ephemeral world of actors and the theatre, of courtesans and the glamor of the Yoshiwara, of changing fashions in dress or hair-do, occasionally of sweet and lovely genre scenes, glimpses of domestic life, and later of familiar landscapes, the landmarks of Japan. This "transient world" was portrayed with power and grace and poetic charm by the artists of the Ukiyo-ye School. The "eternal world," the pure contemplation of nature, the invocation of religious emotion, and all the themes regarded as lofty and idealistic by Chinese precedent, were still the prerogative of the classical or aristocratic schools of painting. During the seventeenth century, various painters began to react against the growing decadence and stereotyped themes of the Kanō and Tosa painting schools in favor of more vital and realistic subject-matter. The germ of Ukiyo-ye was in the air. The real founder of the School was Hishikawa Moronobu (1625-1694). It was he who around 1660 first had the idea of using the woodcut medium for making Floating-World pictures and thus channeling Ukiyo-ye into a popular art. Most of his work as a print designer appeared in books (illustration 115) or in albums, such as *Shungwa* (illustration 117a). He may thus be accounted the father of Japanese book illustration, since the art before his time was crude and lacking in character and variety (illustration 114b). The difference in woodcut technique between his early and late work points up the advance made by the artisans of knife and chisel during the same period. The earliest works are clumsily engraved. In the later works, one feels, the brush stroke in all its idiosyncracies has been translated to the wood. Henceforth the self-effacing skill of the woodcutter interposed no barrier to the perfect rendering of an artist's style. Moronobu's prints have a heavy-handed vigor and boldness of characterization in contrast to the almost feminine sensibility and grace apparent in the designs of his younger contemporary Nishikawa Sukenobu, who also worked almost exclusively for books (illustrations 115a, 117). Both were trained as painters in the classical schools, and both exerted considerable influence on succeeding artists in spite of the fact that they designed relatively few single prints. Indeed, book illustration was as much a medium for Ukiyo-ye as was the separate woodcut; and many great artists, such as Shunshō, Kiyonaga, Shigemasa, Utamaro, and Hokusai, were also prolific and distinguished illustrators.

The first artist, perhaps, to design single prints *(ichimai-ye)* in great numbers was Torii Kiyonobu I (1664-1729). Most of his work was connected with the theatre: he painted signboards for theatres and designed programs. After some experience as a book illustrator, he started, around 1695, to design single prints of actors, which were hawked about on the streets. Their immediate success started the fashion for theatrical subjects (illustration 514). His draughtsmanship—as was consistent with his poster training—was bold and vigorous, emphasizing large masses by exuberant lines. Kiyonobu was the founder of the Torii School which was active for six generations in carrying on a tradition more or less connected with the theatre. The second head of the Torii clan was his son, or possibly son-in-law, Torii Kiyomasu (illustrations 512, 540). A detailed study of the work of Kiyonobu and Kiyomasu and of the meagre family records and other extant sources, reveal problems which have agitated scholars for many years. It has been discovered, for instance, that there are variations of style and treatment and also chronological discrepancies in different phases of their work. The existence of prints signed Kiyonobu after his death in 1729 postulates the activity of a second Kiyonobu. The similarity between certain prints of Kiyomasu and Kiyonobu II suggests that they were designed by one person. There also exist certain differences between the early, middle, and late periods of Kiyomasu's oeuvre which imply the existance of possibly three artists of the name. Several theories have been offered to solve the problem. Some scholars maintain that there were only two artists involved: Kiyonobu-Kiyomasu I and Kiyonobu-Kiyomasu II who used the two names interchangably. Another school asserts that such simultaneous use of two names is contrary to all Japanese custom, and has advanced an ingenious theory reconstructing Kiyomasu I, II, and III, and Kiyonobu I and II (the latter having first been Kiyomasu II but after his father's retirement or death having adopted his name). The latter hypothesis has much to recommend it, though neither theory completly reconciles all the known facts. The whole question is brought up as an example of the problems encountered in tracing the history of a folk art such as Japanese prints.

Around the beginning of the Hōyei period, or 1704, several other important artists, Kwaigetsudō and Masanobu, began to issue prints. Relatively little is known about Kwaigetsudō; the name probably represents not a single person but rather a workshop or clan. Their production was meagre and their works are very rare. All of the 23 subjects which have come down to us are *Bijin-ye* or pictures of courtesans. They are among the greatest of Japanese prints for sheer vitality of brush stroke, power of curving line, and monumental three-dimensional design. A large *sumi-ye* of a stately Oiran, superbly designed with swirling drapery, and signed Kwaigetsudō Doshin, is reproduced as illustration 511.

The third great figure of the early period was Okumura Masanobu (1691-1768). As an artist he probably was self taught; he undoubtedly studied the works of his elder contemporaries, Moronobu, Sukenobu, and Kwaigetsudō. He was a book seller and print publisher as well as an artist. As a consequence, no doubt, of his interest as a publisher in questions related to wood cutting and printing, his name has been associated with a number of important technical innovations. But beyond all technical considerations, he was a designer of great distinction. His figures convey the impression of elegance, reserve strength, and mellow integration (illustration 513), He further extended the range of Ukiyo-ye subject-matter to include, beside actors and women, portraits and out-door scenes suggesting landscape. In keeping with his self-taught background and open-minded response to different forms of art, he must have had some familiarity with Chinese art (see his self portrait in the guise of the Chinese magician *Chokwarō*, (illustration 522). He must also have seen some European pictures and have studied the conventions of European perspective. He was the first to make *Uki-ye*, or perspective prints, in which these conventions were employed. This tradition, though not common, did run through all periods of Japanese printmaking. Other well-known artists who made *Uki-ye* were Shiba Kokan, Shunshō, Toyoharu (illustration 548) and Hokusai. Masanobu is credited with having invented a special form, or rather shape, of Japanese woodcut, *hashira-ye* or pillar print. The shape is very tall and narrow; and such prints were made to be hung on columns in Japanese houses. An unusually large *naga-ye* (tall picture) by Masanobu, though not the exact proportions of a *hashira-ye*, is reproduced as illustration 520. This woodcut was undoubtedly used as a pillar print, for is portrays *Shōki*, the equivalent of the Chinese *Chung K'uei* the Demon Queller, whose effigy was placed by the door to ward off evil spirits. Many later artists including Kiyomitsu, Toyonobu, Harunobu, Koryūsai (illustration 553), Kiyonaga (illustration 554), Shunchō, Chōki, and others, designed pillar prints to supply popular demand, fascinated no doubt also by the challenge of the unusual proportions to their powers of invention and compostition.

The earliest Japanese prints were in black and white only (*sumi-ye*). Kiyonobu is supposed to have been the first to add color by hand. Among the colors used in early times were a red or orange pigment called by the Japanese *tan*, sometimes a yellow pigment used with *tan*, sometimes a rose-red called *beni* in combination with a greenish yellow or with low-toned blues and purples. Masanobu first had the idea of mixing a little lacquer, *urushi*, with some of the pigments to give them brilliance and also of dusting gold powder on them, thus creating another classification of hand-colored prints, the *urushi-ye*.

At the beginning of Kwanpo (1741), true color prints, in which the colors are printed from separate color blocks and not added by hand, made their appearance. It is not known with certainty who was responsible for this important innovation. Masanobu, if not the actual inventor, was one of the first to sense its possibilities. Though a veteran of the primitive black and white era, he was flexible and inventive enough to master the conventions of a two-color compositional scheme, and design some of the most charming *benizuri-ye* ever made (illustration 517). At first the *beni* color scheme, rose and green, with a black key block, was used. Later other color combinations and even three color blocks with black were employed, thus leading up to the inception of the full polychrome print in the Meiwa era. In addition to Masanobu and Shigenaga a group of very able younger artists—Toyonobu, Kiyohiro, and Kiyomitsu—fully exploited the possibilities of the two and three color-block woodcut (illustrations 518, 519, 521).

The artists whom we have hitherto been considering are generally classified as the Primitives. They are primitives with reference to technique and not to treatment, since Japanese prints were from the beginning highly sophisticated. The black and white prints and those colored by hand may be considered the first phase in the development of the Japanese print; to the second or transition stage belong the two and three color prints—thus covering the periods in history from Genroku through Hōreki (1688-1763). The earlier prints, monumental or heraldic in character, display a boldness of execution and a dynamic interplay of linear rhythms. The designs were mostly of single figures; and little attempt was made at pictorial composition except in book illustrations or in *Shungwa* albums and other series. At the beginning of the Meiwa period, or about 1765, a farther improvement in the printing process was made, which rendered possible polychrome effects with as many as eight to eleven blocks (later many more blocks were used), thus inaugurating the era of the "Brocade Picture" (*nishiki-ye*) or full color print, which was to hold sway ever after. Harunobu was the first of the great designers to take advantage of this improvement, and it gave scope to his exquisite and lovely sense of color, in some of the most beautiful prints ever made (illustrations 523, 524, 525, 526). Harunobu first used color-printed backgrounds, and was also the first to make effective use of *gauffrage*, blind stamping, the impress of a woodblock without ink to make embossed patterns on the paper, thus giving textural variety. This device was used by many succeeding artists, notably Utamaro, and particularly on the kind of print known as *surimono*. The use of mica colors has been ascribed with no great certainty to Harunobu and even Masanobu. The fullest exploitation of mica pigments, particularly as backgrounds in a range of yellow, pink, or silver grey, came later with Utamaro and Sharaku. Their use was forbidden after 1794. With the mention of "gradation printing," first used by Toriyama Sekiyen in his book *Sekiyen Gwafu* 1773, and later most effectively employed by Hokusai and Hiroshige, the account of the technical innovations in Japanese prints is fairly complete. But beyond and overshadowing questions of technique is the chronicle of the various artists' approach to the perennial problem of self-expression.

Suzuki Harunobu (1725-1770) was the dominant figure of the Meiwa period (1764-1772). He broke away from the Torii tradition of actor prints, and, following the lead of Sukenobu, devoted himself to genre scenes of idyllic charm. There is magic in his girlish figures, exquisite in their sensitive gestures. It is astonishing how much feeling and sensibility can be expressed by the pose, the gesture, the outline of the figure, for in these woodcuts, as in all Japanese prints, the faces are like masks, expressionless according to Western ideas. Louis V. Ledoux has beautifully summed up Harunobu's salient quality:

He is the artist of young girlhood, the poet of youth. His figures, untouched by sorrow, move through an earthly paradise, a fairyland of loveliness, the world that might be rather than the world that is. He has caught and rendered for us the evanescent charm of youth; he has sought to preserve, with the freshness of the morning on it, that fleeting moment between the opening of the bud and the fall of the first petal, in which alone beauty is perfect, unalloyed.

After the death of Harunobu and during the Anyei period (1772-1781), though there was no all-pervading personality such as his, there was nevertheless no dearth of distinguished designers. Isoda Koryūsai, the Samurai pupil and friend of Harunobu, carried on his tradition, yet with an individual touch in his coloring and later in his style. He was famous for his bird and pillar prints (illustrations 116, 553). Kitao Shigemasa (1739-1820), equally renowned as a calligrapher, draughtsman, and illustrator, unfortunately designed relatively few single prints. He collaborated with Shunshō in the illustrations to *Seiro Bijin Awase Sugata Kagami*, Mirror Reflecting the Forms of Fair Women of the Green-Houses, 1776, one of the most beautiful of Japanese color print books. Another famous illustrated book is the *Yehon Butai Ogi*, Picture Book of Stage Fans of 1770, in which Bunchō and Shunshō collaborated. Samurai-born Ippitsusai Bunchō, whose life exhibited elements of a strange psychological conflict, combined, one might say, the exquisite sensibility (particularly as regards color) of Harunobu with the form and subject-matter of Shunshō (illustration 537). The most important artist, perhaps, who came to full maturity during the Anyei period, was Katsukawa Shunshō. He was a prolific designer for books, *Shungwa* albums, and theatrical prints, chiefly in *hoso-ye* shape (illustrations 535, 555). His actor portraits display an intensity unknown to the Torii masters, an emotional *timbre* conveyed by superb draughtsmanship, placement, and conscious use of color. In Ficke's words: "all his figures are dynamic—the storehouses of volcanic forces whose existence he suggests by restless line-conflicts. . . . In repose they are like statues; in action they have the vigor of those natural forces—waves, river currents, storms of thunder—which so often form their backgrounds."

222

Shunshō has an austere and possibly limited appeal, for he concentrated not on beauty but on dramatic effect. At his best he is unsurpassed.

The Temmei period (1781-1789) was dominated by Torii Kiyonaga (illustrations 527, 528, 531, 554). He was a pupil of, though little influenced by Torii Kiyomitsu. At his death, Kiyonaga became head of the clan as Torii IV, and did much to restore its waning prestige. Of the younger generation, Shunchō, Chōki, Shunman, Yeishi, and Toyokuni, all fell under the spell of his style. Before Kiyonaga retired around 1790, he had designed, beside numerous book illustrations, a total of approximately eight hundred prints—figure and genre pieces from daily life, courtesans, as well as theatre subjects, *joruri* plays, actors in character, and actors in private life. He represented the full flowering of the Ukiyo-ye School—the stage at which Phidias, for example, summed up Greek sculpture—by a perfect fusion of strength and refinement. His is an art of balance, of idealized grandeur, not the tumultuous grandeur of the Primitives, but a calm and poised serenity, static withal, in its conscious symmetry. "Kiyonaga," in Binyon's words, "rarely invents motives beyond the simplest to relate his figures to one another; and his most characteristic women are proudly impassive. He is content with the solid pose of his majestic forms, as if to bend or sway them toward or away from each other would mar their dignity. But out of these so simple harmonies what a magnificent whole he creates, consummate in its equilibrium and authority! If his resources as a designer are strangely limited and easily exhausted, within those limits he is perfect, and he is a splendid draughtsman." Kiyonaga was one of the first to explore the possibilities of the diptych, triptych, and pentaptych forms of composition on separate blocks, each unit functioning as a separate composition yet so tied together in design as to form part of an over-all picture. The diptychs of the *Minami Juniko* series are justly famous (illustration 531), and so are such triptychs as *Boating Party on the Sumida, Visitors to Emoshima, Party Viewing Moon across The Sumida River.*

Utamaro and the meteoric Sharaku were the leading artists of Kwansei (1789-1801), but again they were not alone in the field. Katsukawa Shunyei (illustration 536) carried on the tradition of his

223

teacher Shunshō. Hosoda Yeishi, Samurai born, and trained in the classical Kanō school, carried over a certain nobility of treatment into his popular productions, particularly when under the sway of Kiyonaga's style (illustration 549). Like him he was an accomplished designer of triptychs (see the *Genji* series and illustration 532) and of such delightful pentaptychs as *Yoshitsune playing before Joruri-hime*. When, however, Yeishi lapsed into the taste of the day in order to vie with Utamaro, he was apt to become mannered and overly sweet. The *surimono* by Shunman (illustration 543) is an example of a kind of print in vogue from the time of Moronobu onwards, a greeting card for special occasions such as the New Year, and usually commissioned by private individuals. Generally smaller in size than the average print and on thicker paper, they were sumptuously printed with many blocks and elaborate *gauffrage*. Kubo Shunman himself, as described by Fenollosa, "is, like Shigenaga and Bunchō, one of those strange personalities who infuse their art with a nameless individual charm. Everything he does has a strange touch. The Kiyonaga face becomes distorted with a sort of divine frenzy; trees grope about with their branch tips like sentient beings; flowers seem to exhale unknown perfumes." A poet as well as an artist, he designed relatively few prints, but of rare distinction, restrained in color and with an intriguing complexity of rhythm, as in the six sheet *Tamagawa* or the triptych *Cup Floating Game*. The eclectic, Yeishōsai Chōki, in a style compounded of Kiyonaga, Yeishi, Sharaku, and Utamaro, designed some prints with a haunting beauty of coloring, *New Year's Sunrise* and *Fireflies* (illustration 542).

In Tōshūsai Sharaku we meet one of the most extraordinary figures in Japanese art. We know little about him other than he was a *Nō* dancer in the service of the Daimyo of Awa. In the last ten months of the year 1794 he designed about 136 prints of actors, which have survived, including 23 bust portraits with mica backgrounds (illustrations 538, 539). We do not know how or why he suddenly burst in, full fledged as it were, upon the print world with his terrific characterizations, nor why he ceased in so short a time, to be heard of no more. His prints evidently were not popular, yet he must have had some measure of contemporary appreciation, since his work, issued by one of the most discriminating publishers of the time, Tsutaya, influenced Chōki and was imitated by Toyokuni and Kunimasa. It was not that the form of his work was new and strange, for much of it was in conventional *hoso-ye* shape, and his use of the bust portrait had been anticipated by Shunyei. It is possible that the public and the actors vaguely sensed in his pictures something that cut deeper than the mere re-creation of a dramatic role, and penetrated behind the actor's mask to lash at the being underneath. Brutally realistic satire, though occasionally met with, as in Shunshō's *Two Wrestlers*, is nevertheless fairly rare in Japanese art. Sharaku's mood may have been something different and more akin to that of Goya or Grosz, a savage irony directed against a whole class or even the human race. His work disturbed or repelled. A critic wrote of Sharaku but a few years after his brief appearance: "He drew portraits of actors, but exaggerated the truth, and his pictures lacked form. Therefore he was not well received, and after a year or so he ceased to work." On the other hand another critic, not later than 1802, wrote: "The power of his brush strokes and of his taste is praiseworthy." It is likely that his work, though not popular, was appreciated by the discriminating few. And it may well be, as Ledoux has pointed out, that the cessation of Sharaku's activity as a print designer was caused not by his unpopularity but by the ban of his feudal lord, as an occupation unworthy of his rank as a *Nō* dancer. These biographical speculations may add a dash of mystery to the Sharaku legend, but are in the last analysis subordinate to the timeless appeal of his great artistic creations. His delineations of actors in their roles transcend the confines of the Kabuki stage and become awe-inspiring personifications of demonic forces, of baleful passions and odious instincts—brutality, duplicity, vainglory, bestiality, lust, and revenge. His designs, for all their disturbing effect, have a haunting impressiveness, a kind of fearsome beauty. The lines are restrained but powerfully intense, and display an inspired grasp of the essentials of physiognomy and character. Seldom have the depths of human emotions been revealed with such objective yet expressive power.

Kitagawa Utamaro was discovered by the West in the 1880's and 1890's, and was endowed with *fin de siècle* decadent tendencies by some

225

of the critics. Utamaro was not, in my opinion, a decadent at all, but an artist of great sensibility and sensitiveness to the currents of his time, a restless and daring experimenter in the same sense that Picasso is today. In a print *oeuvre* totaling about a thousand pieces he showed himself a designer of unusual inventiveness and a master of complex rhythm. Only one year younger than Kiyonaga, Utamaro did not reach the maturity of his style until about 1790 when the Torii artist retired. For a decade he reigned supreme. His work was immensely popular, On several of his prints he indulged in boastful and disparaging remarks about his rival contemporaries. He had many imitators, forgers even, during his lifetime. He gave to the perennial theme of woman a new significance and form. "It is this seizure," as Binyon has said, "of the aboriginal, the essential, the instinctive, in feminine humanity that distinguishes Utamaro among all the artists of the world." The types he designed were varied: the *petite* grace of *Okita the Tea-House Waitress*, the stateliness of *The Hour of the Snake*, the willowy languor of the *Woman Seated on a Veranda*. In some, the characteristics were exaggerated almost to the breaking point; but the series of half-length figures and large heads with silver or yellow or pink mica backgrounds (illustration 529) display to the full his rare power of draughtsmanship and subtle coloring. But there was more to Utamaro than his projections of feminine beauty: there were the snow and moonlit landscapes, the fusion of scientific precision and esthetic style in the illustrations to the *Insect Book* and *Gifts of the Ebb Tide* (shells and rocks), the great set in twelve sheets of *Silk Culture*, the consummately designed triptychs, *Awabi Fishers* (illustration 533), *The Printmakers, The Dressmakers, The Summer Storm, The Women on the Bridge, The Fishing Party on the Sumida*, and finally the tender domestic scenes, mothers and children, including the powerful *Yamauba and Kintoki* series (illustration 530) inspired by the legend of the boy giant of the mountains.

The rare large woodcut *Four Beauties Enacting the Ox Cart Scene* (illustration 534) is an example of a kind of subject fairly common in Ukiyo-ye. It is called a "Brother Picture", that is to say a scene from a play or well-known legend (in this case Scene 6 of the Sugawara tragedy) brought up to date or re-enacted by courtesans or sometimes

226

by children. It is no doubt a form of parody, not so much of manner as of content; and gives a fair indication of the cultural level of the audience for whom Japanese prints were made. The treatment is in terms of everyday life, brought down to earth as it were, and sometimes with a touch of irreverence or "spoofing." But the implication is plain that the artists, the courtesans, and public were familiar with the allusions contained in these and many other prints referring to themes and parables in Chinese and Japanese philosophy and poetry. It is as if a movie magazine of today were to publish regularly impersonations of episodes from Shakespeare, Milton, or Homer. A further measure of popular culture is given by the many illustrated anthologies of poetry that were published from Moronobu onwards, and by the frequency with which poems of incomparable beauty appeared on prints.

Utamaro was a many-sided artist, constantly trying out new effects, uneven in production. His best work, which is rare, ranks among the masterpieces of Ukiyo-ye. His mediocre productions, combined with those of his imitators, have given a distorted picture of his genius. His total work must be judged in relation to the taste of his age, which he both reflected and, to a certain extent, dominated. The times had indeed changed since the austere grandeur of the Primitives was popular; now the populace, somewhat blasé and already accustomed to complicated colorings from twenty to thirty blocks, demanded novelty in any form. Unrest and revolutionary ferment, too, were stirring, agitation against the continued usurpation of power by the Shoguns, which was suppressed but eventually culminated in their overthrow in 1867. In 1804 Utamaro published, in spite of the censorship, several satiric prints which gave offense to the Shogun. He suffered imprisonment, and died in broken health in 1806. After his death there was a marked decline in the quality of figure design. The leading artist, Toyokuni I, who had made some notable prints in rivalry with—and imitation of— Utamaro, succumbed to the general deterioration of taste, reflected also in banal textile patterns and overladen coiffures. The later Toyokuni, his pupils and namesakes (there were four who bore his name) lost their mastery in exaggerated and meaningless gestures, in elaboration of unessential detail, in uninspired realism, and in inferior coloring. It

227

is most unfortunate that these are the prints most commonly known in the West, for they give a false idea of the true worth of Ukiyo-ye. Even their subject-matter became stereotyped and trivial: these artists were most successful when they did not aim too high, but contented themselves with still life arrangements on *surimono* or such fanciful semi-humorous compositions as Utagawa Kuniyoshi's *Goldfish Story* (illustration 541) and other fish or bird-and-flower designs.

In one branch of printmaking only was there any sign of freshness and vitality—landscape. After 1800 a shift of interest away from the figure is noticeable. A landscape school arose, which portrayed the land—as others had portrayed the people—the city and the country, its streets and highways, its harbors and landmarks, the ever-changing aspects of the great mountain, Fuji. The landscapists gained favor with the populace. A landscape tradition of long standing had been laid down by the classical Kanō and Tosa Schools; and to a certain degree it influenced the new movement. But the new Ukiyo-ye artists gave it a character of their own: not the mood of lofty communion with nature, but an intimate, localized, and human touch; not the mountain as a symbol of sublimity, but the mountain seen from a spot famous for its view. And thus arose the many series of *Yedo Views;* or the scenes along the highways between Yedo and Kyōto (*The Fifty-three Stations of the Tokaido or Eastern Highway, The Sixty-nine Stations of the Kisokaidō via Kiso Gorge*); or *The Thirty-six Famous Views of Fuji.* Several figure designers of the Utagawa School, Kunisada I and Kuniyoshi, also made a few notable landscapes, but the two greatest designers were Hokusai and Hiroshige. Each had pupils and followers who carried on but never equalled their performances.

Katsushika Hokusai, "the Man Mad about Painting," as he sometimes signed himself, was born in 1760. He was a pupil of Shunsō, but in his final development was largely self-taught, drawing upon many sources including the European and Chinese. He was always poor, always changing his name and his lodging, and he was always drawing. No artist has ever shown a more unflagging and a more undiscriminating delight in the delineation of humanity and all natural objects. The thirteen volumes of his sketch books, *Mangwa* (illustration 545), were a

228

veritable encyclopedia of graphic representations of birds, insects, animals, fish, flowers, trees, rocks, mountains, architecture, ghosts, and every possible trade and craft and expression and gesture of man. In his celebrated epilogue to the first volume of the *Hundred Views of Fuji*, 1834, he spoke of his own artistic development, saying that as early as his sixth year he felt the impulse to draw the form of things; when he was fifty he had already published innumerable sketches. At seventy-three he began to comprehend approximately the true form and nature of birds, fish, and plants; consequently he hoped to make great progress after the age of eighty, and when he should have reached the age of one hundred and ten, every dot and every line would be alive. Hokusai was a fecund, tirelessly inventive artist who had to digest the entire visible world before he could arrange it in the hierarchy of its importance. His work is a triumph of extrovert externalization. In his later phase he somewhat overcame his unselective lack of taste to produce magnificent designs in landscape. Justly renowned are his *Thirty-six Views of Fuji* (illustration 546) portraying the majestic mountain in various aspects, often in contrast with the puny occupations of man. This set and the ten supplementary plates are remarkable for their originality of composition and the sprightly counterpoint of their linear rhythms. Other famous series are the *Waterfalls*, the *Bridges*, the *Lu Chu Islands*, and the *Flowers* (illustration 547). Early and late he designed *surimono*, a class of print in which his pupils, Hokkei, Gakutei, and Shinsai, also excelled. His other great masterpiece, one in which he for once undertook, successfully, a lofty theme, is the rare set of ten *Images from the Poets of China and Japan*.

Where Hokusai, one might say, approached landscape as a draughtsman in stressing linear structure with a limited palette of color blocks, Hiroshige looked at the problem more with the eye of a painter in playing off color against color. Few artists have ever portrayed such a range of atmospheric effects, day and night, wind and sun, snow and rain; or controlled such delicate manipulations of aerial perspective with so limited a means as the flat color block. Hiroshige accomplished this by stylization and suggestion, by the unerring selection of essential details and by the subtle juxtaposition or blending of colors. The most

229

successful realization of the artist's intention is to be seen only in the rare early impressions. Among his most famous series were *Eight Views of Lake Biwa*, several Tokaido sets including the great *Tokaido* of 1834 (illustration 552), the *Thirty-six Views of Fuji* (illustration 544), and the many sets of *Yedo Views* (illustration 550). He was a prolific designer, and made, beside countless landscapes, a *Chūshingura* set, numerous bird and flower prints (*kwachō*) in narrow upright *tanzaku* form, which may have some relation to the paintings of the Shijo School, some charming fan-shaped compositions or *uchiwa-ye* (illustration 551), and several notable triptychs, including *Kiso Gorge in Snow* and *Banks of the Sumida in Winter*. After Hiroshige's death in 1858 even the landscape school suffered a decline, and Japanese prints in general ceased to have esthetic significance. To be sure, one sometimes encounters a later print of lovely quality, a *Crow* by Kyōsai, *White Mice* by Zeshin, or in modern times a *Nude* by Goyo, but they are definitely exceptions. The opening of Japan to the world in 1854 unloosed a torrent of Western influences which overwhelmed what was left of a stylistic tradition.

Hokusai and Hiroshige were the two artists whom the occidental world found easiest to understand and appreciate. Recognition of Utamaro, Harunobu, and Kiyonaga came later, and of the Primitives and Sharaku last of all. Hokusai's prints were among the first to reach Europe. The story is told that Bracquemond in 1856 had acquired from the printer Delâtre a little volume of Hokusai's *Mangwa* which had been used for packing china, and which he was wont to show with great enthusiasm to Whistler, Degas and all his artist friends in Paris. The artists, particularly the Impressionists, were early and eager collectors of Japanese prints, both landscapes and figure pieces, fascinated by their often daringly assymetrical compositional schemes and their frank reliance on stylization and design to carry the burden of their message. Some even found inspiration for their own work in them. The influence on Whistler can be traced in much of his work, but is most obvious in his etchings and lithographs of the Putney and Battersea Bridges. Degas had a collection of Japanese prints, including the rare *Nude Bathers* of Kiyonaga. Gauguin owned Hokusais and Utamaros, and was influenced by their flat color patterns, and so was Van Gogh, who painted a portrait of Père Tanguy, dealer in artists' colors and Japanese prints, against a background of Japanese pictures. Mary Cassatt, who had in her possession some choice Utamaros, made color prints directly inspired by Japanese woodcuts. Toulouse-Lautrec was perhaps most akin to Ukiyo-ye in choice of subject and sense of style; the *Japonisme* which pervaded his work was perhaps most evident in such lithographs as the cover to *Estampe Originale*, the posters, and the set of *Elles*. Thus the esthetic qualities of Japanese prints were discovered by the artists and critics of Paris (and to a lesser degree those of London) beginning about the middle of the nineteenth century. From there, recognition spread through Europe and America and eventually back to Japan, where Ukiyo-ye had originally been held in little esteem by collectors. These prints of popular and ephemeral appeal have at last been found to have enduring value. The painter, Camille Pissarro, writing of an exhibition of Japanese prints in 1883, has summed up their quality: "I find in the art of this astonishing people a repose, a calm, a grandeur, an extraordinary unity, a rather subdued radiance which is nevertheless brilliant. What astounding balance, and what taste!"

CHINESE DYNASTIES

Han	206 BC — 220 AD
Six Dynasties	220 AD — 618
(including Wei 386-534)	
T'ang	618 - 906
Five Dynasties	907 - 960
Sung	960 -1279
Yüan	1280 -1368
Ming	1368 -1644
Ch'ing	1644 -1911
Republic	1912

JAPANESE CHRONOLOGY

Tenna	1681-1683	Temmei	1781-1788
Jōkyō	1684-1687	Kwansei	1789-1800
Genroku	1688-1703	Kyōwa	1801-1803
Hōyei	1704-1710	Bunkwa	1804-1817
Shōtoku	1711-1715	Bunsei	1818-1829
Kyōhō	1716-1735	Tempō	1830-1843
Gembun	1736-1740	Kokkwa	1844-1847
Kwampō	1741-1743	Kayei	1848-1853
Yenkyō	1744-1747	Ansei	1854-1859
Kwanyen	1748-1750	Manyen	1860
Hōreki	1751-1763	Bunkyū	1861-1863
Meiwa	1764-1771	Genji	1864
Anyei	1772-1780	Keiō	1865-1867

Bibliography

This bibliography is chiefly for the beginner or intelligent layman, who wishes to learn more about prints, and not for the specialist who would require a whole library of reference works. For this reason it is summary and brief.

INTRODUCTION TO THE STUDY OF PRINTS

Ivins, William M., Jr. Prints and Books, Informal Papers (taken from the Metropolitan Museum Bulletin), Cambridge, 1926.

—— Notes on Prints, being the Text of Labels for an Exhibition of Prints at the Metropolitan Museum, N.Y., 1930.

—— How Prints Look, magnified photographs of details of prints with commentary on techniques, Metropolitan Museum, N.Y., 1943.

These three books form an excellent introduction for the intelligent amateur, and can be re-read with profit by the specialist. The clarity of the author's style and the unpedantic freshness of his point of view more than make up for the lack of systematic treatment. Essays by a great scholar who carries his learning lightly.

Hind, A. M. Guide to the Processes and Schools of Engraving, British Museum, 1933.
A well-ordered and invaluable syllabus of 52 pages.

Weitenkampf, Frank. How to Appreciate Prints, New York, 1927.
A useful introduction for the average layman, arranged by techniques.

GENERAL HISTORIES

Bock, Elfried. Geschichte der Graphischen Kunst von ihren Anfängen bis zum Gegenwart, Berlin, 1930.
The best anthology of European prints in all mediums from the beginnings to the present, with over 500 excellent reproductions.

Kristeller, Paul. Kupferstich und Holzschnitt in vier Jahrhunderten, Berlin, 1921.
The standard book in German, and indispensable to the serious student of prints up to 1800.

Glaser, Curt. Die Graphik der Neuzeit, Berlin, 1923.
A profusely illustrated survey of 19th and 20th century European prints. Scholarly but not pedantic. The best book on the period.

Rosenthal, Leon. La Gravure, Paris, 1908.
A short and sound history of all mediums up to 1900, a standard work in French.

Mongan, Elizabeth, and Schniewind, Carl O. The First Century of Printmaking, Chicago, 1941.
Catalogue of an exhibition with excellent illustrations and informative notes.

Lugt, Frits. Les Marques de Collections, Amsterdam, 1921.
The great book on collector's marks with many sidelights on the history of collecting and the mutations of taste.

The Print Collector's Quarterly 1911-1942, edited by Fitz Roy Carrington, Campbell Dodgson, and J. H. Bender.
Contains a wealth of information on all periods and aspects of printmaking for both the amateur and the specialist, as well as an invaluable corpus of handy illustrations.

STUDIES OF SINGLE MEDIUMS

Hind, A. M. Introduction to a History of Woodcut with a Detailed Survey of Work Done in the Fifteenth Century, 2 vols, Boston, 1935.
A mine of information with many illustrations, also extensive bibliographies.

Bliss, Douglas Percy. History of Wood-engraving, London, 1928.
Charmingly written, and with a fresh point of view, touching upon subjects usually ignored, such as Livres d'Heures, Chapbooks, Imagerie, Herbals, etc. From the beginnings to the present. A delightful work by a literate practitioner of the craft.

Friedländer, Max J. Der Holzschnitt, Berlin, 1921.
Handbook of the Berlin Museum and an excellent summary of woodcuts through the 16th century.

Hind, A. M. History of Engraving and Etching, Boston, 1927.
The standard work in English. Very informative, but not light reading. Useful lists, bibliographies, and other scholarly apparatus.

Furst, Herbert. Original Engraving and Etching, London, 1931.
An anthology of good reproductions with page long commentaries, often containing penetrating and original criticism.

Lippmann, Friedrich. Engraving and Etching, London, 1906.
Handbook of the Berlin Museum, written by one of the early authorities, gives sound history up to 19th century.

Pennell, J. and E. R. Lithography and Lithographers, London, 1898.
A breezy and somewhat unorthodox history with many illustrations. The only comprehensive work in English.

Prideaux, S. T. Aquatint Engraving, London, 1909.
Devoted chiefly to early 19th century English aquatint books: travel, topography, sport, natural history, caricature, etc.

MONOGRAPHS ON SEPARATE COUNTRIES

Bock, Elfried. Deutsch Graphik, Berlin, 1922.
The best illustrated survey of German printmaking in all periods.

Courboin, François, La Gravure en France, Paris, 1923.
The best short survey of French printmaking in all branches up to 1900. Excellent illustrations accurately captioned. The result of great knowledge tempered by humane understanding.

Gray, Basil. The English Print, London, 1937.
A well-written accurate account from early times to the present, the best short study on the subject. The few illustrations are excellent in quality.

A FEW SPECIAL MONOGRAPHS ON ARTISTS

Panofsky, Dr. Erwin. Albrecht Dürer, 2 vols., Princeton, 1943.
The last word on Dürer and his work, profusely illustrated.

Hind, A. M. Rembrandt's Etchings, 2 vols, London, 1923.
Catalogue Raisonné arranged chronologically, with illustration of each plate. The standard authority in English, also notes and bibliography.

Holmes, C. M. Notes on the Art of Rembrandt, London, 1911.
An illuminating study of Rembrandt as artist and creator with special reference to the etchings.

Poore, Charles. Goya, N.Y., 1938.
A very readable study of Goya with considerable notice of his prints.

Dobson, Austin. William Hogarth, London, 1907.
A monograph by the famous scholar on 18th century culture.

Mack, Gerstle. Toulouse-Lautrec, N.Y., 1938.
A well-written study of Lautrec and the Paris of his time.
Museum of Modern Art, New York.
The monographs issued by the Museum give considerable information on certain modern printmakers: Modern Painters and Sculptors as Illustrators, Fantastic and Surrealist Art, Cubism and Abstract Art, Latin American Collections, Art in Our Time, Photography, and special works on Picasso, Chagall, Matisse, Miro, Dali, Rouault, Feininger, Marin, and Stuart Davis.

OLDER AMERICAN PRINTS

Dreppard, Carl W. Early American Prints, N.Y., 1930.
A chatty informal introduction to the subject, containing, nevertheless, much pertinent information.
Weitenkampf, Frank. American Graphic Art, N.Y., 1924.
A very useful reference work, crammed with information collected over a lifetime of association with prints.
Peters, Harry T. Currier and Ives, Printmakers to the American People, N.Y., 1929.
—— America on Stone, The Other Printmakers to the American People, N.Y., 1931.
Sumptuously illustrated records of American lithographs in the 19th century. A pioneer work in this field.
Bland, Jane Cooper. Currier and Ives, A Manual for Collectors, N.Y., 1931.
A complete checklist of prints and auction prices.
Murrell, William. History of American Graphic Humor 1747-1938, 2 vols, N.Y., 1933-1938.
A monumental work on caricature and humor with many illustrations.

CHINESE PRINTS

The references in this section are somewhat more numerous, since the literature itself is so scanty.
Carter, Thomas F. The Invention of Printing in China, N.Y., 1925.
An admirable piece of research and presentation. Unfortunately the author touches upon woodcut and illustration only indirectly.
Binyon, L. Catalogue of Japanese and Chinese Colour Prints in the British Museum, 1916.
Brief list of Chinese prints, including the Tung Huan finds and the Kaempfer purchase.
Bernoulli, R. Meisterwerke Ostasiatischer Graphik, Plaven, 1923.
Excellent reproductions with commentary on Chinese and Japanese prints in the Kunstgewerbe Museum in Berlin.
Fischer, Otto. Ausstellung Chinesicher Steinabklatsche, Zurich, 1944.
The best short historical survey of stone rubbings, written with feeling and understanding.
Wang, Chi-chen. The Technique of Chinese Rubbings and Its Application, N.Y., 1938.
An authoritative though short exposition with some excellent large reproductions of rubbings.
Wu, K. T. Colour Printing in the Ming Dynasty, in T'ien Hsia Monthly, August 1940.
Important study by a Chinese scholar.
Tschicold, Jan. L'Estampe Chinoise Ancienne en Couleurs, Basle, 1940.
—— Chinesische Farbendrucke aus dem Lehrbuch der Malerei des Senfkorngartens, 1941.
Excellent facsimiles and scholarly notes with bibliographies on Chinese color prints. The last word on Chinese color prints.
Kurth, Julius. Der Chinesche Farbendruck, Plauen, 1922.
The conclusions in this pioneer study have been somewhat superseded by later scholarship.
Metzgar, Judson D. Chinese Color Prints, Los Angeles, 1943.

An annotated catalogue of an exhibition chiefly of Ten Bamboo Studio and Mustard Seed Garden.

Ferguson, J. C. Outlines of Chinese Art, Chicago, 1919.
An excellent summary, treating incidentally of stone rubbings.

Waley, Arthur. Introduction to the Study of Chinese Painting, London, 1923.
The best book on Chinese painting, with philosophical background based on Chinese sources.

Siren, Osvald. The Chinese on the Art of Painting: Translation and Comment, Peiping, 1936.
Chinese writings on art from the Han through Ch'ing Dynasties.

JAPANESE PRINTS

Ficke, Arthur Davison. Chats on Japanese Prints, London, 1915.
A charmingly written introduction to the subject by a poet and life-long student of Japanese prints. Important.

Gookin, F. W. Japanese Color-prints and Their Designers, Japan Society, New York, 1913.
An introductory essay by one of the great authorities, with 24 excellent reproductions.

Binyon and Sexton. Japanese Colour Prints, London, 1923.
The best all-around work on the subject, well written, sound in its judgment, and largely accurate in its facts. It has excellent tables of chronology and of actor's crests and publisher's seals.

Binyon, L. Catalogue of Japanese and Chinese Colour Prints in the British Museum, 1916.
A most useful work for its lists of prints, though of course far from complete, and for its technical introduction. Has facsimiles of signatures.

Ledoux, Louis V. Catalogue of an Exhibition of Japanese Figure Prints, Grolier Club, 1924.
———— Catalogue of an Exhibition of Japanese Landscape Prints, Grolier Club, 1924.
———— An Essay on Japanese Prints, Japan Society, N.Y., 1938.
———— Japanese Prints of the Ledoux Collection: The Primitives, N.Y., Volumes I-V, 1942-1950.
A series of beautifully presented works with superb reproduction. The charm of the author's style, his vast knowledge, poetic understanding, and sound taste, give distinction to his writings, and make him a most felicitous interpreter of Japanese prints.

Stewart, Basil. Subjects Portrayed in Japanese Colour-prints, N.Y., 1922.
Extensively illustrated, strong on Hokusai and Hiroshige and theatre prints. Facsimiles of signatures, crests, and publishers' seals.

Strange, E. F. Japanese Colour Prints, London, 1931.
Handbook of the Victoria and Albert Museum with facsimiles of signatures, notes on chronology, and numerous illustrations. Strong on the Utagawa School.

Henderson and Ledoux. The Surviving Works of Sharaku, N.Y., 1939.
This and the following work by Hirano are admirable examples of patient and enlightened research. In addition to much useful and accurate information on related topics, each book furnishes a catalogue raisonné of all known prints.

Hirano, C. Kiyonaga, A Study of His Life and Works, 2 vols, Boston, 1939.
One volume of text and one volume of reproductions of all known prints.

Rumpf, Fritz. Meister des Japanischen Farbenholzschnittes, Berlin, 1924.
Though more or less a specialist's book, based on long familiarity with Japanese language and sources, it is useful in correcting mistakes by Kurth and other writers.

Toda, K. Catalogue of Japanese and Chinese Illustrated Books in the Ryerson Library of the Chicago Art Institute, Chicago, 1931.
A scholarly work giving detailed information, illustrated, an indispensable book.

Brown, Louise Norton. Block Printing and Book Illustration in Japan, London, 1924.
A pioneer work not always accurate, illustrated.

236

ORNAMENT AND ARCHITECTURAL PRINTS

Jessen, P. Der Ornamentstich, Berlin, 1920.
By far the best concise and systematic account of ornament and architectural prints. Very useful introduction.
Guilmard, D. Les Maitres Ornemanistes, Paris, 1880-1881.
A pioneer work on ornament, but still useful. Illustrated.
Berlin Museum. Katalog der Ornamentstich-sammlung, 2 vols, Berlin, 1936.
An indispensable work for the study of ornament; the most complete and accurate listing of works on the subject.
Blomfield, R. Architectural Drawing and Draughtsmen, London, 1912.
One of the few instructive surveys on architectural prints, written by an architect.

ILLUSTRATED BOOKS

Pollard, A. W. Early Illustrated Books, London, 1893.
A survey by one of the great authorities.
Worringer, W. Die Altdeutsche Buchillustration, Munich, 1919.
Illustrated survey of German woodcuts in books up to the middle of the 16th century.
Hardie, Martin. English Colored Books, London, 1906.
A delightful work incorporating much research.
Mahoney, Latimer, and Folmsbee. Illustrators of Children's Books, Boston, 1948.
A wealth of information on illustrated books, old and new, with many pictures.
Rümann, Arthur. Das Illustrierte Buch des XIX Jahrhunderts, Leipzig, 1930.
Well illustrated and documented work on 19th century book illustration.
Skira, Albert. Anthologie du Livre Illustré par les Peintres et Sculpteurs de l'Ecole de Paris, Genève, 1946.
Excellent bibliography, with illustrations, of modern editions de luxe.

THREE LANDMARKS OF TECHNIQUE

Bosse, A. Traicté des Manières de Graver en taille-douce, Paris, 1645. And later editions revised by Cochin, Paris, 1745 and 1758.
A famous technician codifies for the first time the technical basis of etching and engraving.
Papillon, J. M. Traité Historique et Pratique de la Gravure en Bois, 3 vols, Paris, 1766.
The great eighteenth century woodcutter sums up the theory and practices of his art.
Senefelder, Aloys. Lehrbuch der Steindruckerey, Munich, 1818.
Technical exposition of lithographic procedure with autobiographical notes on its invention, also examples printed from stone.

THE TECHNIQUES OF PRINTMAKING AND RESTORING

Plenderleith, H. J. Conservation of Prints, Drawings and Manuscripts, London, 1937.
Sound instruction on cleaning and restoring prints.
Mayer, Ralph. The Artist's Handbook of Materials and Techniques, N.Y., 1940.
An invaluable work on techniques including those of prints and picture restoration.
Curwen, Harold. Processes of Graphic Reproduction in Printing, London, 1934.
A clear and concise exposition of graphic techniques including photo-mechanical processes.
Lumsden, E. The Art of Etching, Philadelphia, n.d.
The technique in all its details, with an illuminating and appreciative historical survey. An important and readable book.

237

Chatto and Jackson. A Treatise on Wood Engraving Historical and Practical, London, 1861.
Out of date except for Bewick and reproductive wood-engraving of the nineteenth century.

Gusman, Pierre. La Gravure sur Bois, Paris, 1916.
An authoritative technical and historical treatise, with excellent illustrations including a number printed from the original blocks. Also a short notice on oriental work.

Müller, H. A. How I Make Woodcuts and Wood-engravings, N.Y., 1945.
Written by a famous teacher and engraver, with examples.

Sternberg, Harry. Silk Screen Color Printing, N.Y., 1942.
A pioneer work on serigraphs with photographic illustrations of various steps of the process and other illustrations.

Shokler, H. Artist's Manual for Silk Screen Print Making, N.Y., 1946.
A full account of serigraphy with technical notes by an artist.

NEW BOOKS

Conningham, F. A. Currier and Ives Prints, N.Y., 1949.
An illustrated check list with auction prices.

Michener, James A. The Floating World, N.Y., 1954.
A fresh interpretation based largely on Japanese sources. Informative on theatre and actors, commerce of prints, contemporary artists, etc.

Sternberg, Harry. Modern Methods and Materials of Etching, N.Y., 1949.
Photographic illustrations of various steps.

Hayter, S. W. New Ways of Gravure, N.Y., 1949.
An exposition of modern methods of engraving with highly personal comment.

Buckland-Wright, John. Etching and Engraving, Technique and the Modern Trend, N.Y., 1953.
An excellent technical treatise with a wide range of illustrations.

Dehn and Barrett. How to Draw and Paint Lithographs, N.Y., 1950.
The best technical book on lithography by a famous lithographer and printer.

Schweidler, Max. Die Instandsetzung von Kupferstichen, usw. Stuttgart, 1950.
An authoritative exposition on print restoration by one of the most famous restorers of the century.

Schraubstadter, Carl. Care and Repair of Japanese Prints, Cornwall on Hudson, 1948.
The care of Japanese prints by a great authority. Useful for other prints, too.

Sachs, Paul J. Modern Prints and Drawings, N.Y., 1954.
A delightful introduction to XIX and XX century graphic art.

PLATES

1. From Turrecremata, *Meditationes*, Rome, 1467

2. From Valturius, *De Re Militari*, Verona, 1472

3. From Boccaccio, *Decameron*, Venice

4. From *Hypnerotomachia Poliphili*, Venice, 1499

6. From Ingold, *Guldin Spil*, Augsburg, 1472

5. From Bible, Cologne, 1479

8. From Bible, Lübeck, 1474

7. From Boccaccio, *De Claris Mulieribus*, Ulm, 1473

10. From Savonarola, *Compendio di Revelazione,*
Florence, 1496

12. From Boccaccio, *Ninfale Fiesolano,* Florence

9. From Forestis, *De Claris Mulieribus,*
Ferrara, 1497

11. From *Contrasto di Carnevale,* Florence

13a. From *Aesopi Fabulae*, Verona

13. From Gafurius, *De Re Musica*, Milan, 1492

14. From Ketham, *Fasciculus Medicinae*, Venice, 1493

15. From *Missale Parisiense*, Paris

16a. From *Horae B.V.M.*, David and Bathsheba

16. From *Horae B.V.M.*, Dives and Lazarus

18. German School. Gossip during Mass, 15th Century (manière criblée)

17. From *Usatges de Barcelona*, Barcelona, 1495

19. German school. St. Christopher, 1423 (woodcut)

20. From *Buch der Weisheit*, Ulm, 1483

21. From Terence, Lyon, 1493

22. From Terence, Ulm, 1486

23. From *Le Chevalier Delibéré*,
Gouda, 1488

24. Dürer. From Brant, *Narrenschiff*,
Basel, 1494

25. Dürer. Four Riders of the
Apocalypse, 1498 (woodcut)

26. Dürer. Christ Appearing to Magdalen,
1511 (woodcut)

27. From Bartholomaeus Anglicus

29. Dutch School. Canticum Canticorum, 15th Century (woodcut)

28. Reuwich. Group of Syrians

30. From *Historie van Trojen*, Haarlem, 1485

33. Altdorfer. Death of the Virgin (woodcut)

32. Holbein. Ruth and Boaz, Lyon, 1538 (woodcut)

31. Holbein. Death and Ploughman

35. Baldung Grien. The Fifth Commandment (woodcut)

34. From Marchant, *Danse Macabre*, Paris, 1485

36. Graf. Soldiers and Death
(woodcut)

37. Cranach. Soldier and Woman (woodcut)

38. Burgkmair. St. Luke Painting the
Virgin

38a. Dürer School. Pieta

39. Titian. Landscape with Milkmaid

40. Baldung Grien. Horses, 1534 (woodcut)

42. Weiditz. From *Calixtus und Melibea*, Augsburg, 1520

43. Weiditz. From Petrarch. *Consolation*, Augsburg,

41. Altdorfer. Fountain (woodcut)

45. Boldrini, after Titian. Venus and Amor (woodcut)

44. Cranach. Venus (woodcut)

47. De Nanto, after Titian. Portrait of Ariosto, 1532 (woodcut)

46. Baldung Grien. Portrait of Brunfels (woodcut)

48. From de' Medici, *Nencia de Barberino*, Florence

49. From Dante, *Divina Commedia*, Florence, 1506

50. From *Bible en Françoys*, Paris

51. Graf. Arms of Unterwalden (wood engraving)

52. Baldung Grien. Nativity
(woodcut)

53. Baldung Grien. Ascension of
Christ (woodcut)

54. Baldung Grien. Adam and Eve
(woodcut)

55. Baldung Grien. The
Bewitched Groom
(woodcut)

56. Dale. Playing Card,
    15th Century

57. Weiditz. From Brunfels,
    Herbal, Strassburg, 1530

58. Flöttner. Playing
    Card (woodcut)

59. Viator. Interior, Toul 1505 (woodcut)

60. Tory. From *Horae*, Paris, 1525

61. Vicentino. From *Modo de Scrivere*, Rome, 1522

62. Flöttner. Bed (woodcut

63. From Vecellio, *Corona delle Nobili Donne*, Venice, 1592

64. Jegher, after Rubens. Temptation of Christ (woodcut)

65. Goltzius. Landscape (woodcut)

66. Deny, after Pillemont. Ornament
(engraving)

67. Foin, after Lalonde.
Barometer (engraving)

68. From Chapbook, *Robinson
Crusoe*, 18th century

69. Papillon. Notre Dame de Bonne
Déliverance (woodcut)

71. Image Populaire. World Upside Down, 18th century

72. Image Populaire. The Day of the Fall of Bastille, 18th century

70. Menzel. Voltaire and Frederick the Great (wood engraving)

74. Grandville. The Porcupine

73. Busch. Adagio

75. Calvert. The Return Home (wood engraving, enlarged)

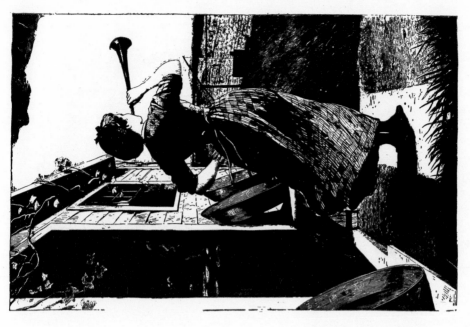

76. Homer. The Dinner Horn

75a. Daumier. Auction Showroom

77. Bewick. Angler in Rain

78. Bewick. Hanging out Clothes

79. Daumier. Le Bourgeois Campagnard, 1840 (wood engraving)

80. Busch. The Visit

81. From *Saint-Pièrre, Paul and Virginia*, Paris, 1838

82. Richter. Harvest Dance (wood engraving)

83. Doré. London Slum

84. Burne-Jones. Adam and Eve

85. Gill. Nowell (wood engraving)

86. Weber. Mother and Child (woodcut)

87. Murphy. Adoration of the Shepherds

90. Galanis. Still Life (wood engraving)

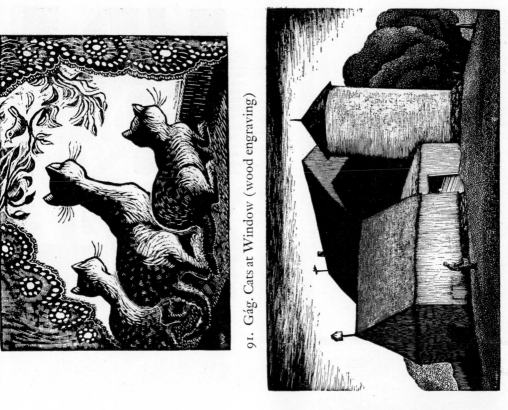

91. Gág. Cats at Window (wood engraving)

92. Skoczylas. Village Square (woodcut)

93. Nason. Ipswich Barns (wood engraving)

94a. Albers. Aquarium

94c. Léger. Abstraction

94. Feininger. Village Church

94b. Sager. Ice Floes

96. Murphy. Morning Gossip (wood engraving)

97a. Holgate. Bather

95. Marcks. Cats (woodcut)

97. Maillol. The Spring

96a. Matisse. Nude

98. Sakhnovskaya. Women in the 1905 Revolution (wood engraving)

99. Masereel. The Strike (wood engraving)

DIE LEBENDEN DEM TOTEN . ERINNERUNG AN DEN 15. JANUAR 1919

99a. Kollwitz. Liebknecht Memorial

100. Kravchenko. Dnieprostroi (wood engraving)

100a. Konstantinov. Collective Farm

102. Rethel. Death the Victor (woodcut)

103. Posada. Calavera (relief etching)

101. Lynd Ward. Spring Idyll (wood engraving)

104. Vallotton. At Twenty Years (woodcut)

105. Chinese School. Procession, Wei Dynasty (stone rubbing)

106. Chinese School. Buddhist Image, 10th century (woodcut)

107. Coptic School. Textile Design, 6th century (woodcut)

108. Chinese School. Manju-sri (woodcut)

109. Chinese School. Playing Card (woodcut)

110. K'uei Hsing. Ideograph of Chung K'uei

111. Chinese School. Ho Huan Tree

112. Chinese School. Portrait of Confucius

113. Su Tung P'o. God of Fortune (stone rubbing)

113a. Chia Li. Bamboo

113b. Chinese School. Plum Tree

113c. Wang Wei. Wang Wei's Villa

114. Chinese School. Kuan-yin

114a. Ch'ung Huan. The
Waterfall

114b. Japanese School. From
Ise Monogatari

114c. Kanō Tanyu. Chinese Sage

115. Moronobu. A Garden

115a. Sukenobu. Yuya Gozen in Modern Dress

116a. Korin. Crows in Moonlight

117a. Moronobu. The Lovers

116. Koryūsai. Crane among Pines

117. Sukenobu. Women Sketching

118. Mantegna. Bacchanal (engraving)

119. Pollaiuolo. Battle of the Naked Men (engraving)

ECCE VENIENTEM DIEM
ET LATENTIA APERIEN
TEM TENEBIT GREMIO
GENTIVM REGINA.

SIBYLLA LIBI
CA

120. Florentine School. Libyan Sibyl (engraving)

121. Italian School. Primum Mobile

123. Botticelli School. Assumption of the Virgin
(engraving)

122. Florentine School. The Planet Mercury (engraving)

125. Veit Stoss. Madonna and Child (engraving)

124. Master of the Playing Cards. Cyclamen Queen
(engraving)

127. Master of the Amsterdam Cabinet. The Lovers (engraving)

126. Mantegna School. Entombment with Four Birds (engraving)

129. van Meckenem. Birth of the Virgin (engraving)

128. Schongauer. Nativity (engraving)

131. de' Barbari. Apollo and Diana

130. Master E. S. Madonna and Child of Einsiedeln
(engraving)

132. German School. St. Onuphrius (woodcut)

133. French School. Nativity
(woodcut)

133a. German School. Madonna and Child with Three Saints

134. Meckenem. Portrait of Self and Wife

135. Pollaiuolo School. Profile of
a Lady (engraving)

136. Da Vinci School. Profile of
a Lady (engraving)

136a. Mantegna. Virgin and Child

137. Meister der Weibermacht. Satire on the Power of Women (engraving)

137b. Robetta. Allegory of Abundance

137a. Campagnola. St. John the Baptist

140. Master I. A. M. Design for Baldachin

139. Peregrino. Orpheus (niello engraving)

138. Peregrino. Ornament (niello engraving)

141. Master F. S. Ornament (engraving)

144. Florentine School. Ornament (engraving)

143. Master E. S. Grotesque Letter Q

142. Romanesque School. Nativity (engraving)

146. Raimondi. Two Fauns (engraving)

145. Schongauer. Griffin (engraving)

148. Dürer. Virgin and Child with Monkey (engraving)

147. Dürer. Adam and Eve (engraving)

150. Dürer. Melancholia (engraving)

149. Dürer. Christ on Mount of Olives (etching)

152. Cranach. Portrait of Luther (engraving)

BILIBALDI·PIRKEYMHERI·EFFIGIES
AETATIS·SVAE·ANNO·L·iii·
VIVITVR·INGENIO·CAETERA·MORTIS·
·ERVNT·
·M·D·XX·iv·

151. Dürer. Portrait of Pirkheimer (engraving)

153. Agostino Carracci. Portrait of Titian (engraving)

154. van Leyden. Portrait of Maximilian (etching and engraving)

155. Hirschvogel. Landscape (etching)

156. Dürer. The Cannon (etching)

157. D. Hopfer. Broadsheet against Hoarding

158. van Leyden. Milkmaid (engraving)

159. Cousin. Entombment (engraving)

160. G. Campagnola. Christ and the Woman of Samaria (engraving)

161. Raimondi, after Raphael. Judgment of Paris (engraving)

162. Raimondi, after Raphael. Massacre of the Innocents (engraving)

164. Duvet. Wine Press of the Wrath of God

163. Duvet. Marriage of Adam and Eve (engraving)

166. Parmigiano. St. Thais (etching)

165. Baroccio. Annunciation (etching)

167. Da Carpi, after Parmigiano. Chronos

168. Da Carpi, after Raphael. Draught of Fishes (chiaroscuro woodcut)

170. Cranach. St. Christopher (chiaroscuro woodcut)

169. Baldung Grien. The Witches (chiaroscuro woodcut)

171. Altdorfer. Virgin and Child
with St. Anne (engraving)

172. Vellert. Faun upon Wine
Barrel

173. H. S. Beham. Drummer and
Standard Bearer (engraving)
(enlarged)

174. Master I. B. Luna
(engraving)

175. B. Beham. Bookplate
(engraving)

176. Delaune. Ornament
(engraving)

177. Aldegrever. Ornament with Lettering (engraving)

179. From *Nuremberg Chronicle*, 1493

180. Ortelius Map of America, 1580 (engraving)

178. Fontana. Obelisk (engraving)

182. Balducci. Marriage of the Duke of Tuscany (etching)

181. Serlio. Corinthian Capital

181a. Primaticcio. Diana

Iulius, Augustus, nec non et Iunius Aestas ·   AESTAS *Adolescentis imago)*   Frugiferas aruis fert Aestas torrida messeis ·

183. Bruegel. Summer (engraving)

184. Bruegel. Justice (engraving)

185. Bruegel. Luilekkerland (engraving)

186. Bruegel. Kermesse (engraving)

188. Rembrandt. Portrait of His Mother (etching)

187. Rembrandt. Self-Portrait Leaning on Stone Sill (etching)

190. Rembrandt. Woman with Arrow (etching)

189. Rembrandt. Dr. Faustus (etching)

191. Rembrandt. Landscape with Trees, Farm Buildings, and Tower (etching)

192. Rembrandt. Three Trees (etching)

193. Rembrandt. Christ and Woman of Samaria (etching)

194. Rembrandt. Christ Preaching (etching)

195. Seghers. Rocky River Landscape with Road (etching)

196. Seghers. The Three Books (etching)

197. Ribera. Drunken Silenus (etching)

198. Goudt, after Elsheimer. Philemon and Baucis (engraving)

200. Buytewech. The Lovers

199. van Ostade. The Family (etching)

NICOLAVS CLAVDIVS FABRICIVS
DE PEIRESC SENATOR AQVENSIS

G. F. Mellan G. del. et fecit

202. Mellan. Portrait of Peiresc (engraving)

201. van Dyck. Portrait of de Momper (etching)

203. Gelée. Rape of Europa (etching)

204. Bolswert, after Rubens. Village Dance (engraving)

205. Gelée. Dance by the Waterside (etching)

206. De Bry. Cruelty to the Indians

207. Rembrandt. Beggar Warming
His Hands (etching)

208. Callot. Beggar with Head and
Feet Bare (etching)

209. Callot. Parterre at Nancy (etching)

210. Callot. The Marauders

211. Callot. Pillage of a House

Au bout du comte ils treuuent pour deisin
Qu'ils sont uenus d'Aegipte a ce festin

212. Callot. Gypsies

213. Bega. The Drinker

213a. Blooteling. The Smoker

214. Teniers. Kermesse (etching)

215. Bosse. Hearing (etching)

216. Bosse. Visite à l'Accouchée (etching)

218. Simonin. Molière as Sganarelle (engraving)

217. Callot. Pantaloon (etching)

He could not endure to be pinch'd with cold

For a smoother skin at night

Embraceth her with more delight

220. Hollar. Winter (etching)

HERCVLES VICTOR

219. Goltzius. Farnese Hercules (engraving)

222. Rubens. St. Catherine (etching)

221. Guercino. St. Anthony (etching)

224. Salvator Rosa. St. William the Hermit (etching)

223. Cantarini. Flight into Egypt (etching)

225. Waterloo. The Linden Tree (etching)

226. van Ruysdael. The Wheat Field (etching)

227. Both. The Wooden Bridge

228. van Ostade. The Fisherman (etching)

228a. J. van de Velde. June

228b. Potter. Cowherd

228c. Zeeman. Vessels of Amsterdam

228d. Backhuysen. Marine with Distant View of Amsterdam

230. Woeiriot. Design for Ring (engraving)

229. Tutin. Ornament (engraving)

231. Della Bella. Cartouche (etching)

232. Jacquinet. Gunsmith's Shop

233. Le Pautre. Ornament (engraving)

234. Le Clerc. Galerie des Gobelins (engraving)

235. Le Pautre. Grottoes and Fountains (engraving)

237. Leoni. Portrait of Galileo (engraving)

236. Goltzius. Portrait of Henri IV (engraving)

237b. Morin after Champaigne. Portrait of Vitré

AMELIA ELISABETHA, D.G. HASSIÆ LANDGRAVIA &c.
COMITISSA HANOVIÆ MVNTZENB:

237a. Siegen. Portrait of the Landgravin of Hesse

238a. Nanteuil. Portrait of Loret

238. Nanteuil. Portrait of Louis XIV (engraving)

239a. Wille after Toqué. Portrait of de Marigny

239. Drevet, after Rigaud. Portrait of de Cotte
(engraving)

240. Fragonard. Bacchanal (etching)

241. Demarteau, after Boucher. Venus Desarmée par les Amours (engraving)

242. Le Prince. O Fortunatos Nimium (aquatint)

243. Tardieu, after Watteau. Embarquement pour Cythère (engraving)

245. Cars, after Lemoyne. Rape of Europa (engraving)

244. Cars, after Watteau. Fêtes Vénitiennes (engraving)

247. Simonet, after Baudouin. Soirée des Tuileries (engraving)

246. De Launay, after Fragonard. Les Hazards Heureux
d'Escarpolette (engraving)

249. De Launay, after Lavreince. Le Billet Doux (engraving)

248. De Launay, after Baudouin. Le Carquois Epuisé (engraving)

251. Lepicié, after Chardin. La Gouvernante (engraving)

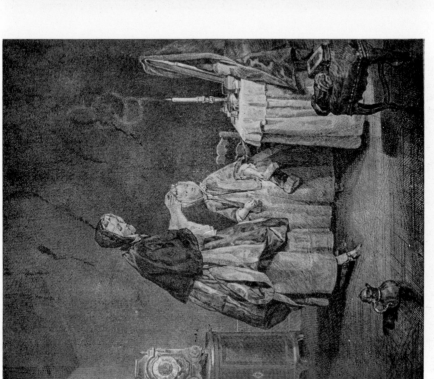

250. Le Bas, after Chardin. Le Negligé (engraving)

253. Malbeste, after Moreau. Sortie de l'Opera (engraving)

252. Helman, after Moreau. Les Délices de la Maternité (engraving)

255. De Launay, after Moreau. Les Adieux (engraving)

254. Helman, after Moreau. Le Souper Fin (engraving)

256. G. St. Aubin. Spectacle de Tuileries (etching)

257. G. St. Aubin. Les Nouvellistes (etching)

258. Hogarth. Marriage à la Mode (engraving)

259. Hogarth. The Enraged Musician (engraving)

261. G. St. Aubin. Théâtre Italien (etching)

260. Delafosse, after Carmontelle. The Mozart Family (engraving)

263. Cars, after Boucher. Tartuffe (engraving)

262. Hogarth. Laughing Audience (engraving)

265. Bonnet, after Boucher. Femme à la Rose

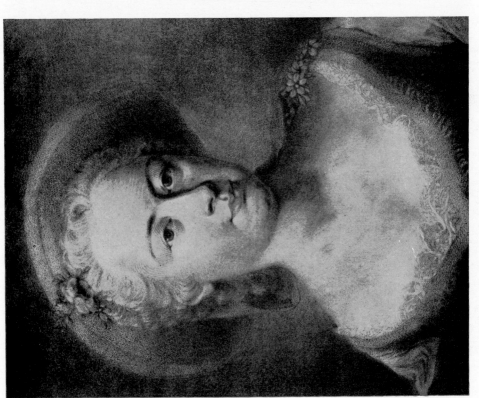

264. Pitteri. Portrait of Pompadour (engraving)

BENJAMIN FRANKLIN.

Né a Boston dans la nouvelle Angleterre le 17 Janvier 1706.

267. A. St. Aubin, after Cochin. Portrait of Franklin (engraving)

266. Hogarth. Portrait of Lord Lovat (etching)

268. G. St. Aubin. Académie Particulière

269. Chodowiecki. Cabinet d'un Peintre (engraving)

270. Choffard. The Shop of Basan (engraving)

271. Aveline, after Watteau. The Shop of Gersaint (engraving)

272. Gaucher, after Moreau. The Crowning of the Bust of Voltaire (engraving)

273. Berthault, after Fragonard *fils*. Revolutionary Committee under the Terror (engraving)

274. Vue d'Optique. View of Lammerk

275. Revere. Boston Massacre (engraving)

276. Bibiena. Galeria Reale

277. Piranesi. The Baths of Titus (etching)

278. Piranesi. Via del Corso (etching)

279. Piranesi. Carcere (etching)

280. Canaletto. The Prison (etching)

281. Canaletto. The Terrace (etching)

282. G. B. Tiepolo. Caprice (etching)

283. D. Tiepolo. Flight into Egypt (etching)

287. Monnoyer. Flowers (engraving)

285. Chrétien. Portrait (engraving)

286. St. Memin. Portrait of Jefferson
(engraving)

Desk & Bookcase

284. Chippendale. Furniture Design
(engraving)

289. Janinet after Hoin. Mme. Dugazon in the Role of Nina

288. Moreau-le-Jeune. The Fair of Gonesse

290. Jukes, after Rowlandson. Vauxhall (aquatint)

291. Debucourt. Promenade Publique (aquatint in color)

291a. Le Mire after Gravelot.
Illustration to Corneille

291b. de Longeuil after Eisen.
Illustration to La Fontaine

291c. Daullé after Pesne. Portrait of Jean Mariette

291d. Bartsch. Self Portrait

LA LIBERTÉ

293. Copia, after Prud'hon, La Liberté (engraving)

292. Sergent-Marceau. Les Peuples Parcourant les Rues

295. Smith, after Reynolds. Mrs. Carnac (mezzotint)

294. Turner, after Hoppner. Viscount Nelson (mezzotint)

297. Doughty, after Reynolds. Dr. Johnson (mezzotint)

296. Meyer, after Romney. Lady Hamilton (mezzotint)

299. Bartolozzi, after Cosway. Mrs. Abington (stipple engraving)

298. Earlom, after Huysum. Fruit Piece

299a. Constable. Milford Bridge

299b. Gainsborough. Landscape

300. Turner. Source of the Arvernon

301. Lucas, after Constable. Summer Evening (mezzotint)

302. Pugin and Rowlandson. Christie's Auction Rooms

303. Rowlandson. Sign of the Four Alls (etching)

304. Rowlandson. Ballad Singers (etching)

305. Rowlandson. The Bottom of Mr. Figgs' "Whiskey" Broke Through

306. Reeve, after Newhouse. False Alarm on the Road to Gretna Green (aquatint)

307. Reeve, after Hodges. Hare Hunting (aquatint)

308. Langlois, after Redouté. Rose

309. Havell, after Audubon. Trail's Flycatcher

310. Currier, after Palmer. Clipper Ship "Contest" (lithograph)

311. Goya. Porque Fue Sensible
(aquatint)

312. Goya. Subir y Balar (aquatint)

313. Goya. Flying Men (aquatint)

314. Goya. Bravo Torro (lithograph)

315. Goya. Disparate de Bestia (aquatint)

316. Goya. Gracias à La Almorta (aquatint)

317. Goya. Y no hay Remedio (aquatint)

318. Raffet. Revue Nocturne (lithograph)

319. Goya. Estragos de la Guerra (aquatint)

321. Boilly. Portrait of Susemihl (lithograph)

320. Quaglio. Portrait of Senefelder (lithograph)

323. Delacroix. La Soeur de Dugesclin (lithograph)

322. Delacroix. Faust (lithograph)

324. Kriehuber. Une Matinée chez Liszt (lithograph)

325. Géricault. Boxers (lithograph)

326. Denon. Denon Drawing a Portrait (lithograph)

327. C. Vernet. Delpech's Printing Shop (lithograph)

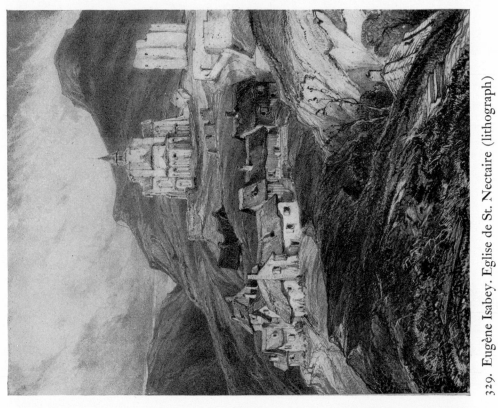

329. Eugène Isabey. Eglise de St. Nectaire (lithograph)

328. Bonington. Tour du Gros Horloge (lithograph)

330. Boys. Hôtel de Cluny (lithograph in color)

331. Bonnard. Paris Night (lithograph in color)

332. Daumier. Ventre Législatif (lithograph)

333. Daumier. Rue Transnonain (lithograph)

334. Daumier. Croquis d'Eté (lithograph)

335. Daumier. Cab Shortage at the Exposition

337. Daumier. Les Témoins (lithograph)

336. Daumier. European Equilibrium (lithograph)

339. Daumier. Mlle Constitutionelle (lithograph)

338. Daumier. Steps of the Palace of Justice (lithograph)

341. Meryon. Stryge (etching)

340. Meryon. The Morgue (etching)

343. Ensor. Cathedral (etching)

342. Legros. Mort de Vagabond (etching)

345. Blake. Tyger, Tyger (relief etching)

344. Blake. The Morning Stars (engraving)

345d. Blake. Union of the Soul with God

345a. Blake. Storm-Blasted Tree

345b. Blake. Sabrina's Flood

345c. Calvert. Chamber Idyll

347. Redon. L'Aile (lithograph)

346. Bresdin. Comédie de la Mort (lithograph)

348a. Gavarni. A Montmartre

348. Delacroix. The Blacksmith (aquatint)

350. Buhot. Débarquement en Angleterre
(etching)

349. Whistler. Limeburner (etching)

351. Palmer. The Sleeping Shepherd (etching)

350a. Palmer. Opening the Fold

350b. Legros. The Pit and the Pendulum

352. Whistler. Nocturne (lithograph)

353. Whistler. Nocturne (etching)

354. Haden. Egham Lock (etching)

355. Jongkind. Porte d'Honfleur (etching)

357. Manet. Le Printemps (etching)

356. Cassatt. Femme se Coiffant (aquatint in color)

359. Whistler. Annie Haden (drypoint)

358. Degas. Au Louvre (aquatint)

360. Millet. The Diggers (etching)

361. Corot. Paysage Normande (etching)

362. Jacque. Pastoral (etching)

363. Pissarro. The Goose Girl (etching)

365. Lautrec. Portrait of Yvette Guilbert (lithograph)

364. Goya. Self-Portrait (etching and aquatint)

367. Bracquemond. Portrait of Meryon (etching)

366. Van Gogh. Portrait of Dr. Gachet (etching)

369. Lautrec. Etude de Femme (lithograph)

368. Degas. Sortie de Bain (etching)

371. Chassériau. Venus Anadyomène (lithograph)

370. Renoir. Bather (lithograph in color)

372. Cézanne. Bathers (lithograph in color)

373. Gauguin. Mahna No Varua Ino (wood engraving)

374. Ingres. Odalisque (lithograph)

375. Manet. Olympia (etching)

379. Lautrec. Jane Avril (lithograph)

378. Degas. Mlle Bécat aux Ambassadeurs (lithograph)

381. Steinlen. Lait Stérilisé (lithograph poster)

380. Lautrec. Jockey (lithograph)

383. Fantin. Siegfried and the Rhine Maidens (lithograph)

382. Zorn. The Waltz (etching)

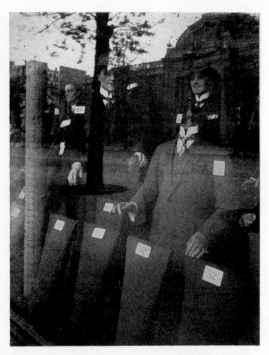

384. Hill. Mrs. Jameson (photograph)

385. Atget. Avenue des Gobelins
     (photograph)

386. Stieglitz. The Hand of Man (photograph)

387. Dix. Dance of Death

388. Gag. Stone Crusher

389. Baker. Religion

390. Handforth. Lili

391. Bacon. Patroness

392. Forain. Témoins à l'Audience

394. Lepère. July in Picardie

396. Bauer. The Visit

393. Young. Tewa

395. Segonzac. Cure de Soleil

397. Bone. Ballantrae Road

398. McBey. Dawn

399. Arms. La Colegiata, Toro

400. Cameron. Doge's Palace

401. Sickert. Gaité, Montparnasse

402. Benson. Mallards at Evening

403. Bone. Spanish Good Friday

404. Griggs. The Almonry

406. Ganso. Nude at Mirror

405. Brockhurst. Adolescence

408. Siporin. Fisher Folk

407. Cook. Mexican Interior

410. Bone. Ship Building

409. Pennell. Pedro Miguel Lock, Panama

412. Cook. Lower Manhattan

411. Marin. Woolworth Building

413. Wickey. Bathers

414. Sloan. Woman's Page

415. Kent. Pinnacle

416. Soyer. Back Stage

417. Bellows. A Stag at Sharkey's

418. Davies. Nocturne   419. Shannon. Bathers

420. Soyer. The Mission

415. Kent. Pinnacle

416. Soyer. Back Stage

417. Bellows. A Stag at Sharkey's

418. Davies. Nocturne

419. Shannon. Bathers

420. Soyer. The Mission

421. Pascin. Cinderella

422. Dwight. Queer Fish

423. Gág. Lamplight

424. Benton. Going West

425. Hopper. American Landscape

426. Dehn. Garden of the Gods

427. Becker. Drummer

428. Covarrubias. Lindy Hop

429. Stuart Davis. Barbershop Chord

430. Barlach. Judgment Day

431. Schanker. St. George

432. Hecht. Mont Saint Michel

433. Signac. Bords de la Seine

434. Twohv. Indian Village

436. Hermes. Through the Windscreen

437. Marin. Downtown New York

438. Spruance. Road from the Shore

439. Spencer. Roof Tops

440. Gropper. For the Record

441. Bettelheim. Assembly Line

442. Sternberg. Coal Miner and Wife

443. Huntley. Coke

444. Sternberg. Dance of the Machine

445. Lozowick. Tanks

447. Kollwitz. Beggars

446. Grosz. Street Scene

449. Kollwitz. The Strike

451. Jules. Nightmare

448. Gropper. The Judge

450. Dehn. All for a Piece of Meat

452. Dix. Airplane Raid

453. Nevinson. Airplane

454. Gorelick. Bombing

455. Grosz. The Robbers

456. Kollwitz. Killed in Action

457. White. Cave, Saipan

458. Kollwitz. Woman between Life and Death

459. Castellon. Rendezvous in a Landscape

460. Rouault. By the Sea

461. Spruance. Fathers and Sons

462. Orozco. Mouths

466. Rouault. "Love Ye One Another"

465. Rouault. The Beggar

468. Kahn. Judith on her Way to Holophernes

467. Munch. The Cry

470. Kokoschka. The Resurrection

471. Munch. The Kiss

469. Beckmann. The Curtain Rises

472. Velonis. Decoration: Empire

473. Pytlak. Rockport

474. Morley. Execution

475. Gwathmey. End of Day

476. Lasansky. Self Portrait

477. Siqueiros. Head of Woman

478. Orozco. Requiem

479. Mendez. Dream of the Poor

480. Posada. Calavera Huertista

481. Rivera. Fruits of Labor

482. Charlot. First Steps

483. Matisse. Liseuse

484. Derain. Head

485. Kuniyoshi. Café

486. Matisse. La
Persanne

487. Picasso. Repas Frugal

88. Picasso. Pierrot et Harlequin

489. Miró. The Singers

490. Masson. Génie du Blé

491. Dali. Illustration to *Chants de Maldoror*

492. Chirico. Figure

493. Klee. L'Homme Approximatif

94. Chagall. Grandfather's House

495. Chagall. Jacob's Dream

496. Picasso. Minotauromachia

498. Landacre. Counterpoint

497. Hermes. Adam and Eve

501. Hayter. Pavane

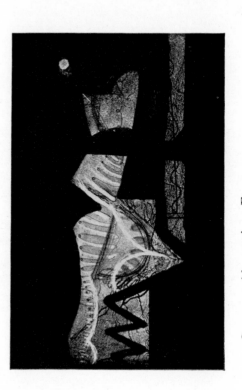

499. Braque. Abstraction

500. Stamper. Abstraction: Energy

503. Wu Tao Tzŭ. Tortoise and Serpent

502. Chinese School. Five Omens of the Frog Pool

506. Chinese School. Buddha

505. Chinese School. Maitreya

504. Kuan Hsiu. Lohan

507. Ten-Bamboo Studio. Persimmon and Oranges

508. Chinese School. Scenes in a Spiral

509. Mustard-Seed-Garden Manual. Squirrel-shrew and Grapes

510. Teng K'uei. Birds in Rain

511. Kwaigetsudō. Oiran

512. Kiyomasu I. Hanjurō
in Woman's Role

513. Masanobu. Kyōto: The Song

514. Kiyonobu I. Takesaburō and Danjurō in the Chūshingura

515. Shigenaga. Women with Camelias

516. Kiyomitsu. Daimyo Procession Game

519. Kiyomitsu. Ichimatsu as Osono in the Chūshin-gura

518. Kiyohiro. Fisherman with Attendants

517. Masanobu. Hanshozuku Bijin Soroi

522. Masanobu. Self Portrait

521. Toyonobu. Oiran in Night Attire

520. Masanobu. Shōki, the Demon Queller

524. Harunobu. Girl with Lantern

523. Harunobu. Girl Watching Frogs

526. Harunobu. Girl Parting with her Lover

525. Harunobu. Girls Playing Cat's Cradle

528. Kiyonaga. Iris Pond

527. Kiyonaga. In a Public Bath House

530. Utamaro. Yamauba and Kintoki

529. Utamaro. Head of Woman

531. Kiyonaga. Terrace by the Sea

532. Yeishi. Fête in Nobleman's Palace

533. Utamaro. Watching Awabi Divers at Enoshima

534. Utamaro. Four Beauties Enacting Oxcart Scene

537. Bunchō. Fox Dance

536. Shunyei. Wrestler

535. Shunsho. Nakamura
Sukegorō as a Samurai

539. Sharaku. Matsumoto Koshirō as Gorobei

538. Sharaku. Ichikawa Ebizō as Kwandayū

540. Kiyomasu. Golden Pheasant

541. Kuniyoshi. Cat and Goldfish

542. Chōki. Catching Fireflies

543. Shunman. Surimono

544. Hiroshige. Fuji from Ichikoku
Bridge

545. Hokusai. Acrobats from *Mangwa*

546. Hokusai. The Wave

549. Yeishi. Ladies and Child at Seashore

547. Hokusai. Iris

548. Toyoharu. Yoshitsune Serenading Joruri Hime

551. Hiroshige. Catching Fireflies

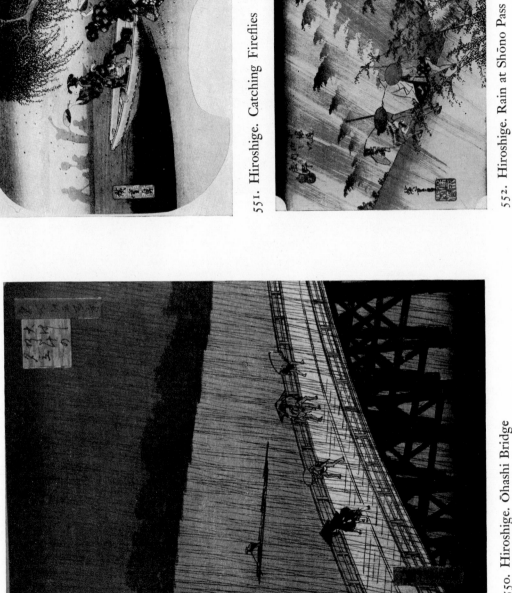

552. Hiroshige. Rain at Shōno Pass

550. Hiroshige. Ōhashi Bridge

553. Koryūsai.
Bather

554. Kiyonaga.
Woman
Smoothing
Eyebrows

555. Shunshō. Woman in
Red

INDEX OF PLATES

INDEX OF PLATES

Dimensions are given in inches, height coming first. Titles of books are given in italics. Some anonymous illustrations are listed under the book title.

Callot, Jacques, The Marauders, etching from the Disasters of War, 1632, 2⅞ x 7⅜, Meaume 571. Philadelphia Museum of Art. 210
———, Pillage of a House, etching from the Disasters of War, 1632, 2⅞ x 7⅜, Meaume 568. Philadelphia Museum of Art. 211
———, Beggar with Head and Feet Bare, etching, ca. 1624, 5⅜ x 3⅜, Meaume 696. Private Collection. 208
Calvert, Edward. English School (1799-1883). Chamber Idyll, wood-engraving, 1831, 1⅞ x 3, Finberg 10. Metropolitan Museum of Art. 345c
———, The Return, wood-engraving, 1830, 1⅞ x 3, Finberg 9. Metropolitan Museum of Art. 75
Cameron, D. Y. British School (1865-1945). Doge's Palace, etching and drypoint, 1902, 10 x 15, Rinder 326. Knoedler Gallery, New York. 400
Campagnola, Giulio. Italian School (1482-after 1513). Christ and the Woman of Samaria, engraving, 5⅛ x 7¼, Bartsch 2. Knoedler Gallery, New York. 160
———, St. John the Baptist, engraving, 13⅜ x 9¼, Bartsch 3. National Gallery of Art, Rosenwald Collection. 137a
Canaletto, Antonio Canale, called. Italian School (1697-1768). The Prison, etching, ca. 1741, 5½ x 8¼, De Vesme 18. Metropolitan Museum of Art. 280
———, The Terrace, etching, ca. 1741, 5½ x 8¼, De Vesme 21, first state. Private Collection. 281
Cantarini, Simone. Italian School (1612-1648). Rest on the Flight to Egypt, etching, 8¼ x 6¾, Bartsch 3. Weyhe Gallery, New York. 223
Canticum Canticorum. Netherlands School (Fifteenth Century). Woodcut from Block Book, ca. 1465, 5 x 6⅝. Morgan Library, New York 29
Carracci, Agostino. Italian School (1557-1602). Portrait of Titian, engraving, 1587, 12¼ x 9⅛, Bartsch 154. National Gallery of Art, Rosenwald Collection. 153
Carmontelle, Louis. French School (1717-1806). The Mozart Family, engraving by Delafosse, 1764. Knoedler Gallery, New York. 260
Carpi, Ugo da. Italian School (1450-after 1525). *See* Raphael and Parmigiano.
Cars, Laurent. French School (1699-1771). *See* Watteau, Lemoyne, and Boucher.
Cassatt, Mary. American School (1845-1926). Femme se Coiffant, aquatint in color, 1891, 14¼ x 10¼. Metropolitan Museum of Art. 356

Castellon, Federico. American School (b. 1914). Rendezvous in a Landscape, lithograph in two tones, 1938, 9⅝ x 15⅛, Philadelphia Museum of Art. 459
Cézanne, Paul. French School (1839-1906). Bathers, color lithograph, 1898, 16¼ x 20, Philadelphia Museum of Art. 372
Chagall, Marc. Russian School (b. 1889). Grandfather's House, drypoint, 1923, 8⅛ x 6¼, from the set of twenty *Mein Leben.* Private Collection. 494
———, Jacob's Dream, etching, 1931-9, 11⅞ x 9⅝, from the unpublished illustrations to the Old Testament. Collection of the artist, courtesy of the Museum of Modern Art. 495

Chapbook. English School, Eighteenth century. Robinson Crusoe, woodcut based on the engraved frontispiece to the first edition, 5⅛ x 3. From *Bliss' History of Wood-engraving.* 68
Chardin, Jean Baptiste. French School (1699-1779). Le Négligé, engraving by Le Bas, 1741, 12⅞ x 9⅞, Bocher 38. Philadelphia Museum of Art. 250
———, La Gouvernante, engraving by Lépicié, 1739, 12⅞ x 10⅛, Bocher 24. Philadelphia Museum of Art. 251
Charlot, Jean. American-Mexican School (b. 1898). First Steps, lithograph, 1936, 13¾ x 9. Philadelphia Museum of Art. 482
Chassériau, Théodore. French School (1819-1856). Venus Anadyomène, lithograph, 1839, 11⅛ x 8⅞, National Gallery of Art, Rosenwald Collection. 371
Chevalier Delibéré. Dutch School. Knight and Death, woodcut, Gouda, 1488, 7⅞ x 5⅜. Kupferstichkabinett, Berlin. 23
Chia Li. Chinese School. Bamboo, stone rubbing, K'ang Hsi period 1661-1723, 104½ x 16½, Philadelphia Museum of Art. 113a
Chinese School. Han Dynasty. The Ho Huan Tree, stone rubbing from the Family Tomb of Wu at Chia Hsiang, Shantung, dated A.D. 147, 18¼ x 17¾. Philadelphia Museum of Art. 111
———, Han Dynasty. Five Omens of the Frog Pool, stone rubbing from the so-called Li Hsi Tablet at Ch'ên-hsien in Kan-su, dated A.D. 171. From *Ferguson's Outlines of Chinese Art.* 502
———, Wei Dynasty (386-535), Buddha under the Bodhi Tree, from the Caves of Yün Kang in Shansi, stone rubbing, 53⅜ x 26. Philadelphia Museum of Art. 506
———, Wei Dynasty. Maitreya in Meditation, stone rubbing from relief at Lung Mên

grotto, dated A.D. 542. From *Ferguson's Outlines of Chinese Art.* 505

——, Wei Dynasty. Procession, stone rubbing from a Buddhist stele, A.D. 524, 9 x 24, now in the University Museum, Philadelphia. 105

——, Five Dynasties (907-960). Manju-sri, woodcut, ca. 950, 6⅛ x 7⅞, British Museum. 108

——, Five Dynasties (907-960). Buddhist Image, woodcut, printed by stamping, 2 x 1½. British Museum. 106

——, Early Ming Dynasty. Scenes in a Spiral, woodcut from a *Shu I Chi* or Record of Marvels, ca. 1375, 11 x 11⅛, the red and yellow colors probably added through stencils. Philadelphia Museum of Art. 508

——, Ming Dynasty, reign of Hung Wu (1368-1393). Kuan Yin, woodcut from the series, *P'u-sa Hsiang-tu,* Boddhisattva Images, 10¾ x 8½. Philadelphia Museum of Art. 114

——, Ming Dynasty. Playing Card, woodcut, ca. 1400, found near Turfan, 3 x 1. From *Carter's Invention of Printing in China.* 109

——, Ming Dynasty. Portrait of Confucius, stone rubbing, based on a T'ang design, 13 x 10. Private Collection. 112

——, Ch'ing Dynasty. Blossoming Plum Tree, stone rubbing, 1848, from Pei Lin (Tablet Grove) Sianfu, 66 x 25. Philadelphia Museum of Art. 113b

Chippendale, Thomas. English School (1709-1779). Design for Desk and Book Case, 1753, plate 84 of *Gentleman and Cabinetmaker's Director,* London 1755 (second edition), engraving by M. Darly, 12¼ x 6½. Philadelphia Museum of Art. 284

Chirico, Giorgio de. Italian School (b. 1888). Figure, lithograph, ca. 1925, 16¼ x 12⅛. Philadelphia Museum of Art. 492

Chodowiecki, Daniel. Polish-German School (1726-1801). Cabinet d'un Peintre, engraving, 1771, 6⅛ x 8¼, Engelmann 75. Philadelphia Museum of Art. 269

Choffard, Pierre Philippe. French School (1730-1809). The Shop of Basan, engraving, ca. 1799, 2½ x 5, Portalis and Beraldi 626. Bibliothèque Nationale, Paris. 270

Chōki, Yeishōsai. Japanese School (fl. 1785-1805). Lady and Child Catching Fireflies, polychrome woodcut, mica background, Ōban. Metropolitan Museum of Art. 542

Chrétien, Gilles Louis. French School (1754-1811). Portrait, engraving with physionotrace. Private Collection. 285

Ch'ung Huan. Chinese School. The Water-

fall, woodcut from *Album of Famous Paintings* edited by Wang Fou Tsao, reign of Ch'ien Lung (1736-1795). 10½ x 7. Philadelphia Museum of Art. 114a

Cochin, Charles Nicolas. French School (1715-1790). Portrait of Franklin, engraving by A. de St. Aubin, 1777, 8 x 5¾. Philadelphia Museum of Art. 267

Constable, John. English School (1776-1837). Milford Bridge near Salisbury, etching, ca. 1829, 4½ x 7. Philadelphia Museum of Art. 299a

——, Summer Evening, mezzotint by David Lucas, 1833, 6⅞ x 9⅞, Shirley 6, trial proof. Philadelphia Museum of Art. 301

Contrasto di Carnevale. Italian School. The Fish-shop, woodcut, Florence, ca. 1500, 2⅞ x 4, Kristeller 85. From *Kristeller's Florentine Woodcuts.* 11

Cook, Howard. American School (b. 1901). Lower Manhattan, lithograph, 1930, 14¼ x 10. Philadelphia Museum of Art. 412

——, Mexican Interior, etching, 1933, 16 x 10⅝. Philadelphia Museum of Art. 407

Copia, Jacques Louis. French School (1764-1799). *See* Prud'hon.

Coptic School. Sixth Century. Textile Design of Birds, woodcut. From *Gusman's Gravure sur Bois.* 107

Corot, Jean Baptiste Camille. French School (1796-1875). Paysage Normande, etching, 1869, 4¾ x 7½, Delteil 9. Philadelphia Museum of Art. 361

Cosway, Richard. English School (1742-1821). Mrs. Abington, stipple engraving by Bartolozzi, 1783. Metropolitan Museum of Art. 299

Courbet, Gustave. French School (1819-1877). The Apostle Jean Journet Setting Out for the Conquest of Universal Harmony, lithograph, 9½ x 6¾. Private Collection. 377

Cousin, Jean. French School (1490-1560). The Entombment, engraving, ca. 1540, 6¾ x 11½. Bibliothèque Nationale, Paris. 159

Covarrubias, Miguel. Mexican School (b. 1904). Lindy Hop, lithograph, 1936, 12⅞ x 9½. Philadelphia Museum of Art. 428

Cranach, Lucas. German School (1472-1553). Portrait of Luther, engraving, 1521, 8⅛ x 5⅞, Bartsch 6, Knoedler Gallery, New York. 152

——, St. Christopher, chiaroscuro woodcut, 1509 (instead of 1506), 11⅛ x 7⅞, Bartsch 58. National Gallery of Art, Rosenwald Collection. 170

——, Venus, woodcut, 1509 (instead of 1506), 10⅞ x 7½, Bartsch 113. Private Collection.

44

ing by Bonifaccio, from the book, *Rome 1589*, 14¾ x 9. Private Collection. 178

Forain, Jean Louis. French School (1852-1931). Témoins à l'Audience, etching, Guerin 33. Knoedler Gallery, New York. 392

Forestis, De Claris Mulieribus. Italian School. Portrait of Paula Gonzaga, woodcut, Ferrara, 1497, 2¼ x 2⅝. Library of Congress, Rosenwald Collection. 9

Fragonard, Jean Honoré. French School (1732-1806). Bacchanal, etching, 1763, 5¼ x 7⅜, Baudicour 6. National Gallery of Art, Rosenwald Collection. 240

——, The Happy Accidents of the Swing, engraving by N. Delaunay, ca. 1768, 20¼ x 16¾. Knoedler Gallery, New York. 246

Fragonard *fils*, Alexandre Evariste. French School (1780-1850). Revolutionary Committee under the Terror, engraving by Berthault, from *Tableaux Historiques de la Revolution Française*, Paris, Didot, 1802, 7⅜ x 9⅞. Private Collection. 273

French School. Fifteenth Century. The Nativity, woodcut, hand colored. Metropolitan Museum of Art. 133

——, *Paul and Virginia*, Curmer, 1838. 81

Gafurius, De Re Musica. Italian School. The Organist, woodcut, Milan 1492, 7⅞ x 4. Library of Congress, Rosenwald Collection, edition of 1518. 13

Gág, Wanda. American School (1893-1946). Lamplight, lithograph, 1929, 10¾ x 8⅜. Philadelphia Museum of Art. 423

——, Cats at Window, wood engraving, 1930, 2⅞ x 3¾. Philadelphia Museum of Art. 91

——, Stone Crusher, lithograph, 1929, 14⅜ x 11⅜. Philadelphia Museum of Art. 388

Gainsborough, Thomas. English School (1727-1788). Landscape, soft ground etching and aquatint, ca. 1760, 11 x 13½, Woodall 12. Private Collection. 299b

Galanis, Demetrios. French-Greek School (b. 1882). Still Life, wood-engraving, ca. 1926. Weyhe Gallery, New York. 90

Ganso, Emil. American School (1895-1941). Nude at Mirror, etching and aquatint, 1930, 12 x 7⅞. Weyhe Gallery, New York. 406

Gaucher, Charles Étienne. French School (1740-1804). See Moreau.

Gauguin, Paul. French School (1848-1903). Mahna no Varua Ino, wood-engraving, ca. 1894, 8 x 13⅞. Philadelphia Museum of Art. 373

Gavarni, Guillaume Sulpice Chevalier, called. French School (1804-1866). A Montmartre,

lithograph from the Series *Les Lorettes*, 1842, 6⅞ x 6⅛. Private Collection. 348a

——, Portrait of the De Goncourt Brothers, lithograph, 1853, 7⅝ x 6⅜, Museum of Fine Arts, Boston. 376

Gelée, Claude, called Lorrain. French School (1600-1682). Dance by the Waterside, etching, ca. 1636, 5 x 7⅝, Blum 19. Philadelphia Museum of Art. 205

——, Rape of Europa, etching, 1634, 7⅝ x 9⅝, Blum 9. Philadelphia Museum of Art. 203

Géricault, Théodore. French School (1791-1824). Boxers, lithograph, 1818, 13⅞ x 16⅜, Delteil 10. Metropolitan Museum of Art. 325

German School. Fifteenth Century. Madonna and Child with Three Saints, woodcut, ca. 1420-1430, 3⅜ x 5¼, Schreiber 1172. National Gallery of Art, Rosenwald Collection. 133a

——, Fifteenth Century. Gossip during Mass, metal engraving, dotted print, ca. 1490, 14⅝ x 10¼, Schreiber 2761. Cincinnati Art Museum. 18

——, St. Christopher, woodcut, 1423, 11 x 8⅛. Rylands Library, Manchester. 19

——, St. Onuphrius, colored woodcut, second half of fifteenth century, 5¾ x 4½. Metropolitan Museum of Art. 132

Gill, Eric. English School (1882-1940). Nowell, wood-engraving, 1916, 2⅛ x 2⅛, Cleverdon 49. Private Collection. 85

Goltzius, Hendrik. Flemish School (1558-1617). Farnese Hercules, engraving, 16 x 11½, Dutuit 143. Metropolitan Museum of Art. 219

——, Portrait of Henri IV, engraving, 12⅜ x 9¾, Dutuit 173. Knoedler Gallery. New York. 236

——, Landscape, woodcut, 7 x 9¾, Dutuit 241. Metropolitan Museum of Art. 65

Gorelick, Boris. American School. Bombing, lithograph, 1939, 11 x 14½, N. Y. Art Project. Philadelphia Museum of Art. 454

Goudt, Hendrik de. Dutch School (1585-1630). See Elsheimer.

Goya, Francisco. Spanish School (1746-1828). Self Portrait, from the series of *Caprices*, etching and aquatint, 1797, 5⅜ x 4⅜, Delteil 38. Metropolitan Museum of Art. 364

——, Porque fue Sensible, Because She Was Sensitive, aquatint, from the *Caprices*, 1797, 7 x 4⅜, Delteil 69. Metropolitan Museum of Art. 311

——, Subir y Bajar, To Rise and Fall, aquatint from the *Caprices*, 1797, 7⅜ x 5⅛, Delteil 93. Metropolitan Museum of Art. 312

486

Hiroshige, Andō, Catching Fireflies at the Ugi River, near Kyōto, from the series *Shokuko Meisho, Views of Various Provinces*, polychrome woodcut, 8¾ x 11½, Uehiwa-ye fan print, Publisher Dansendō. Philadelphia Museum of Art. 551

——, Ōhashi Atake, Storm on the Great Bridge, No. 52 of *Meisho Yedo Hyakkei*, Hundred Views of Yedo, polychrome woodcut, 1857, 14½ x 9⅜, British Museum Catalogue 436, Philadelphia Museum of Art. 550

——, Fuji from Ichikoku Bridge, from the *Thirty-six Views of Fuji*, polychrome woodcut, 1858, 13¼ x 8⅜, British Museum Catalogue 511. Metropolitan Museum of Art. 544

Hirschvogel, Augustin. German School (1503-1553?). Landscape, etching, 1526, 5⅜ x 8¼, Bartsch 74. National Gallery of Art, Rosenwald Collection. 155

Historie van Trojen. Dutch School. Sir Hercules fighting Three Lions, woodcut, Haarlem 1485, 5½ x 4½. From *Bliss' History of Wood-engraving.* 30

Hodges, W. P. English School (fl. early 19th century). Hare Hunting, aquatint in colors by Reeve, 1836. Knoedler Gallery, New York. 307

Hogarth, William. English School (1697-1764). Laughing Audience, engraving, 1733, 6⅞ x 7⅛, Dobson, p. 239. Philadelphia Museum of Art. 262

——, The Enraged Musician, engraving, 1741, 13⅛ x 15¾, Dobson, p. 245. Philadelphia Museum of Art. 259

——, Marriage à la Mode, Plate II, engraving by Baron, 1745, 13⅞ x 17¼, Dobson, p. 246. Philadelphia Museum of Art. 258

——, Portrait of Lord Lovat, etching, 1746, 13⅛ x 8¾, Dobson, p. 248. Philadelphia Museum of Art. 266

Hokusai Katsushika. Japanese School (1760-1849). The Wave, polychrome woodcut from *The Thirty-six Views of Fuji*, 1823-1829, 9¾ x 14½, British Museum Catalogue 127. Metropolitan Museum of Art. 546

——, Iris, polychrome woodcut, ca. 1830, 10 x 15⅛. Metropolitan Museum of Art. 547

——, Acrobats, woodcut from *Mangwa*, Vol. X, 1819, 6¾ x 4⅞, Philadelphia Museum of Art. 545

Holbein, Hans. German School (1497?-1543). Death and the Ploughman, woodcut from the *Dance of Death*, Lyon 1538, 2⅞ x 2. Metropolitan Museum of Art. 31

——, Ruth and Boaz, woodcut from the *Images to the Bible*, Lyon 1538, 2½ x 3½. Metropolitan Museum of Art. 32

Holgate, Edwin. Canadian School (b. 1892). Bather, wood-engraving, ca. 1931, 8½ x 8⅜. Private Collection. 97a

Hollar, Wenzel. Bohemian School (1607-1677). Winter, etching, 1643, 9⅞ x 7¼, Parthey 609. Knoedler Gallery, New York. 220

Homer, Winslow. American School (1836-1910). The Dinner Horn, wood-engraving after his drawing, from Harper's Weekly, 1870, 13¾ x 9. Private Collection. 76

Hopfer, Daniel. German School (c. 1470-1536). Broadsheet against Hoarding, etching, ca. 1525, 7⅞ x 10¾, Bartsch 23. Private Collection. 157

Hopper, Edward. American School (b. 1882). American Landscape, etching, 1920, 7 x 12⅜. Philadelphia Museum of Art. 425

Hoppner, John. British School (1758-1810). Viscount Nelson, Mezzotint by Turner, 1805, Whitman 401. Knoedler Gallery, New York. 294

Horae B.V.M. French School. Dives and Lazarus, metal cut from *Horae*, Pigouchet, Paris 1498, 6¼ x 4¾. Metropolitan Museum of Art. 16

——, David and Bathsheba, metal cut from *Horae*, Kerver, Paris 1505, 6 x 3⅜. Private Collection. 16a

Huntley, Victoria Hutson. American School (b. 1900). Coke, lithograph, 1932, 9⅜ x 13⅜. Philadelphia Museum of Art. 443

Hypnerotomachia Poliphili. Italian School. By the Stream, woodcut, Aldus, Venice 1499, 4⅛ x 5⅛. Library of Congress, Rosenwald Collection. 4

Image Populaire. French School (late 18th century). The World Upside Down, woodcut, published by Leloup at Le Mans, 12¼ x 15¾. From *Duchartre, Imagerie Populaire.* 71

——, The Day of the Fall of the Bastille, woodcut, published by Letourmy at Orléans, ca. 1790, 16½ x 20⅞. From *Duchartre, Imagerie Populaire.* 72

Ingolds Guldin Spil. German School. Playing Cards, woodcut, G. Zainer, Augsburg 1472, 3¼ x 4½, Hain 9187. Library of Congress, Rosenwald Collection. 6

Ingres, Jean Dominique. French School (1780-1867). Odalisque, lithograph, 1825, 5⅛ x 8¼. Private Collection. 374

Isabey, Eugène. French School (1803-1886). Eglise de St. Nectaire, lithograph, 1831,

11 x 9, Beraldi 16. Philadelphia Museum of Art. 329

Italian School. Fifteenth Century. Primum Mobile, No. 49 of the "E" series of so-called Tarocchi Cards, engraving, ca. 1465, 6⅛ x 3¾. Kupferstichkabinett, Berlin. 121

Jacque, Charles. French School (1813-1894). Pastorale, etching, 1864, 3⅞ x 6⅛, Guiffrey 180. Museum of Fine Arts, Boston. 362

Jacquinet, C. French School (fl. middle of 17th century). Gunsmith's Shop, engraving from *Plusieurs Models . . . d'Arquebuzerie,* Paris 1660, 4⅞ x 5, Berlin Catalogue 821. Private Collection. 232

Janinet, François. French School (1752-1813). Mme. Dugazon in the Role of Nina, mixed engraving printed in colors after the design by J. B. Hoin, 1787, 12½ x 9¼, Portalis et Beraldi 35, proof before letters. Hawkes Collection, Philadelphia Museum of Art. 289

Japanese School. Sixteenth Century. Horsemen with Fuji in Distance, woodcut from *Ise Monogatari,* ca. 1575. From *Kurth's Der Japanische Holzschnitt.* 114b

Jegher, Christophe. Flemish School (c. 1578-c. 1652). See Rubens.

Jongkind, Joan Barthold. Dutch School (1819-1891). Sortie du Port d'Honfleur, etching, 1864, 8⅛ x 11⅞, Delteil 11. Metropolitan Museum of Art. 355

Jukes, Francis. English School (1746-1812). See Rowlandson.

Jules, Mervin. American School (b. 1912). Nightmare, lithograph, ca. 1940, 7⅞ x 9⅞. Philadelphia Museum of Art. 451

Kahn, Max. American School (b. 1903). Judith on her Way to the Tent of Holophernes, color lithograph, 1934, 24⅛ x 15⅞. Philadelphia Museum of Art. 468

Kanō Tanyu. Japanese School (1602-1674). Chinese Sage, woodcut from *Gwa-ko senran.* From *Anderson's Japanese Wood Engravings.* 114c

Kent, Rockwell. American School (b. 1882). Pinnacle, lithograph, 1928, 11¾ x 7¼. Philadelphia Museum of Art. 415

———, Twilight of Man, wood-engraving, 1926, 5½ x 7⅞. Philadelphia Museum of Art. 89

Ketham, Fasciculus Medicinae. Italian School. The Plague, woodcut, Venice 1493, 11¾ x 7¾. Library of Congress, Rosenwald Collection. 14

Kiyohiro Torii. Japanese School (1708-1776). Fisherman with Attendants, two-color woodcut, beni-ye, ca. 1750-1760, Ōban 17 x 12⅛, Publisher Maruya. Poem reads: "Birds singing give more power to the arms carrying basket." Philadelphia Museum of Art. 518

Kiyomasu I Torii. Japanese School (1694?-1716?). Fujimura Hanjurō in Woman's Role, hand colored woodcut, ca. 1715, hoso-ye 13 x 6. Philadelphia Museum of Art. 512

Kiyomasu II Torii. Japanese School (1702-1752). Golden Pheasant on Pine Branch, hand colored woodcut, urushi-ye, ca. 1720-1729, hoso-ye, 12⅞ x 6¼. Philadelphia Museum of Art. 540

Kiyomitsu Torii. Japanese School (1735-1785). Sanogawa Ichimatsu I as Osono, wife of Gihei in the Chūshingura, two-color woodcut green and yellow, ca. 1750, hoso-ye 12 x 5⅛, Publisher Yamashiroya. Philadelphia Museum of Art. 519

———, Daimyo Procession Game, polychrome woodcut. Metropolitan Museum of Art. 516

Kiyonaga Torii. Japanese School (1742-1815). Iris Pond, polychrome woodcut, part of a diptych, 1785, Ōban 14⅞ x 10⅛, Hirano 705. Metropolitan Museum of Art. 528

———, Terrace by the Sea, polychrome woodcut, 1784, Ōban diptych from series *Minami Jūni Kō,* Twelve Months in the South, this is the ninth month, Hirano 631. Private Collection. 531

———, In a Public Bath House, polychrome woodcut from series *Fūzoku Azuma no Nishiki,* ca. 1785, Ōban 14¾ x 9⅝, Hirano 585. Clarence Buckingham Collection, Chicago Art Institute. 527

———, Woman Smoothing Eyebrows, polychrome woodcut, 1781, hashira-ye 28 x 5, Hirano 322. Fogg Art Museum, Cambridge, Mass. 554

Kiyonobu I Torii. Japanese School (1664-1729). Nakamura Takesaburō and Ichikawa Danjūro II in a Scene from Chūshingura, hand colored woodcut ca. 1720, 16¼ x 10¾. Philadelphia Museum of Art. 514

Klee, Paul. Swiss-German School (1879-1940). L'Homme Approximatif, etching, 1931, 6¾ x 5¼. Private Collection. 493

Kokoschka, Oskar. German-Czech School (b. 1886). The Resurrection, lithograph, 1916, 11¼ x 12¾. Buchholz Gallery, New York. 470

Kollwitz, Käthe. German School (1867-1945). The Strike, from the series *The Weavers,* etching, 1897, 8⅛ x 11¼, Sievers 32. Collection Erich Cohn. 449

———, Woman Between Life and Death, etch-

Lepère, Auguste. French School (1849-1918). July in Picardie, etching, ca. 1908, 7 x 8¾. Knoedler Gallery, New York. 394

Lepicié, Bernard. French School (1698-1755). *See Chardin.*

Le Prince, Jean Baptiste. French School (1733-1781). O Fortunatos Nimium, aquatint, 1768, Portalis and Beraldi 47. From *Courboin's La Gravure en France.* 242

Longueil, Joseph de. French School (1730-1792. *See* Eisen.

Lozowick, Louis. American School (b. 1892). Tanks, lithograph, 1929, 14 x 8. Philadelphia Museum of Art. 445

Lucas, David. English School (1802-1881). *See* Constable.

Maillol, Aristide. French School (1861-1944). The Spring, woodcut from *Virgil's Eclogues,* 1926, 3⅞ x 4⅛. Weyhe Gallery, New York. 97

Malbeste, Georges. French School (1754-1843). *See* Moreau.

Manet, Edouard. French School (1832-1883). Olympia, etching, 1865, 3⅜ x 7, Guérin 39. Metropolitan Museum of Art. 375

——, Le Printemps, etching, 1882, 6⅛ x 4¼, Guérin 66, first state. Philadelphia Museum of Art. 357

Mantegna, Andrea. Italian School (1431-1506). Virgin and Child, engraving, ca. 1470, 8⅞ x 8⅜, Bartsch 8. National Gallery of Art, Rosenwald Collection. 136a

——, Bacchanal with Winepress, engraving, ca. 1475, 13⅛ x 18¼, Bartsch 19. Knoedler Gallery, New York. 118

Mantegna School. Entombment with Four Birds, engraving, 17⅞ x 14, Bartsch 2. Metropolitan Museum of Art. 126

Marc, Franz. German School (1880-1916). Annunciation, woodcut, ca. 1910, 7⅞ x 10⅛. Private Collection. 88

Marcks, Gerhard. German School (b. 1889). Cats, woodcut, 1921, 9¼ x 15⅛, Philadelphia Museum of Art. 95

Marin, John. American School (b. 1870). Downtown New York, etching, 1921, 7 x 8¾, Benson 119. Private Collection. 437

——, Woolworth Building, etching, 1913, 12⅞ x 10½, Benson 109. Private Collection. 411

Masanobu Okumura. Japanese School (1691-1768). Shōki, the Demon Queller, woodcut, ca. 1725, Kakimono-ye 34 x 13. Philadelphia Museum of Art. 520

——, Kyōto: The Song, from the set of twelve, entitled *Ukiyo Hachi no Ki,* hand colored woodcut tan-ye, Shibui 67. Crozier Collection. 513

——, Self Portrait in guise of Chinese Magician Chōkwarō, hand colored woodcut, urushi-ye ca. 1730-1735, hoso-ye, 12½ x 6. Kurth Collection. 522

—— Hanshozuku Bijin Soroi, portraying the postess Ono no Komachi, from series *Models of Ladies' Costume,* two color woodcut beni-ye, ca. 1745, hoso-ye 12⅝ x 5¾. Philadelphia Museum of Art. 517

Masereel, Frans. Flemish School (b. 1889). The Strike, wood-engraving from the set *Passion of Man,* 1918, 5 x 4¼. Private Collection. 99

Masson, André. French School (b. 1896). Génie du Blé, etching and soft-ground, 1942, 13⅞ x 9¾, Edition Curt Valentin. Philadelphia Museum of Art. 490

Master, E. S. German School (fl. 1440-1467). Madonna and Child of Einsiedeln, engraving, 1466, 8¼ x 4⅞, Lehrs 81. Dresden Museum. 130

——, Grotesque Letter Q, engraving, 5⅞ x 4⅜, Lehrs 298. Graphische Sammlung, Munich. 143

——, Ornament, engraving, ca. 1445, 3⅞ x 5⅜, Lehrs 308, Dresden Museum. 141

Master I.A.M. of Zwole. Netherlands School (fl. c. 1485). Design for a Baldachin, ca. 1485, engraving, 16½ x 11. Berlin Kupferstichkabinett. 140

Master I.B. (Georg Pencz). German School (ca. 1500-1550). Luna, engraving, 1529, 3¼ x 2, Bartsch 17. Knoedler Gallery, New York. 174

Master L.D. (Léonard Davent or Tiry) School of Fontainebleau (fl. 1500-1550). *See* Primaticcio.

Master of the Amsterdam Cabinet. German School (fl. 1480). The Lovers, engraving and drypoint, 6½ x 4¼, Lehrs 75. Coburg Museum. 127

Master of the Playing Cards. German School (fl. 1430-after 1450). Cyclamen Queen, engraving, ca. 1440, 5⅞ x 3¾, Geisberg 55. Dresden Museum. 124

Matisse, Henri. French School (b. 1869). Nu au Fauteuil, linoleum cut, 1906, 12⅛ x 8¼. Philadelphia Museum of Art. 96a

——, La Persanne, etching, 1914, 6¼ x 2⅜. Metropolitan Museum of Art. 486

——, Liseuse, lithograph, 1925, 6⅜ x 9⅝. Private Collection. 483

McBey, James. American-British School (b. 1883). Dawn, Camel Patrol, etching, 1919, 9 x 15, Hardie 181. National Gallery of Art, Rosenwald Collection. 398

Meckenem, Israhel van. German School (c. 1447-1503). Portrait of Self and Wife, engraving, 4⅞ x 6¾, Bartsch 1. National Gallery of Art, Rosenwald Collection. 134
———, Birth of the Virgin, engraving, 10¼ x 7¼, Bartsch 31. National Gallery of Art, Rosenwald Collection. 129
de'Medici, Nencia de Barberino. Italian School. The Gift, woodcut, Florence ca. 1500, 4¼ x 3½, Kristeller 282. Metropolitan Museum of Art. 48
Meister der Weibermacht. German School (fl. middle of 15th century). Satire on the Power of Women, ca. 1450, engraving, 5⅛ x 7⅞, Geisberg 44. Munich Library. 137
Mellan, Claude. French School (1598-1688). Portrait of Peiresc, engraving, 1657, 8⅜ x 5⅜. Museum of Fine Arts, Boston. 202
Mendez, Leopoldo, Mexican School (b. 1893). Dream of the Poor, wood-engraving, ca. 1936, 4⅞ x 4¾. Philadelphia Museum of Art. 479
Menzel, Adolph von, German School (1815-1905). Voltaire and Frederick, wood-engraving from Die Geschichte Friedrichs des Grossen, Berlin 1840, 5½ x 3⅞. Metropolitan Museum of Art. 70
Meryon, Charles. French School (1821-1868). Le Stryge, etching, 1853, 6¾ x 5, Delteil 23. Knoedler Galery, New York. 341
———, The Morgue, etching, 1854, 8⅜ x 7⅜, Delteil 36. Philadelphia Museum of Art. 340
Meyer, Henry. English School (1782-1847). See Romney.
Millet, Jean François. French School (1814-1875). The Diggers, etching, ca. 1855, 8¾ x 12⅜, Delteil 13. Collection Staunton B. Peck. 360
Miró, Joan. Spanish School (b. 1893). The Singers, color pochoir, 1934, 12⅜ x 9⅞. Philadelphia Museum of Art. 489
Missale Parisiense. French School. Celebration of the Mass, woodcut, Jean du Pré, Paris 1481, 10¼ x 7⅛. Bibliothèque Nationale, Paris. 15
Monnoyer, Jean Baptiste. French School (1634-1699). Bouquet of Flowers, hand colored engraving. Weyhe Gallery, New York. 287
Moreau-le-Jeune, Jean Michel. French School (1741-1814). Les Délices de la Maternité, from Le Monument du Costume, engraving by Helman, 1777, 10⅜ x 8½, Bocher 1354. Philadelphia Museum of Art. 252
———, Le Souper Fin, from Le Monument du Costume, engraving by Helman, 1781, 10½

x 8½, Bocher 1370. Philadelphia Museum of Art. 254
———, Les Adieux, from Le Monument du Costume, engraving by Delaunary, 1777, 10⅜ x 8½, Bocher 1357. Philadelphia Museum of Art. 255
———, Sortie de l'Opera, from Le Monument du Costume, engraving by Malbeste, 1783, 10½ x 8¾, Bocher 1369. Philadelphia Museum of Art. 253
———, The Fair of Gonesse, engraving, from de la Borde, Choix de Chansons, 1772, 5⅜ x 3⅞. Metropolitan Museum of Art. 288
———, Crowning the Bust of Voltaire, engraving by Gaucher, 1778, 9⅞ x 11¼. National Gallery of Art, Rosenwald Collection. 272
Morin, Jean. French School (1590-1650). Portrait of Antoine Vitré, engraving after Philippe de Champaigne, 12¼ x 8⅜. Philadelphia Museum of Art. 237b
Morley, Eugene. American School (b. 1909). Execution, color serigraph, 1940, 11¼ x 16⅛. Private Collection. 474
Moronobu Hishikawa. Japanese School (1625-1694). A Garden, woodcut from Tsukiyama Niwa-Tsukuri Den. An account of Landscape Gardening, 1691, 8½ x 13, Toda, p. 99. Philadelphia Museum of Art. 115
———, The Lovers, woodcut sumi-ye from a shungwa series, ca. 1683, 9¼ x 13¼, Ledoux Catalogue 4. Collection Louis V. Ledoux. 117a
Munch, Edvard. Norwegian School (1863-1944). The Cry, lithograph, 1895, 13⅞ x 9⅞, Schiefler 32. National Gallery of Art, Rosenwald Collection. 467
———, The Kiss, two toned woodcut, 1902, 18¼ x 18¼, Schiefler 102. Museum of Modern Art, New York. 471
Murphy, John J. A. American School (b. 1888). Adoration of the Shepherds, wood-engraving, 1920, 2½ x 2⅜. Private collection. 87
———, Morning Gossip, wood-engraving, ca. 1920, 5⅜ x 5⅞. From The Print Collector's Quarterly. 96
Mustard-Seed-Garden Manual. Chinese School. Squirrel-shrew and Grapes, color woodcut supposedly based on a composition by the Sung artist Chao Cháng, in Vol. III, from the Chieh-tzü-yuan Hua-chuan 1679-1701, from a later edition of the early nineteenth century. Philadelphia Museum of Art. 509

Nanteuil, Robert. French School (1623?-1678). Louis XIV, engraving, 1667, 17¾ x 12⅛,

Petitjean and Wickert 139. Philadelphia Museum of Art. 238
——, Portrait of Loret, engraving, 1658, 10 x 7, Petitjean and Wickert 130. Philadelphia Museum of Art. 238a
Nason, Thomas W. American School (b. 1889). Ipswich Barns, wood-engraving, 1930, 3⅜ x 5¼. Private Collection. 93
Nevinson, C. R. W. English School (1889-1946). Airplane, lithograph, 1917, 15⅞ x 12⅜. Philadelphia Museum of Art. 453
Newhouse, C. B. English School (fl. 1830-1845). False Alarm on the Road to Gretna Green, ca. 1840, aquatint in colors by Reeve. Knoedler Gallery, New York. 306
Nuremberg Chronicle. German School. Map of the World, woodcut, Koberger, Nuremberg 1493, 12¼ x 17⅛. Philadelphia Museum of Art. 179

Orozco, José Clemente. Mexican School (b. 1883). Requiem, lithograph, 1928, 11¾ x 15¾. Philadelphia Museum of Art. 478
——, Mouths, lithograph, 1935, 12½ x 16½. Philadelphia Museum of Art. 462
——, Leaders, lithograph, 1935, 13 x 16½. Private Collection. 463
Ortelius, Abraham. Dutch School (1527-1598). Map of America, hand colored engraving, 1589, 13½ x 19½. Weyhe Gallery, New York. 180

Palmer, Samuel. English School (1805-1881). Opening the Fold, etching, 1880, 4⅜ x 7, Hardie 13. Philadelphia Museum of Art. 350a
——, The Sleeping Shepherd, etching, 1857, 3¾ x 3, Hardie 6. Philadelphia Museum of Art. 351
Papillon, Jean Michel. French School (1698-1776). Notre Dame de Bonne Déliverance, woodcut. From *Courboin's L'Estampe Française*. 69
Parmigiano, Francesco Mazzuola, called. Italian School (1503-1540). St. Thais, etching, 5⅛ x 4½, Bartsch 10. Metropolitan Museum of Art. 166
——, Saturn (or Chronos), chiaroscuro woodcut by Ugo da Carpi, 12⅛ x 17, Bartsch 28. Metropolitan Museum of Art. 167
Pascin, Jules. French School (1885-1930). Cinderella, soft-ground etching and aquatint printed in color, 1929, Tremois Paris, 10 x 13⅞. Private Collection. 421
Pennell, Joseph. American School (1860-1926). Pedro Miguel Lock, Panama, lithograph, 1912, 22 x 16¾. Metropolitan Museum of Art. 409

Peregrino da Cesena. Italian School (fl. ca. 1500-1525). Orpheus, engraving, ca. 1525, 2⅜ x 1⅞, Hind 203. Kupferstichkabinett, Berlin. 139
——, Ornament, engraving, ca. 1525, 2¾ x 1¾, Hind 265. British Museum. 138
Picasso, Pablo. Spanish School (b. 1881). Repas Frugal, etching on zinc, 1904, 18¼ x 14¾, Geiser 2. Private Collection. 487
——, Pierrot et Harlequin, poichoir in colors, ca. 1919, 10⅞ x 8⅜. Metropolitan Museum of Art. 488
——, Minotauromachia, etching, 1935, 19½ x 27¼. Collection Henry P. McIlhenny. 496
Pillemont, Jean. French School (1728-1808). Ornament, engraving by Jeanne Deny, 1770, 9½ x 6½. Metropolitan Museum of Art. 66
Piranesi, Giovanni Battista. Italian School (1720-1778). Prison Scene, etching from *Carceri d'Invenzione*, 1760, 16 x 21¼, Hind 15. Philadelphia Museum of Art. 279
——, Via del Corso, etching from *Vedute di Roma*, 1752, 15¾ x 24¼, Hind 24. Weyhe Gallery, New York. 278
——, The Baths of Titus (should be Trajan), etching from *Vedute di Roma*, 1775, 19 x 27⅞, Hind 123. Weyhe Gallery, New York. 277
Pissarro, Camille. French School (1830-1903). The Goose Girl, etching, 1888, 5½ x 7⅞, Delteil 76. Private Collection. 363
Pitteri, Giovanni Marco. Italian School (1703-1786). Portrait of the Marquise de Pompadour, engraving. Knoedler Gallery, New York. 264
Pollaiuolo, Antonio. Italian School (1432?-1498). Battle of the Naked Men, engraving, ca. 1470, 16⅜ x 24⅛. Bartsch 2. Collection Paul J. Sachs. 119
Pollaiuolo School. Profile of a Lady, engraving, ca. 1455, 8⅞ x 5¾. Kupferstichkabinett, Berlin. 135
Posada, José Guadalupe. Mexican School (1851-1913) Calavera, relief etching printed as woodcut, ca. 1910, 5⅜ x 10. Private Collection. 103
——, Calavera Huertista, engraving on zinc, 1913, 8½ x 8½. Private Collection. 480
Potter, Paul. Dutch School (1625-1654). Cowherd, etching, 1644, 7 x 10⅜, Bartsch 14. Philadelphia Museum of Art. 228b
Primaticcio, Francesco. School of Fontainebleau (1504-1570). Diana, etching by Master L.D., ca. 1550, 5¾ x 11. Private Collection. 181a
Prud'hon, Pierre Paul. French School (1758-

493

1823). La Liberté, engraving by Copia, ca. 1795. From *Courboin's La Gravure en France*. 293

Pytlak, Leonard. American School (b. 1910). Rockport, color serigraph, ca. 1941, 13⅜ x 19¼. Philadelphia Museum of Art. 473

Quaglio, Lorenzo. German School (1787-1837). Portrait of Senefelder, lithograph in two tones, 1818, 11⅛ x 8⅞. Private Collection. 320

Raffet, Denis Auguste. French School (1804-1860). Revue Nocturne, lithograph, 1836, 7⅞ x 10¾, Beraldi 429, first state. Philadelphia Museum of Art. 318

Raimondi, Marcantonio. Italian School (ca. 1480-1530). Two Fauns and a Child, engraving after a relief on a sarcophagus in the Naples Museum, 6⅛ x 7⅛, Bartsch 230. Sessler Gallery, Philadelphia. 146

——, *See also* Raphael

Raphael Santi. Italian School (1483-1520). Judgment of Paris, engraving by Raimondi, ca. 1515, 11½ x 17, Bartsch 245. Metropolitan Museum of Art. 161

——, Massacre of the Innocents, engraving by Raimondi, ca. 1515, 10⅞ x 16¾, Bartsch 18. Metropolitan Museum of Art. 162

——, Draught of Fishes, chiaroscuro woodcut by Ugo da Carpi, 9⅛ x 13⅜, Bartsch 13. Metropolitan Museum of Art. 168

Redon, Odilon. French School (1840-1916). L'Aile, lithograph, 1893, 12½ x 9½, Mellerio 122. Art Institute, Chicago. 347

Redouté, Pierre Joseph. French School (1759-1840). Rosa Bullata, colored stipple, 1817-1824, 12¾ x 7¾. Weyhe Gallery, New York. by Langlois. 308

Reeve, R. English School (fl. 1814-1838). *See* Newhouse and Hodges.

Rembrandt van Ryan. Dutch School (1606-1669). Self Portrait Leaning on Stone Sill, etching, 1639, 8⅛ x 6½, Hind 168. National Gallery of Art, Rosenwald Collection. 187

——, Portrait of his Mother, etching, 1631, 5¾ x 5⅛, Hind 52. Knoedler Gallery, New York. 188

——, Dr. Faustus, etching, 1652, 8¼ x 6⅜, Hind 260. National Gallery of Art, Rosenwald Collection. 189

——, Beggar warming his Hands, etching, ca. 1630, 2⅛ x 1⅞, Hind 8. Knoedler Gallery, New York. 207

——, Three Trees, etching, 1643, 8¼ x 11, Hind 205. Metropolitan Museum of Art. 192

Rembrandt van Ryan, Landscape with Trees, Farm Buildings and Tower, etching, 1650, 4⅞ x 12½, Hind 244. Collection A. E. McvVitty. 191

——, Woman with Arrow (or Bed-curtain Rope), etching, 1661, 8 x 4⅞, Hind 303. Collection A. E. McVitty. 190

——, Christ and Woman of Samaria, etching, 1657, 4⅞ x 6¼, Hind 294. Knoedler Gallery, New York. 193

——, Christ Preaching, etching, 1652, 6⅛ x 8⅛, Hind 256. Collection Robert L. Rosenwald. 194

Renoir, Auguste. French School (1841-1919). Baigneuse, lithograph in color, 1896, 16¼ x 13½, Delteil 28. Philadelphia Museum of Art. 370

Rethel, Alfred. German School (1816-1859). Death the Victor, woodcut from the set *Auch ein Totentanz*, 1848. Weyhe Gallery, New York. 102

Reuwich, Erhard. German School (fl. end of fifteenth century). Group of Syrians, woodcut from *Breydenbach's Peregrinationes*, Mainz, 1468, 3¼ x 4½, Hain 3959. Library of Congress, Rosenwald Collection. 28

Revere, Paul. American School (1735-1818). Boston Massacre, hand colored engraving, 1770, 7⅞ x 8⅜, Stauffer 2675. Metropolitan Museum of Art. 275

Reynolds, Sir Joshua. English School (1723-1792). Dr. Johnson, mezzotint by Doughty, 1779, 16 x 13, J. C. Smith 2. Knoedler Gallery, New York. 297

——, Mrs. Carnac, mezzotint by J. R. Smith, 1778, 23⅜ x 15⅜, J. C. Smith 31. Knoedler Gallery, New York. 295

Ribera, Jusepe de. Spanish-Italian School (1588-1652) Drunken Silenus, etching, 1628, 10½ x 13¾, Bartsch 13. Philadelphia Museum of Art. 197

Richter, Ludwig. German School (1803-1884). Harvest Dance, wood-engraving. Weyhe Gallery, New York. 82

Rigaud, Hyacinthe. French School (1659-1743). Portrait of Robert de Cotte, engraving by Pierre Drevet, 1722, 15⅜ x 11¾. Knoedler Gallery, New York. 239

Rivera, Diego. Mexican School (b. 1886). Fruits of Labor, lithograph, 1932, 16½ x 11¾. Philadelphia Museum of Art. 481

Robetta, Christofano. Italian School (1462-1522). Allegory of Abundance, engraving, 9⅞ x 7, Bartsch 18. Knoedler Gallery, New York. 137b

Romanesque School. Twelfth Century. The Nativity, engraving from the Chandelier of the Emperor Barbarossa at Aix-la-Chapelle,

tablet at Ch'ëng-tu in Szechuan, 37 x 19. From *Waley's Introduction to the study of Chinese Painting.* 503

Yeishi Hosoda. Japanese School (1756-1829). Two Ladies and Child by Seashore, polychrome woodcut. Metropolitan Museum of Art. 549
——, Fête in Nobleman's Palace, polychrome woodcut, triptych. Metropolitan Museum of Art. 532

Young, Mahonri M. American School (b. 1877). Tewa, drypoint, 1917, 6 x 8½. Private Collection. 393

Zeeman, Renier Nooms called. Dutch School (1623-ca. 1663). Vessels of Amsterdam, number 4 of series, etching, 4¾ x 9½, Dutuit 90. Private Collection. 228c
Zorn, Anders. Swedish School (1860-1920). The Waltz, etching, 1891, 13¼ x 9. Knoedler Gallery, New York. 382